BRIEF HISTORY OF THE REVOLUTIONARY ACTIVITIES OF COMRADE

KIM IL SUNG

Fredonia Books
Amsterdam, The Netherlands

Brief History of the Revolutionary
Activities of Comrade Kim Il Sung

by
The Party History Institute of the Central
Committee of the Workers' Party of Korea

ISBN: 1-58963-939-1

Copyright © 2002 by Fredonia Books

Reprinted from the 1969 edition

Fredonia Books
Amsterdam, The Netherlands
http://www.fredoniabooks.com

All rights reserved, including the right to reproduce
this book, or portions thereof, in any form.

The great Leader of the 40 million Korean people Comrade Kim Il Sung, peerless patriot, national hero, ever-victorious iron-willed brilliant commander and one of the outstanding leaders of the international communist and working-class movements, has devoted his all to the struggle for the freedom and happiness of the people and the victory of the revolution to this day for more than 40 years ever since he set out on the revolutionary struggle in his early years.

Bearing the destinies of the fatherland and the nation on his shoulders, Comrade Kim Il Sung has led the Korean revolution to victory and scored great shining achievements never known in any period of our country's history.

The history of the revolutionary activities of Comrade Kim Il Sung is a history of sanguinary struggle for the independence of the country and the liberation of the working class and other sections of the people, a glorious history woven throughout with his fervent love for the fatherland and the people and with his boundless fidelity to the revolution.

It is also a history of victories of the Korean people's national-liberation struggle and the communist movement of Korea, a history of creative development of Marxism-Leninism in Korea.

Comrade Kim Il Sung thoroughly established *Juche* in the Korean revolution and thereby opened up a new path for the communist movement and national-liberation struggle in Korea, delivered our country and nation out of the life-and-death crisis, and has led and is leading the Korean people correctly along the road of epoch-making change and prosperity.

Comrade Kim Il Sung applied Marxism-Leninism to the realities of Korea for the first time in the history of our country's communist movement and brought about its new development and, laying down a correct and original line of revolution and ways for its accomplishment, has tirelessly led the Korean revolution to victory.

The Korean people have registered brilliant achievements and great successes in the revolution and construction. All the victories and successes achieved by the Korean people are, without exception, associated with the wise leadership of Comrade Kim Il Sung.

Comrade Kim Il Sung has waged a tireless and unyielding struggle against the most outrageous Japanese imperialists and U.S. imperialists over a long period and given active support and assistance to the peoples of other countries in their revolutionary struggle, holding high the banner of proletarian internationalism.

By his profound and original theoretical and practical activities Comrade Kim Il Sung has made a great contribution to the international communist and working-class movements and the national-liberation struggle of the peoples in the colonial and dependent countries.

It is a boundless honour and bliss for the Korean Communists and people that they learn from the great Leader Comrade Kim Il Sung who is possessed of scientific revolutionary theory, a wealth of experiences, distinguished ability of leadership and high virtues and has led our people along the path of glorious victory through the long drawn-out tempest of revolution and that they live and fight as his faithful soldiers, upholding his leadership.

1

Comrade Kim Il Sung, the respected and beloved Leader of the Korean people, was born into the family of a poor peasant in Mangyongdae of Pyongyang (Nam-*ri*, Kopyong sub-county, Taedong county, South Pyongan Province at the time) on April 15, 1912.

The family of Comrade Kim Il Sung is a patriotic and revolutionary family that have fought from generation to generation for the independence of the country and the freedom and liberation of the people against foreign aggressors.

His great-grandfather Mr. Kim Ung U was a patriot who led the battle for sinking the pirate ship "General Sherman" dispatched by the U.S. aggressors as a feeler for their aggression of our country in 1866.

His grandfather Mr. Kim Bo Hyon and his grandmother Mrs. Li Bo Ik, too, were patriots who, backing the revolutionary struggle of their sons and grandsons, remained profoundly true to their national principles without yielding to the harsh repression and persecution by the Japanese imperialists and fought tenaciously against the aggressors.

His father Mr. Kim Hyong Jik was a pioneer and outstanding leader of the national-liberation movement in our country. He had a strong patriotic anti-Japanese spirit and extraordinary talents and noble qualities.

Having embarked on the road of revolution with "Lofty Aims", he led the anti-Japanese struggle already in his secondary-school days and formed the Korean National Association in March 1917.

The Korean National Association raised the fighting task of firmly rallying broad patriotic anti-Japanese forces and achieving Korea's independence through the efforts of the Koreans themselves whenever there would be created a favorable revolutionary situation. It was a revolutionary organization most steadfast in the anti-imperialist stand and an underground anti-Japanese revolutionary organization biggest in the size and the sphere of activity, too, in the period prior to the dissemination of Marxism-Leninism in our country.

The Korean National Association under the guidance of Mr. Kim Hyong Jik spread its organizations extensively in different parts of the homeland and even abroad, and actively organized and mobilized the masses of the people to the anti-Japanese struggle, properly combining legal with illegal activities.

He, together with over 100 persons connected with the Korean National Association, was arrested by the Japanese imperialist police in the autumn of 1917.

With no amount of brutal torture and appeasement measure could the Japanese imperialist police break his lofty revolutionary constancy and fervent revolutionary spirit for the restoration of the fatherland.

Upon his release from prison, he moved his theatre of struggle to the northern borderland of our country and northeast China, and energetically unfolded revolutionary activities as the leading spirit of the anti-Japanese movements at home and abroad.

Mr. Kim Hyong Jik resolutely repudiated the futile attempt of the bourgeois nationalists to achieve "independence" by means of "petitioning" the Japanese imperialist rogues or with the "help" of the imperialist powers and, firmly adhering to the position that the restoration of the country should on all accounts be realized independently through the enlistment of the broad patriotic forces of the Korean people, conducted energetic activities for the union of anti-Japanese revolutionary forces and the unity and cohesion of their ranks.

Sensitive to progressive ideas, he always went deep among the working people to induce the revolutionary awakening of the masses for the new advancement of the anti-Japanese national-liberation movement in our country, and fought resolutely in defence of the interests of the people.

He set up schools in many places and made every effort to educate and train the rising generation in patriotism and new knowledge. Meanwhile, he devoted all his energies to bringing up his sons into ardent patriots, into fine revolutionaries.

He always told his sons about the beautiful mountains and rivers of the country and the struggle of its patriotic people, about the October Socialist Revolution in Russia and the latest world events.

Mr. Kim Hyong Jik was thus not only an indomitable anti-Japanese revolutionary fighter who devoted his whole life to the struggle for the independence of the country and the freedom and liberation of the people and a patriotic, revolutionary educator, but also an outstanding leader of the anti-Japanese national-liberation movement in our country.

Mrs. Kang Ban Sok, mother of Comrade Kim Il Sung, was also endowed with remarkable talents, a kind heart and strong character, and she was an anti-Japanese revolutionary fighter who fought unyieldingly against the foes.

In defiance of the abject poverty and the persecution by the Japanese imperialist police, she actively helped Mr. Kim Hyong Jik in his revolutionary activities, reared her sons steadfastly into ardent revolutionaries and Communists, and devoted her all to the education of the rising generation in pursuance of her late husband's will.

While operating as a member of the secret revolutionary circle organized by Comrade Kim Il Sung with Communists in the Fusung area, she formed an anti-Japanese women's organization and, extending its organization to many areas, energetically organized and unfolded a struggle for the independence of the country and the social emancipation of women.

Though she was suffering from poverty and infirmity, she undertook to carry out difficult missions of underground work without regard to her own person, solely for the sake of revolution. Particularly, she devoted herself body and soul to helping Comrade Kim Il Sung in the work for founding the anti-Japanese guerilla army.

Thus, Mrs. Kang Ban Sok was an ardent Communist and prominent female political figure who devoted her all to victory of the Korean revolution as the wife of a revolutionary, as the mother who gave birth to and brought up Comrade Kim Il Sung, the great Leader of the Korean people.

Mr. Kim Hyong Gwon, uncle of Comrade Kim Il Sung, too, was an ardent revolutionary fighter and a staunch Communist who joined in the revolutionary struggle in his early years for the restoration of the fatherland.

He joined the Korean Revolutionary Army which had been organized by Comrade Kim Il Sung in preparation for the anti-Japanese armed struggle, and dauntlessly conducted armed operations in the northern areas of Korea in command of one of its details in the summer of 1930, and dealt mortal blows to the Japanese imperialists.

He was arrested by the Japanese imperialist police and imprisoned under a 15-year sentence. He died in prison, where he fought with an indomitable will to the end of his life for the victory of the Korean revolution without yielding to the brutal torture and any conciliatory measure of the enemy.

The two younger brothers of Comrade Kim Il Sung were

also Communists who took part in the anti-Japanese struggle in their early years and fought stoutly.

His younger brother Comrade Kim Chol Ju was an indefatigable revolutionary fighter who organized and conducted political work energetically among the masses as the leader of a local Young Communist League organization, sent to the Anti-Japanese Guerilla Army many fine youths trained in the YCL organization, and died a heroic death in 1935 fighting in arms against Japanese imperialism.

His cousin Comrade Kim Won Ju, too, was a determined anti-Japanese revolutionary fighter who, in response to the anti-Japanese armed struggle organized and waged under the leadership of Comrade Kim Il Sung, formed underground revolutionary organizations with factory workers, youth and students, and fought energetically against Japanese imperialism.

Mr. Kang Don Uk, grandfather of Comrade Kim Il Sung on the mother's side, and Mr. Kang Jin Sok, his uncle on the mother's side, were also anti-Japanese fighters who fought fiercely for the restoration of the fatherland.

As seen above, the family and relations of Comrade Kim Il Sung, the outstanding Leader of the Korean revolution and great Leader of the Korean people—from great-grandfather, grandfather, grandmother, father, mother, uncle, younger brothers to grandfather and uncle on the mother's side—fought passionately from generation to generation for the independence of the country and the freedom and liberation of the people.

Born in a revolutionary home, Comrade Kim Il Sung grew up in rough storms and tribulations when the whole country was pervaded with the indignation and agony of national ruin, while being educated in patriotism by his parents from his childhood.

He was inspired with patriotic ardor by the March First Uprising which was a nation-wide anti-Japanese resistance struggle of the Korean people; nourished a fighting will to annihilate the enemy when he saw repeated brutal arrests of his father by the Japanese imperialist police; and, influenced by his father's indomitable revolutionary activities, fostered strong patriotic anti-Japanese ideas and revolutionary class consciousness from unusually early years.

From his childhood Comrade Kim Il Sung was broad-minded and kind-hearted and, besides having unusual talents, was diligent and vigorous by nature.

Comrade Kim Il Sung always carried books in his hand. He eagerly read the biographies of famous patriotic generals of our country and great men of the world and regularly read newspapers already in his primary-school days.

Thus, he not only gained the highest mark for every subject of study but also acquired a large store of knowledge about society in particular, thanks to the education by his father.

When he was 14 Comrade Kim Il Sung, nursing a burning desire and firm resolve to fight the Japanese imperialists and attain independence for the country at all costs, went to northeast China where his father was engaged in the revolutionary struggle.

Looking back to that time, Comrade Kim Il Sung said as follows:

"I crossed the River Amnok-gang when 14, firmly resolved not to return before Korea won independence. Young as I was at the time, I could not repress my sorrow as I, singing the 'Song of the River Amnok-gang' composed by someone, wondered when I should be able to tread on this soil again and when I should return to this land where I had grown up and our ancestors lay in their graves."

Comrade Kim Il Sung helped his father in his revolutionary activities, creditably carrying out missions of conveying secret messages, and energetically inspired students and the masses with patriotic anti-Japanese ideas.

Unable to suppress his indignation at the fact that the fatherland was lost and the fellow countrymen were going through a miserable lot, he called the masses to the anti-Japanese struggle by fervent speeches filled with wrath.

His logical and passionate anti-Japanese propaganda always stirred the audience.

The profound political knowledge and great magnanimity of Comrade Kim Il Sung brought large numbers of children and youths to rally around him.

Children and youth followed him with boundless respect and liked to be in his company at all times.

Thus, already at that time Comrade Kim Il Sung was widely known among the masses and their attention was focussed on him.

On June 5, 1926 Mr. Kim Hyong Jik who had devoted his whole life to the struggle for the restoration of the fatherland passed away to the deep regret of the people. The father's death was a strong mental shock to Comrade Kim Il Sung.

Comrade Kim Il Sung firmly pledged to devote himself to the revolutionary struggle in pursuance of the lofty will of his father who had said that the country had to be restored at all costs even if the bones were broken and the body was torn to pieces.

In the summer of 1926 Comrade Kim Il Sung entered the Hwasong Uisuk School in Huatien county.

This school had been set up by the nationalists for the purpose of training cadres for the Independence Army.

The contents of education at the Hwasong Uisuk School tinted throughout with nationalistic ideas could hardly satisfy Comrade Kim Il Sung who aspired to things new.

Comrade Kim Il Sung zealously read books on socialism in secrecy and came to acquire the socialist and communist ideas.

Comrade Kim Il Sung who was seeking a new way to deliver the country and the people from under the oppression of Japanese imperialism, was convinced that the road of Marxism-Leninism was the only road leading to the genuine salvation of the country and the people.

Comrade Kim Il Sung formed an illegal revolutionary organization—the Down-With-Imperialism Union (T.D.—abbreviation from the Korean pronunciation)—in the autumn of 1926.

Concerning the aims of this Union, Comrade Kim Il Sung said to the following effect:

...**The aims of the "T.D." are to struggle for building socialism and communism in Korea in the future and, for the present, to defeat Japanese imperialism and achieve the liberation and independence of Korea....**

This was a Marxist-Leninist programme of action, the first of its kind to lay down most correctly the ultimate goal and immediate fighting tasks of the Korean revolution.

The Down-With-Imperialism Union opened up a bright opportunity to unite progressive youths and students who aimed to overthrow Japanese imperialism and build a socialist and communist society in Korea, and to organize and mobilize, through their medium, broad sections of the youth to the anti-Japanese struggle. The Down-With-Imperialism Union under the guidance of Comrade Kim Il Sung waged a struggle to rear progressive youths and students into Communists through the dissemination of revolutionary Marxist-Leninist ideas among the youth and students and persistent ideological education for raising their class awakening.

Indeed, the formation of the Down-With-Imperialism Union was an epoch-making event in the development of the communist and the national-liberation movement in our country.

This marked the beginning of the revolutionary activities of Comrade Kim Il Sung and it was then that he emerged as a leader of the revolutionary youth and student movement.

Comrade Kim Il Sung left the Hwasong Uisuk School

resolutely in mid-course with the lofty aim of studying scientific communism more profoundly and extending and strengthening the organization of the Down-With-Imperialism Union.

In this way Comrade Kim Il Sung paved a new path, the right path of revolution, by himself with a firm faith in the truth he was searching after and with a spirit of enterprise and resolution which could not be dampened by anything when justice was concerned.

In the winter of 1926 Comrade Kim Il Sung formed the Saenal (New Day) Juvenile Union with children and youths in Fusung and published its newspaper "Saenal" (New Day) with a view to educating and training them in the patriotic anti-Japanese ideas and socialist and communist ideas.

In the spring of 1927 Comrade Kim Il Sung moved the centre of his revolutionary activities to Kirin.

While a student at the Kirin Yuwen Middle School, Comrade Kim Il Sung was secretly absorbed in reading the *Communist Manifesto, Capital* and other works of the founders of Marxism-Leninism and works of revolutionary literature.

Comrade Kim Il Sung learned Marxism-Leninism not merely as a current thought or simply as a theory but regarded it as a weapon of struggle and a means of practical activity.

Comrade Kim Il Sung organized reading circles secretly and expounded and propagated Marxism-Leninism energetically among the youth and students.

In disseminating Marxism-Leninism, Comrade Kim Il Sung rejected the old dogmatic and quotation-mongering method, saw to the profound understanding of its essence and linked it closely with the practical problems of the Korean revolution.

The studies of Marxism-Leninism conducted among the youth and students under the guidance of Comrade Kim Il Sung became living studies not only to have a deep understanding of its ideas and theory but also to grasp clear ways of the practical struggle at the moment.

With regard to the need to arm the broad sections of the masses including the youth and students with Marxism-Leninism and unite them gradually and firmly in the revolutionary organizations, Comrade Kim Il Sung said in the following vein:

...If we are to crush the Japanese villains and restore the independence of the country, we need first of all to unite the masses who love the country.... Let all of us unite forces and rise in a revolutionary struggle.... In future, the youth should all be embraced in the youth organizations, the boys and girls in the juvenile organizations and the women in the women's organizations and fight with greater determination against the Japanese imperialists and the class enemies....

In the summer of 1927, Comrade Kim Il Sung changed the name of the Down-With-Imperialism Union into the Anti-Imperialist Youth League to rally broad progressive youths and students and united in it progressive youths and students who came from different regions. The Anti-Imperialist Youth League was an illegal mass revolutionary organization of youth and students.

Comrade Kim Il Sung, while uniting the progressive youths and students and expanding their organization in this way, formed the Young Communist League of Korea with the core elements of those youths and students in the summer of 1927.

Under the guidance of Comrade Kim Il Sung the Young Communist League and the Anti-Imperialist Youth League extended their organizations to the Kirin Yuwen Middle School and many other schools in the city such as the Wenkuang Middle School, Middle School No. 1, Middle School No. 5, the Kirin Normal School, Kirin Girls' Middle School, Kirin Law and Politics School, and even to many urban and rural areas, among them Tunhua, Chiaoho, Huatien, Fusung, Panshih, Changchun, Shenyang, etc., and thus they developed into

Comrade Kim Il Sung
in his Yuwen Middle School days

militant revolutionary organizations embracing a large number of youths and students.

In the meantime, Comrade Kim Il Sung, with a view to educating and training broad sections of children and youth, organized in the spring of 1927 a legal children and youth organization, the Association of Korean Juveniles in Kirin, and reorganized the Ryogil Association of Korean Students in Kirin which was under the influence of the nationalists into the Ryugil Association of Korean Students in Kirin and guided it.

Comrade Kim Il Sung, through the medium of the Association of Korean Juveniles in Kirin and the Ryugil Association of Korean Students in Kirin, enhanced the national and class consciousness of the children and youth, and educated and trained them gradually to aspire after communism.

Comrade Kim Il Sung extended the scope of his revolutionary activities not only among the students and youth but also among the masses in wide urban and rural areas.

From 1928 Comrade Kim Il Sung sent many Young Communist League and Anti-Imperialist Youth League members to the towns and rural villages in the district east of Kirin and along the Kirin-Changchun railway line to carry on activities, while he himself proceeded to those areas and worked energetically to revolutionize the masses.

Leading the members of the Young Communist League and the Anti-Imperialist Youth League, Comrade Kim Il Sung set up schools in rural villages and educated and cultivated the children and youths and, with these schools as the bases, organized and conducted mass political work extensively. And by putting out various publications, he infused the masses with patriotic anti-Japanese ideas and united broad sections of the masses in the revolutionary organizations.

Under the leadership of Comrade Kim Il Sung the youth and students were growing up reliably into an organized force conscious of the lofty revolutionary missions entrusted to them, into true performers of the communist movement and the national-liberation struggle in our country, and the national and class awakening of the broad masses in towns and the countryside was enhanced, and their revolutionary spirit heightened rapidly.

Comrade Kim Il Sung did not confine himself to firmly uniting the youth and students in the revolutionary organizations and educating them. He organized and mobilized their organized forces to the struggle against Japanese imperialism and the reactionary warlords, thus tempering them in the practical struggle.

Drawing on the triumphant experience in the organization of school-strike struggle against reactionary teachers in the summer of 1928, Comrade Kim Il Sung organized and led a vigorous anti-Japanese demonstration of youths and students in Kirin against the building of the Kirin-Hoeryong railway line started by the Japanese imperialists for the purpose of seizing Manchuria and a struggle to boycott Japanese goods in the autumn of the same year.

Through these struggles Comrade Kim Il Sung dealt heavy blows to Japanese imperialism and to the reactionary warlords, and trained the members of the Young Communist League and the Anti-Imperialist Youth League in the practical struggle and boosted their confidence in victory, rallying broad sections of youth and students more firmly in the revolutionary organizations.

Gathered in Kirin from different places in and outside the country in those days were a large number of persons styling themselves "leaders" of the communist and the nationalist movement.

As the leader of the youth and student movement, Comrade Kim Il Sung had many occasions to come in contact with them.

In the course of this contact he acquired a detailed inside

knowledge of the communist and nationalist movements and became able to see through their chronic defects.

Most of those who styled themselves "leaders" of the communist and the nationalist movement at the time were, without exception, factionalists or narrow-minded, conservative nationalists, and they were engaged in factional strife for "hegemony" by aligning a few persons of their respective groupings without any mass foundation or were engrossed in Rightist and Leftist utterances and empty talks alien to the specific realities of our country.

The factionalists behaved themselves each as "theoretician" and "leader" and tried to mislead the youth and students by advancing Right and Left sophistries such as "The Korean revolution is a proletarian revolution" or "The Korean revolution being a bourgeois democratic revolution, the hegemony in the revolution should be held by the national bourgeoisie."

Comrade Kim Il Sung trenchantly exposed and criticized the true nature of such opportunist theories of the factionalists and smashed their manoeuvrings in good time.

Comrade Kim Il Sung frequently arranged forums of youths and students on political issues, where he put forward for extensive discussions such questions as "On the Japanese imperialist policy of aggression," "On the present stage in the Korean revolution," and "How to conduct the Korean revolution?" and offered right conclusions on them, thus crushing the opportunist "theories" of the factionalists and enabling the youth and students to see the path ahead of the Korean revolution correctly and advance unwaveringly along that path.

The struggle waged by Comrade Kim Il Sung against factionalism and Right and Left opportunism was a struggle for the revolutionary Marxist-Leninist principle to get the upper hand of opportunism and for the revolutionary forces to overcome the machinations of the factionalists for the first time within the communist movement of our country.

Also, Comrade Kim Il Sung scathingly exposed and criticized the acts of the bosses of the nationalist organizations who, holding each his own sphere of influence in different areas, did not care for the independence of the country but were engrossed in the scramble for the hegemony among them, squandering the "funds for the movement" collected from the patriotic fellow countrymen, and the true nature of the principle of non-resistance and national nihilism advocated by the national reformists, thus awakening and uniting in the revolutionary organizations the youth and students who were under their influence or nursing illusions about them.

As seen above, from the early days of his revolutionary activities, Comrade Kim Il Sung clearly saw through the true colours of the factionalists and national reformists who did enormous harm to the Korean revolution, shattered in good time ideologically, theoretically and in practice the unsound trends of thoughts spread by them and led the youth, students and the masses along the right path of the Korean revolution.

Thus, Comrade Kim Il Sung became widely known as the recognized leader who held an unchallenged authority and prestige among the youth, students and masses, and came to enjoy the deep love and high respect of them.

The course Comrade Kim Il Sung had covered in blazing the trail for the revolution was not smooth.

As his reputation was enhanced as days went by, he was always shadowed and watched by the Japanese imperialists and their lackeys, the reactionary warlords.

Seeing that the anti-Japanese movement of the youth and students was unfolded vigorously under the guidance of Comrade Kim Il Sung, the Japanese imperialists bribed and abetted the reactionary Chinese warlords to make a big round-up in the autumn of 1929 of Koreans engaged in the anti-Japanese movement.

At that time Comrade Kim Il Sung, too, was arrested by the reactionary police and thrown into the Kirin prison together with his comrades.

Around this time Comrade Kim Il Sung was apprehended three times by the enemy.

The firm faith of Comrade Kim Il Sung in the victory of the revolution and his fervent revolutionary passion, his firm revolutionary principle and strong fighting spirit could not be broken by the repeated arrests and tortures of the enemy, however brutal.

Even behind the bars of the Kirin prison, Comrade Kim Il Sung gave continued guidance to the revolutionary organizations and elaborated his great plans for the Korean revolution.

In the spring of 1930 Comrade Kim Il Sung left the Kirin prison at the expiration of his term.

The course of the early revolutionary activities unfolded by Comrade Kim Il Sung with Kirin as the centre was a course in which he completely shaped the Marxist-Leninist world outlook and struck out a unique revolutionary path by applying Marxism-Leninism to the realities of Korea, and a course in which he reared innumerable youths and students into reliable performers of the Korean revolution, into ardent Communists.

And it was a course of preparation for advancing the Korean revolution onto a higher plane of development.

In this course Comrade Kim Il Sung constructed the guiding theory for the Korean revolution and grew up into an outstanding Marxist-Leninist, into the great Leader of the Korean revolution equipped with unwavering fidelity to revolutionary principle, an indomitable will, remarkable organizing ability, extraordinary revolutionary sweep, revolutionary methods of work and popular work style, and superb art of leadership.

In this way the right path for the Korean revolution was carved out by Comrade Kim Il Sung and new revolutionary forces were being prepared free from all the evils and filth chronic with the communist movement in its early period.

The dawn was breaking in the Korean revolution.

Comrade Kim Il Sung receives his late father's revolvers from his mother

2

In the early 1930's, Comrade Kim Il Sung opened up a new, historic stage which marked a great turn in the anti-Japanese national-liberation struggle and communist movement in our country.

The Japanese imperialists intensified the fascist oppression and plunder of the Korean people as never before, while frantically hurrying with their preparations for a war of aggression to tide over the catastrophic economic crisis that had been sweeping their country between the late 1920's and the early 1930's.

As a result, the national and class contradictions between the Korean people and the Japanese imperialists were aggravated to the extreme, and the workers, peasants and other sections of the broad popular masses were compelled to resist the tyrannical oppression of Japanese imperialism by violence.

At the time when the antagonism between revolution and counter-revolution grew so acute, the factionalists, far from drawing serious lessons from the dissolution of the Korean Communist Party, persisted in factional strife, and most of them succumbed to the reactionary offensive of Japanese imperialism, surrendering, turning their coat or being reduced to philistines in pursuit of an easy life.

The Korean people had gone through many turns and twists in the communist movement and anti-Japanese national-liberation struggle in our country in the preceding period on account of the absence of a genuine leader who could lead the revolutionary struggle correctly by a revolutionary Marxist-Leninist line and strategy and tactics. They, therefore, craved for the appearance of an outstanding leader who would deliver the fatherland and the nation from the crisis, illumine the path for the Korean revolution and lead it to a sure victory.

It was just at that time that Comrade Kim Il Sung, peerless patriot and outstanding Marxist-Leninist, most correctly discerned the demands of the revolutionary situation and stood in the forefront of the revolution to lead the Korean people along the road of sure victory.

The situation was very tense when Comrade Kim Il Sung was released from the Kirin prison. The Left adventurist May 30th Riot staged by the factionalists left grave consequences on the development of the revolutionary movement. Following this riot, the Japanese imperialists and reactionary warlords intensified their brutal suppression of the communist movement, arresting numerous revolutionary people and destroying their organizations.

In this grim situation, Comrade Kim Il Sung regarded it as an urgent task to set forth a correct line of struggle, rehabilitate and readjust the revolutionary organizations, rally and revolutionize the masses, and went among the broad masses in towns and villages to start underground activities on a full scale.

In the summer of 1930, Comrade Kim Il Sung went to Kalun and there he called a meeting of the leading members of the Young Communist League and the Anti-Imperialist Youth League.

At the meeting Comrade Kim Il Sung set forth the most correct revolutionary Marxist-Leninist line and policy for the victory of the Korean revolution. Comrade Kim Il Sung clarified that the character of the Korean revolution was of an anti-imperialist, anti-feudal democratic revolution, and gave a scientific definition of its motive force and objects.

He said that the basic motive force in the anti-imperialist, anti-feudal democratic revolution consisted of the working class and the peasantry, its most reliable ally, and petty bourgeoisie, and an alliance could be formed with the national bourgeoisie, too. And he made it clear that the objects of the revolution were Japanese imperialism and its accomplices—landlords, comprador capitalists, pro-Japanese elements and traitors to the nation, and clearly pointed out that our revolutionary task was to overthrow Japanese imperialism, liberate the country and build socialism and communism subsequently to the anti-imperialist, anti-feudal democratic revolution in our country and, further, to carry out the world revolution.

Comrade Kim Il Sung said to the following effect:

...We are Korean people and youths. We Korean youth cannot merely sit and remain an onlooker to our beautiful land and beloved compatriots, brothers and sisters being trampled underfoot and persecuted by the Japanese imperialists. We must drive out the Japanese imperialists from the soil of our country, liberate Korea and win independence. We cannot stop only at this, however. We are Communists. Communists cannot leave alone the knavish landlords and capitalists who oppress and exploit the proletarian masses.

We, therefore, must overthrow the capitalist system and build socialist and communist society, the cherished desire of the proletarian masses. And these two revolutionary tasks are not foreign to each other.... To make the proletarian revolution, it is essential to crush Japanese imperialism and achieve the liberation and independence of Korea before anything else, and then to build socialist and communist society in our land and carry out the world revolution as well....

Comrade Kim Il Sung made a profound Marxist-Leninist

analysis of the realities of our country and gave a scientific definition of the character and tasks of the Korean revolution, its motive force and objects of struggle.

Thus, the Communists and the revolutionary masses became able to push ahead with the revolutionary struggle unwaveringly towards the correct goal of the struggle indicated by Comrade Kim Il Sung.

Also at the meeting Comrade Kim Il Sung put forward the line of the anti-Japanese armed struggle, a *Juche*-motivated revolutionary line for the Korean revolution, which was the creative development of the Marxist-Leninist theory concerning the armed struggle.

Comrade Kim Il Sung said to the following effect:

...Our immediate aim is to crush the Japanese imperialist aggressors and attain the liberation and independence of Korea. And Japanese imperialism, the target of our struggle, is a burglar armed to the teeth.... Therefore, Japanese imperialism will not withdraw of its own accord. Who, then, should win independence for Korea!? It is absolutely impossible to achieve independence with foreign aid....

The only way is for us Koreans to fight and defeat the Japanese imperialists by our own strength. To do so, an armed struggle must be waged....

The line of the anti-Japanese armed struggle set forth by Comrade Kim Il Sung was the only correct revolutionary line run through with the steadfast idea of *Juche* that the Korean revolution should be accomplished by the Koreans independently by their own strength and struggle.

Also, this line was the most thoroughly anti-imperialist revolutionary line implying that the counter-revolutionary violence should be countered by the revolutionary violence in the national-liberation struggle in colonies and that the armed counter-revolution could be defeated only through an armed struggle.

Further, it was the most correct revolutionary line which defined an organized anti-Japanese armed struggle waged by standing armed forces as the main form of struggle in the anti-Japanese national-liberation movement of the Korean people and which was aimed at vigorously expediting the victory of the Korean revolution by effecting, through this struggle, an all-round guidance of all other forms of struggles of the masses of the people.

Comrade Kim Il Sung, elucidating the great line of the anti-Japanese armed struggle, clearly indicated concrete ways of implementing the line—how to train nuclear pivots of the armed struggle, lay the mass foundation, accumulate military experiences and so on, first of all.

Comrade Kim Il Sung said in the following vein:

...**We should neither overestimate the enemy's strength nor underrate it on any account. To fight and defeat the wicked enemy, we should cultivate our strength quickly.... Of course, we should avoid meaningless conflicts and sacrifices, for we are now in the stage of preparing revolutionary forces. Nevertheless, it is important for us to harden ourselves through actual struggle and also study strategy and tactics.... We cannot merely sit and wait, hoping for victory to come of itself. We must crush Japanese imperialism by force of arms and, to this end, must build up our strength quickly....**

The line of the anti-Japanese armed struggle and all the measures for its implementation clarified by Comrade Kim Il Sung were worked out on the basis of a scientific analysis of the bitter lessons of the communist movement and national-liberation struggle of the preceding period and the revolutionary situation in our country and, particularly, they expressed most correctly the aspirations of the masses who were making a violent advance.

At the meeting, Comrade Kim Il Sung not only elucidated the original line of the anti-Japanese armed struggle but also set forth the line of the united anti-Japanese national front to organize and mobilize all the patriotic anti-Japanese forces of the Korean people on the basis of the worker-peasant alliance under the leadership of the working class.

Comrade Kim Il Sung taught that with the strength of a few Communists alone it was impossible to overthrow the Japanese imperialists and win victory in the revolution, and for victory in the revolution the main forces of the revolution should be firmly built up and, at the same time, all the anti-imperialist, anti-feudal forces that were interested in this revolution should be united closely in the ranks of struggle against Japanese imperialism.

The line of the united anti-Japanese national front advanced by Comrade Kim Il Sung was a wise line reflecting the ardent aspirations of the patriotic Korean people and was the most correct line which made it possible to organize and mobilize all the anti-imperialist classes and circles to routing and wiping out Japanese imperialism, the national and class enemy of the Korean people, and thus tip the scale of forces between the enemy and us in favour of the revolution so as to win the decisive victory in the revolution.

At the meeting Comrade Kim Il Sung also set forth the line of founding a Korean Communist Party.

In those days the factionalists, prompted by the sinister desire to seize hold of the "hegemony," put up the signboard of "Party reconstruction" and made haste allegedly to found the Party each without any preparations for its founding.

Comrade Kim Il Sung taught that a revolutionary Party should be founded on the basis of overcoming those machinations of the factionalists and making full organizational and ideological preparations for the founding of the Party. He instructed that for this purpose it was essential to rear the core elements of worker and peasant origins into Communists and expand their ranks to firmly build up the organizational backbone for the founding of the Party, and overcome factionalism and Right and Left opportunism to achieve the unshakable organizational and ideological unity of the ranks of Communists through the struggle. He also taught that political work should be strengthened among the working people to rally broad sections of the masses in the organizations and lay the firm mass foundation.

The line of founding the Korean Communist Party set forth by Comrade Kim Il Sung was a wise line which he mapped out by analyzing and reviewing the revolutionary situation in those days and the serious lessons of the communist movement in the 1920's and by creatively and most correctly applying and developing the Marxist-Leninist theory concerning the building of the revolutionary party in conformity to the specific conditions of the communist movement in our country.

Comrade Kim Il Sung thus clearly indicated the strategic way of developing the Korean revolution as a whole by closely combining and simultaneously pushing forward the united anti-Japanese national front movement and the preparatory work for the founding of the Korean Communist Party with the anti-Japanese armed struggle as the axis.

Thanks to the *Juche*-motivated revolutionary line for the Korean revolution put forth by Comrade Kim Il Sung, an outstanding Marxist-Leninist and the great Leader of the Korean people, the Communists and the revolutionary people were able to march forward unwaveringly, guided by the great revolutionary ideas originated by him.

Having elucidated the correct line and policy for the conduct of the Korean revolution, Comrade Kim Il Sung organized and mobilized the young Communists and the masses to the practical struggle to put them into effect.

In the summer of 1930, Comrade Kim Il Sung formed the Korean Revolutionary Army with the nuclear members of the Young Communist League and the Anti-Imperialist Youth League in Kuyushu of Itung county.

The Korean Revolutionary Army was a political and paramilitary organization of the Korean Communists formed in preparation for the anti-Japanese armed struggle.

Comrade Kim Il Sung formulated the political and military organizational system of the Korean Revolutionary Army and dispatched its small groups to vast urban and rural areas.

The small groups of the Korean Revolutionary Army explained and inculcated on the broad masses the *Juche*-motivated line of Comrade Kim Il Sung for the Korean revolution, and, under his leadership, energetically conducted political and military activities in preparation for the anti-Japanese armed struggle.

The formation of the Korean Revolutionary Army by Comrade Kim Il Sung was a correct measure of great practical significance in rearing the nuclear pivots of the armed ranks, in giving them political and military training and laying the mass foundations through the rallying of the broad patriotic anti-Japanese forces, that is, in making preparations for a fullscale anti-Japanese armed struggle and in founding the anti-Japanese guerilla army.

While organizing and guiding the activities of the Korean Revolutionary Army, Comrade Kim Il Sung went out personally to farm villages in Changchun, Itung and Huaite counties and other areas to lay the mass foundation of the revolutionary struggle, setting an example in revolutionizing those areas.

Comrade Kim Il Sung set up schools in many villages to give revolutionary education to the rising generation and promoted the national and class awakening of the popular masses through diverse mass political activities—discussion and lecture meetings, political training course, issue of revolutionary publications such as newspaper "Bolshevik" and magazine "Nongu" (Fellow Peasants), the activities of art propaganda troupes, etc.

Heightening the patriotic spirit of the masses and their revolutionary class consciousness in this way, Comrade Kim Il Sung gradually united children, youths, women and peasants in mass anti-Japanese organizations on an extensive scale corresponding to their social standings, thereby building up revolutionary farm villages everywhere.

In August 1930 when the suppression of urban revolutionary organizations by the Japanese imperialists and the reactionary warlords grew more rampant, Comrade Kim Il Sung personally came out in a struggle to defend those organizations in disregard of the risks involved.

Braving the constant dangers threatened to him by the enemy's obstinate shadowing and pursuit, Comrade Kim Il Sung organized and directed the work of the revolutionary organizations in Kirin, Hailung, Chiaoho, Harbin, Tunhua and many other towns and tided over the created difficulties.

Comrade Kim Il Sung who had been directing the work of the urban revolutionary organizations on the spot, again toured the rural areas from one village to another to guide the activities of the Korean Revolutionary Army and to expand and strengthen the revolutionary positions in the rural areas.

He knew neither fatigue nor rest, he worked day and night.

In the daytime he educated and guided the peasants while helping them in their field work, and at night he would issue revolutionary publications or make a long trip to guide the work of the members of small groups of the Korean Revolutionary Army he had sent out to various districts.

Comrade Kim Il Sung, the outstanding Leader of revolution who fought like this with all his devotion, shouldering the heavy burden of the Korean revolution, enjoyed the infinite trust and respect of his comrades and the masses.

From that time on, his comrades and the revolutionary masses called him Comrade Kim Il Sung (previously Comrade Kim Song Ju). At first they called him Comrade Il Sung (Il for One, Sung for Star) or Comrade Han Byol in the sense that they wished him to be the morning star leading the Korean people out of darkness to the dawn of liberation and, later, renamed him Comrade Il Sung (Il for Sun, Sung for Attainment) in the hope that he would become the bright sun of Korea, as so great a leader of the nation like him could not be compared merely to the morning star.

This was a manifestation of the Korean people's unbounded trust in and reverence for Comrade Kim Il Sung, the outstanding Leader of the people and great Leader of the revolution.

Entering 1931, the Japanese imperialists openly revealed their designs for Manchurian invasion and stepped up preparations for it.

Keeping abreast of the fast-changing situation, Comrade Kim Il Sung pushed ahead more actively with the preparatory work for armed struggle.

Early in 1931 Comrade Kim Il Sung planned to organize and unfold an armed struggle in the areas with the basin of the River Tuman-gang, which had favorable conditions both geographically and in the composition of the population, as the centre, and moved the theatre of activity to those areas.

In Tunhua he dispatched members of the Korean Revolutionary Army and of the Young Communist League and the Anti-Imperialist Youth League to different localities to actively promote the preparatory work for armed struggle, and he also personally toured various areas to direct the work.

In September that year, the Japanese imperialists at last invaded Manchuria and intensified their reactionary offensive on a full scale against the Korean people, particularly against the revolutionary forces, to assure the security of their "rear." The Japanese imperialists suppressed the revolutionary advance of the Korean people by force of arms and murdered innocent people in masses everywhere.

To counter the bloody white terrorism of Japanese imperialism by revolutionary armed forces was a pressing question whose solution brooked not a moment's delay.

On the basis of the experiences gained in forming the Korean Revolutionary Army and guiding its activities and of the successes in the preparations for the armed struggle, Comrade Kim Il Sung set forth concrete measures for organizing and unfolding the anti-Japanese armed struggle at the Myongwolgu Conference in November 1931.

At the conference Comrade Kim Il Sung defined guerilla warfare as the basic form of the anti-Japanese armed struggle and clearly pointed out that an anti-Japanese guerilla army should be founded as a standing revolutionary armed force.

He also taught that since the anti-Japanese armed struggle was to be waged in the form of guerilla warfare, the armed struggle could be successful for a long time even in the enemy encirclement on all sides only when the guerilla bases were established for the anti-Japanese guerillas to rely on and the broad mass foundation of the armed struggle laid in and around the bases.

And he set forth the line of strengthening the revolutionary solidarity with the people of the neighbouring country who were suffering from Japanese imperialist aggression and of forming a joint anti-imperialist front with their anti-Japanese armed forces in order to rapidly expand and develop the anti-Japanese armed struggle, isolate the enemy forces to the maximum and deal stunning blows to them.

After the Myongwolgu Conference, Comrade Kim Il Sung exerted all his efforts, first of all, to found an anti-Japanese guerilla army which would become the leading force of the revolutionary movement in Korea.

From the outset the organization of the anti-Japanese guerilla force and the starting of its operations were beset with manifold difficulties.

It was no easy task to organize armed forces and secure weapons under the conditions in which there was no state power nor the foundation of a national army and the whole country was covered with the network of Japanese imperialist oppression setup and the enemy's brutal suppression was rampant.

Comrade Kim Il Sung energetically pushed forward this difficult task with an indomitable revolutionary will and extraordinary revolutionary sweep.

He closely combined the work of founding the anti-Japanese guerilla army with the revolutionary advance of the masses of the people, enlisted fine progressive elements tested in this course as members of the armed force and aroused the broad revolutionary masses to the struggle for securing arms.

Comrade Kim Il Sung taught to the following effect:

...It is no easy task for us to take up arms. The situation obtaining today, however, compels us to take up arms....

The question will not be solved if we merely sit and lament or wail at the sight of the enemy's bestial atrocities.

We must rise and fight in arms. Where should we get arms from? We can buy them if we have money or can make them. But the shortest way is to capture the enemy's weapons. If everyone strains his wits, chooses a place and takes action fearlessly at risk of life, he can get a weapon to arm himself....

Immensely inspired by this teaching, the revolutionary masses, whether men or women, young or old, turned out in the struggle to obtain arms, frustrating the suppressive manoeuvres of the enemy. They wrested weapons from the enemy at the risk of their lives and, at the same time, manufactured weapons by themselves to arm progressive youths.

Difficulties in the work of founding the anti-Japanese guerilla army did not come only from the brutal suppression of the revolutionary organizations and revolutionary masses by the Japanese imperialists. The hostile acts of the anti-Japanese units against the Korean Communists and Korean people also presented a grave obstacle.

The Chinese anti-Japanese units, a nationalist armed force that had risen against the Japanese imperialist invasion of Manchuria at the time, taken in by the false propaganda of the Japanese imperialists against communism and by their attempts at national estrangement, not only regarded the Korean Communists with unconditional hostility but also murdered at random in various places those Korean youths who were coming to join the anti-Japanese armed forces being organized by Comrade Kim Il Sung.

It was the most urgent task to check the hostile acts of the anti-Japanese units against the Korean Communists and revolutionary masses and join hands with them in order to organize the anti-Japanese guerilla army and wage the armed struggle. But in the conditions at that time, it was a difficult job even to make contact with them, which required readiness to sacrifice one's life.

Under these circumstances, Comrade Kim Il Sung negotiated directly with the command of the anti-Japanese units at the risk of his life solely in the interests of revolution, and patiently persuaded them who had been infected with obstinate anti-communist and national chauvinist ideas and perpetrating gross outrages, and thus finally succeeded in unfolding a joint anti-Japanese struggle together with them.

The difficulties in the early stage of the founding of the anti-Japanese guerilla army were thus surmounted.

After overcoming all obstacles lying in his way, Comrade

Kim Il Sung founded on April 25, 1932 the Anti-Japanese Guerilla Army, the first Marxist-Leninist revolutionary armed force of the Korean people, with progressive workers, peasants and patriotic youths, with the members of the Korean Revolutionary Army and of the Young Communist League and the Anti-Imperialist Youth League he had reared over a long period as its nuclear backbone.

Comrade Kim Il Sung said as follows:

"In the darkest period of Japanese imperialist rule the staunch Communists of our country, guided by the Marxist-Leninist theory, organized the Anti-Japanese Guerilla Army, the first contingent of the revolutionary people's armed forces in our country, with the progressive workers and peasants and patriotic youths who set themselves against Japanese imperialism for the national independence and social emancipation of the Korean people."

The Anti-Japanese Guerilla Army was a revolutionary armed force of the working class equipped thoroughly with the idea of *Juche*, the great revolutionary idea of Comrade Kim Il Sung, and fighting for the national independence and social emancipation of the Korean people; it was a people's army maintaining blood ties with the people and fighting with full, single-hearted devotion for the interests of the people.

The Anti-Japanese Guerilla Army was also a revolutionary army of proletarian internationalism that fought for the world revolution, holding high the revolutionary slogan "Workers of the whole world, unite!"

The founding of the Anti-Japanese Guerilla Army by Comrade Kim Il Sung was a great historic event which brought about an epochal turn in the development of the revolutionary movement of the Korean people. It ushered in a new, higher stage of development in the communist movement and the anti-Japanese national-liberation struggle in Korea under the wise leadership of Comrade Kim Il Sung.

The Korean people under the leadership of Comrade Kim Il Sung, peerless patriot, national hero and ever-victorious iron-willed brilliant commander, came out in the sacred struggle for the restoration of the fatherland and for freedom and liberation, with their genuinely revolutionary armed forces for the first time in their history.

As Comrade Kim Il Sung founded the Anti-Japanese Guerilla Army and unfolded the anti-Japanese armed struggle, the communist movement in our country and the anti-Japanese national-liberation struggle of the Korean people entered the most glorious period.

Being the most active and decisive struggle to defeat the Japanese imperialist aggressors who were armed to the teeth and to lead the Korean revolution to victory and, at the same time, the most powerful form of struggle vigorously inspiring and encouraging all other forms of struggles of the masses of the people, the anti-Japanese armed struggle definitely formed the centre of the anti-Japanese national-liberation movement and the communist movement in our country.

In organizing and unfolding the anti-Japanese armed struggle, Comrade Kim Il Sung opened up a broad avenue, indeed, for the vigorous advancement of the Korean revolution as a whole embracing the united anti-Japanese national front movement and the work of founding a Korean Communist Party, which pivoted on the armed struggle.

The anti-Japanese armed struggle, a great struggle which organically combined the task of national liberation with the task of social revolution by correctly and fully reflecting the fundamental interests of the working class and the peasant masses and the national aspirations of our people, inspired the entire Korean people with the hope of national resurrection and confidence in the victory of the revolution and roused them to a nation-wide anti-Japanese resistance struggle.

Being the first armed struggle to be waged for national

and social emancipation in the colonial countries under the banner of Marxism-Leninism, the anti-Japanese armed struggle organized and unfolded by Comrade Kim Il Sung was of great significance in the development of the world revolution as well.

Aimed at dealing a decisive blow to the military-fascistized Japanese imperialists at a time when fascism made its appearance on the international scene and the reactionary offensive of the imperialists was being intensified generally, the anti-Japanese armed struggle exerted a great revolutionary influence on the world people fighting for social progress and national independence.

The anti-Japanese armed struggle organized and waged against the bandit Japanese imperialism that grew strong through aggression and colonial plunder of other countries and possessed millions-strong army of aggression equipped with up-to-date weapons, was an unprecedentedly arduous struggle from the outset.

The Anti-Japanese Guerilla Army had to secure weapons, food and all necessary for the armed struggle by itself through a bloody struggle against the enemy and had to put up a protracted fight, surmounting manifold difficulties and obstacles beyond human imagination.

However, Comrade Kim Il Sung, the brilliant Leader of revolution, mapped out a correct line, strategy and tactics of struggle in each period and each stage of the struggle and, with his excellent leadership, overcame all these difficulties and obstacles and guided the Korean revolutionary movement as a whole centering on the anti-Japanese armed struggle to victory.

Comrade Kim Il Sung worked out intelligent solutions for all problems, always basing himself strictly on the steadfast idea of *Juche* and revolutionary spirit of self-reliance that the Korean revolution should be carried out by the Korean Communists and the Korean people by their own efforts.

Following the founding of the Anti-Japanese Guerilla Army, Comrade Kim Il Sung organized and directed the work of setting up guerilla bases, one of the important strategic questions for guaranteeing the development of the armed struggle and the triumph of the Korean revolution.

He taught that the guerilla base should be a military strategic base for the Anti-Japanese Guerilla Army and, at the same time, an operational base for the Korean revolution to suit the situation at that time and the requirements of the development of the revolution.

The establishment of such bases alone could provide the Anti-Japanese Guerilla Army with bases of military operations and rear bases and enabled it to unremittingly carry on the anti-Japanese armed struggle which assumed a protracted and arduous nature. And only by establishing the bases was it possible to protect the revolutionary forces against the atrocities of indiscriminate slaughter by the Japanese imperialists in those days, and strengthen them, lay the solid mass foundation of the armed struggle, lead various forms of anti-Japanese struggle of the masses along the right path and vigorously inspire and encourage the entire Korean people to the revolutionary struggle.

Comrade Kim Il Sung gave the right orientation also in the work of choosing the forms and locations of the guerilla bases, an important question in the consolidation of the guerilla bases and the development of the armed struggle.

Comrade Kim Il Sung taught that if the guerilla bases were to carry out their role satisfactorily as military strategic bases of the Anti-Japanese Guerilla Army and, at the same time, as operational bases for the Korean revolution, there had to be a correct definition of the forms of bases such as perfect guerilla base and semi-guerilla base corresponding to the ideological and political preparedness of the inhabitants and specific conditions of the base areas. And he stated that a revolutionary government embracing the workers, peasants and all other classes and circles that were against Japanese imperialism, had to be established in the perfect guerilla base assuming the form of a liberated area.

On the basis of a close calculation of the balance of forces between the enemy and our side and of all conditions of the armed struggle, Comrade Kim Il Sung set forth the line of establishing guerilla bases in the areas along the River Tuman-gang bordering on the northern frontier of Korea.

In those days the areas along the River Tuman-gang had favorable conditions for the establishment of guerilla bases.

In those areas more than 80 per cent of the inhabitants were Korean poor peasants and farm hands who had emigrated there after having had enough of the tyrannical oppression and exploitation by the Japanese imperialists, and there was a mass foundation hardened in the protracted anti-Japanese struggle.

And the greater part of these regions was forests extending over steep mountains and deep ravines, which afforded topographical conditions disadvantageous to the enemy for attack and advantageous to the Anti-Japanese Guerilla Army for defence.

The line of establishing guerilla bases laid down by Comrade Kim Il Sung represented the most active and sagacious step designed to vigorously advance the whole Korean revolution with the anti-Japanese armed struggle as the axis by building strong bastions of revolution, placing faith entirely in the strength of the masses of the people and turning all possible conditions to full account in the most adverse situation of the time when the armed struggle had to be waged with neither state support nor any military and economic aid from outside.

The work of setting up guerilla bases in the areas swarming with the heinous Japanese imperialist aggressor troops was attended from the beginning with a fierce fight against the enemy.

In an attempt to obstruct the establishment of guerilla bases, the Japanese imperialists mobilized huge armed forces comprising the army and the police, set fire to the revolutionary rural villages and killed the inhabitants right and left, and made every desperate attempt to sever the ties between the guerillas and the people. With no amount of suppression and vicious manoeuvrings, however, could the enemy break the revolutionary spirit of the anti-Japanese guerillas and the popular masses who rose holding aloft Comrade Kim Il Sung's line of establishing guerilla bases, or put out the raging flames of struggle.

Fighting many battles with the active support of the revolutionary masses, the Anti-Japanese Guerilla Army contained the enemy who frenziedly suppressed the people and, at the same time, went on building guerilla bases. Thus vast liberated areas entirely free from the enemy's ruling system were established in the regions adjacent to the River Tuman-gang in only a few months. In those areas were concentrated people from all walks of life including workers, peasants and progressive intellectuals, who had come out in resistance to Japanese imperialism's fascist suppression.

It was most important to solidly build up the bases into strong bases of revolution politically, economically and militarily after their establishment. But it was by no means an easy job.

Comrade Kim Il Sung reinforced the bases into strong fortresses of the revolution, while organizing and waging a serious struggle to crush the enemy's desperate offensives from without and shatter all the subversive activities of the factionalists and Left opportunists from within.

In the guerilla bases which had now been built a struggle was waged to expand and strengthen them, liquidate the old ruling system and establish a new, revolutionary order.

In the first days of the establishment of the guerilla bases the factionalists and the Left opportunists who knew nothing about the armed struggle insisted upon the building of only perfect guerilla bases in the form of liberated areas, and opposed the building of semi-guerilla bases around them. To make matters worse, they discriminated between the liberated areas and the enemy-controlled areas, labelling them as Red districts and white districts respectively, and regarded the people in the enemy-controlled areas with hostility or kept them away, thus bringing the liberated areas into isolation cut off from the outside world.

Also, the factionalists and Left opportunists who were imbued with flunkeyism and dogmatism, sought to carry out socialist policies right away, insisting on setting up a Soviet form of government in the bases in disregard of the character and immediate tasks of the revolution of our country. This gave rise to a complex situation in the guerilla bases.

Without overcoming such Left deviation the guerilla bases could not be built up into strong bases of the revolution, nor could broad anti-Japanese revolutionary forces be united.

Comrade Kim Il Sung worked energetically to tide over the confusions caused by the Left opportunists.

He scathingly denounced the reckless attempts of the factionalists and Left opportunists who regarded the people in the enemy-controlled areas with hostility and kept them at a distance; he formed underground revolutionary organizations in the vast regions around the liberated areas, rallied and revolutionized the masses of the people and thus set up semi-guerilla bases which came under the ruling system of the enemy in appearance, but, in reality, rendered material and moral support to the Anti-Japanese Guerilla Army.

With the establishment of semi-guerilla bases and the strengthening of political work among the people in the enemy-controlled areas, the Left tendency to separate the people in the liberated areas from the people in the enemy-controlled districts and pit them against each other was overcome and the mass foundation of the armed struggle was widened further.

Rigorously opposing and rejecting the dogmatic, Left opportunist attempts of the factionalists and flunkeys to imitate others blindly without an independent stand and establish a Soviet power because others did so, Comrade Kim Il Sung elucidated the original line on the people's revolutionary government which was best suited to the anti-imperialist, anti-feudal democratic character of the Korean revolution and the immediate task of national liberation.

Comrade Kim Il Sung said to the following effect:

...**The government we are going to set up will neither be run by any king, nor will serve the interests of landlords, capitalists or any individuals, but will be the government of our people that will work for the rights and happiness of the people and for freedom and independence, and this government will give the peasants land, grant the women equal rights with men and enable everyone to learn, work and live well....**

Comrade Kim Il Sung taught that at the stage of the revolution where the task of opposing imperialism and liberating the nation came to the fore as the immediate task, it coincided with the objective demands of the development of the Korean revolution to establish a people's revolutionary government based on the worker-peasant alliance led by the working class and relying on a united front of broad anti-Japanese forces. He also elucidated that this people's revolutionary government should set it as its immediate task to overthrow the colonial rule of Japanese imperialism and achieve national liberation, and should pursue democratic policies correctly expressing the interests of not only the workers and peasants but also all the other social sections that were against imperialism and feudalism.

The people's revolutionary government, as a power organ resting on a united front embracing all the anti-imperialist, anti-feudal sections of the population which was based on the worker-peasant alliance under the leadership of the Communists, was the most revolutionary, popular form of power capable of protecting the interests of the working people thoroughly and winning social emancipation for the broad masses of the people including the workers and peasants.

The line of people's revolutionary government set forth by Comrade Kim Il Sung proved a fatal blow to the factionalists and Left opportunists, and presented a beacon and programmatic guide for the genuine Communists and the masses of the people, that illumined their road of struggle ahead more brightly.

Thanks to the active struggle of the popular masses who, upholding the distinguished leadership of Comrade Kim Il Sung and his correct line on the people's revolutionary government, rose in the implementation of the line, the Left deviation of insisting on the establishment of a Soviet type of government was overcome thoroughly and the people's revolutionary government was set up in the perfect guerilla bases.

Under the leadership of Comrade Kim Il Sung, the people's revolutionary government successfully carried out all democratic reforms—it confiscated land from the Japanese imperialists and pro-Japanese landlords and distributed it to the peasants without compensation, proclaimed the eight-hour day and the minimum wage system, abolished exacting taxes and levies, enforced the law on the equality of the sexes and the compulsory free education system. Thus there were established new socio-economic relations free from exploitation and oppression and a revolutionary order in the perfect guerilla bases.

The line of people's revolutionary government which was set forth by Comrade Kim Il Sung and carried into effect brilliantly in the guerilla bases under his leadership, a line most correctly expressing the objective demands of the development of the Korean revolution and the will of our people, served as a revolutionary banner which closely rallied the broad masses to strengthen the revolutionary forces and aroused the masses of the people vigorously to the anti-Japanese struggle.

And the line on the people's revolutionary government, which developed and enriched anew the Marxist-Leninist theory on the state and the revolution to suit the changed historical conditions, exerted a great revolutionary influence on the oppressed and exploited peoples of the world fighting for sovereignty and for national independence and social emancipation.

With the implementation of the line of people's revolutionary government under the leadership of Comrade Kim Il Sung, the guerilla bases turned into powerful bases of the revolution.

The people in the bases who came to lead a new, free life for the first time under the people's government led by Comrade Kim Il Sung, did farming to secure provisions, and set up armories and clothing factories to manufacture and supply weapons and various war supplies needed in the armed struggle, bravely overcoming all trials and adversities resulting from the enemy's repeated "punitive expeditions" and economic blockade.

Comrade Kim Il Sung also formed organizations of the Communist Party and the Young Communist League and various mass organizations in the guerilla bases, and, through these organizations, educated and trained the people in the bases. Thus, the people in the bases were reared into ardent revolutionaries and Communists. In the guerilla bases many revolutionary publications including newspapers and pamphlets were put out for the ideological, political and cultural education of the masses of the people. These publications were widely distributed not only in the guerilla bases but also in the areas in enemy hands and different parts of the homeland to awaken the people and organize and mobilize them to the anti-Japanese struggle.

Indeed, the guerilla bases set up and consolidated by Comrade Kim Il Sung played a great role as mighty rear bases giving support, material and manpower, to the Anti-Japanese Guerilla Army and as revolutionary bases instilling in the masses of the people a firm conviction of victory in the revolution, inspiring and encouraging them to the anti-Japanese struggle.

The broad sections of patriotic people in our country including workers and peasants had an immense yearning for the revolutionary government and new system in the guerilla bases, defended them with their whole hearts and waged a vigorous indefatigable anti-Japanese struggle, drawing great strength from their achievements.

While strengthening the guerilla bases into strong fortresses of the revolution, Comrade Kim Il Sung waged an energetic struggle to promote the organizational and ideological preparations for the founding of a Marxist-Leninist Party, firmly build up the main force of the revolution, develop the united anti-Japanese national front movement and form a joint anti-imperialist front.

In the course of the anti-Japanese armed struggle Comrade Kim Il Sung adhered with all consistency to the line of steadily expanding the revolutionary ranks by training a new generation of Communists to firmly reinforce the organizational backbone for the founding of a Marxist-Leninist Party and, at the same time, winning the broad masses of the people over to the side of revolution.

Comrade Kim Il Sung taught in the following vein:

...The most important thing in the preparations for the foundation of the Party is to foster and expand the ranks of Communists through the anti-Japanese armed struggle. The Communists tried and tested in the practical struggle will al-

ways and everywhere play the nuclear role in the conduct of our revolution. If we form the core with them and rally the revolutionary masses closely around it, we can found a Marxist-Leninist Party and carry out the complex revolutionary tasks in hand correctly in whatever difficulties.

So, in the course of the anti-Japanese armed struggle we should constantly expand and strengthen our armed ranks and foster and train Communists in battles against the enemy....

To build up a strong organizational backbone for the foundation of the Party, Comrade Kim Il Sung formed organizations of the Communist Party and the Young Communist League in the Anti-Japanese Guerilla Army, the leading force of the Korean revolution, and energetically carried on day-to-day political work among the guerillas, thereby rearing them into indomitable Communists, competent political workers armed thoroughly with the revolutionary idea of *Juche*.

While strengthening his leadership of the Communist Party and Young Communist League organizations in the guerilla bases, Comrade Kim Il Sung also sent anti-Japanese guerillas and many political workers to the areas in enemy hands to organize and expand underground revolutionary organizations and bring up progressive workers and peasants into Communists.

Along with this, he organized and carried on a resolute struggle against factionalism, flunkeyism, and Right and Left opportunism within the ranks of the anti-Japanese armed struggle, thereby achieving the organizational and ideological unity of the Communists.

Comrade Kim Il Sung closely combined the work of making organizational and ideological preparations for the foundation of the Party with the struggle for firmly building up the internal revolutionary forces and forming a united anti-Japanese national front.

Comrade Kim Il Sung solidly built up the main force of

the revolution with the Communists reared in the revolutionary practice as its leading force and on the basis of consolidation of the alliance of the working class and the peasantry, organized and expanded various types of anti-Japanese mass organizations and united broad anti-Japanese forces of all social strata through the medium of those organizations.

Comrade Kim Il Sung devoted his energies to overcoming Right and Left deviations expressed in the work with the masses and to establishing the revolutionary work method and popular style of work in order to rally the revolutionary forces.

In his address delivered in March 1933 to political workers operating among youth, Comrade Kim Il Sung criticized the machinations of the factionalists—their Left tendency towards neglecting political work among the workers, peasants and youths and hindering the expansion of the revolutionary organizations under the pretext of "keeping secrecy" and their Right deviation expressed in their unprincipled attempt to throw open the doors of the revolutionary organizations—and indicated concrete ways for the rapid expansion and strengthening of the revolutionary organizations and the improvement of work with the masses.

He taught that political workers operating among youth should know clearly that they were faithful servants of the people and go deep among the masses of the people to share sweets and bitters with them, have a correct understanding of the movements and demands of the masses of various social sections, awaken them by the method of explanation and persuasion, thereby organizing and enlisting them in the revolutionary struggle.

Comrade Kim Il Sung also taught that the reserve forces of the revolution should be solidly built up for victory in the arduous and protracted anti-Japanese armed struggle.

Comrade Kim Il Sung said to the following effect:

...Every member of the Young Communist League should always remember that an army which has no reserve forces is bound to suffer a reverse. At the present stage the anti-Japanese national-liberation struggle calls for an armed struggle, and the anti-Japanese armed struggle calls for the direct participation of the broad masses of the youth. The political workers operating among youth, therefore, should always bear in mind that victory can be won only when broad sections of the youth are aroused in an organized way to continually strengthen the revolutionary forces and reserve forces....

This teaching of Comrade Kim Il Sung served as an infallible guide for the Communists in the struggle for expanding and strengthening the revolutionary forces.

Under the wise leadership of Comrade Kim Il Sung, the Right and Left deviations and old bureaucratic method of work manifested in the work with the masses were remedied and new revolutionary work method and popular style of work took shape and, as a result, the broader masses were united in the revolutionary ranks.

Comrade Kim Il Sung took the lead in the struggle to cement the revolutionary solidarity with the people of the neighbouring country and, particularly, to materialize a joint anti-imperialist front with the armed anti-Japanese forces on a full scale in the struggle against the common enemy, Japanese imperialism.

It acquired a very great significance to exert revolutionary influence actively on the anti-Japanese units and draw them into the common struggle against imperialism at that time when the combat power of the Anti-Japanese Guerilla Army grew and strengthened and the internal forces of revolution were built up firmly.

The anti-Japanese units that had been acting in concert with the Anti-Japanese Guerilla Army in the common struggle against Japanese imperialism as a result of the active efforts of Comrade Kim Il Sung wandered into a wrong path again owing to the vicious machinations of Japanese imperialism for national estrangement and the reckless Leftist acts on the part of the factionalists in those days.

The anti-Japanese units, frightened by the enemy's ever-intensified military and political offensives, wavered extremely in the struggle and, taken in by Japanese imperialism's national estrangement policy and pernicious propaganda, failed to distinguish between the just struggle of the Korean Communists and the reckless moves of the factionalists and the Left opportunists. The upper crust of the anti-Japanese units were hostile to Koreans, labelling them as "agents of Japanese imperialism" and "people seeking to communize Manchuria," and went so far as to murder the guerillas.

In this situation, it was the most urgent problem for the development of the anti-Japanese armed struggle to awaken the anti-Japanese units and form a joint front with them. But it was indeed a difficult and complicated problem, which nobody could readily solve.

Only Comrade Kim Il Sung, a great Marxist-Leninist and outstanding strategist, could indicate the correct solution and successfully undo the problem.

Comrade Kim Il Sung adhered to the strategic line of forming a joint front with the anti-Japanese units and consolidating and developing it even when there arose any complicated situation in the relations between the Anti-Japanese Guerilla Army and those units, and proceeded from partial coalition to general coalition, from a lower form of common struggle to a higher form. And he overcame the Right and Left deviations in the work with the anti-Japanese units which were expressed in separating the unity with their rank and file from the unity with their upper crust and absolutizing or laying one-sided stress on one of these unities, and set forth and skilfully applied the tactical principle of properly combining the unity with the upper crust and the unity with the rank and file masses of the anti-Japanese units with the main stress on the latter, and of linking struggle with unity by clearly distinguishing the dual character of their upper crust.

In June 1933, Comrade Kim Il Sung at his own risk held negotiations boldly with the command of the anti-Japanese units to form a joint front.

The resolute stand and stubborn fighting spirit of Comrade Kim Il Sung against the Japanese imperialists and the great successes made in the armed struggle by the Anti-Japanese Guerilla Army under his leadership, his lofty revolutionary spirit and great capacity for tolerance, sound logic and convincing explanation, compelled even the so unbendingly antagonistic upper crust of the anti-Japanese units to agree to form a joint anti-imperialist front.

The relations with the anti-Japanese units that were disturbed due to the tricks of Japanese imperialists for national estrangement and to the reckless, ultra-Leftist acts of the factionalists, were improved successfully thanks to the devoted efforts and strenuous struggle of Comrade Kim Il Sung and thus the enemy's crafty tricks were frustrated and the revolutionary situation took a turn for the better.

The successful formation of a joint front with the anti-Japanese units represented a brilliant victory for the line of Comrade Kim Il Sung on the joint anti-imperialist front and furnished another example in surmounting obstacles in the way of the anti-Japanese armed struggle.

In September 1933, Comrade Kim Il Sung victoriously conducted a large-scale battle on the Tungning county seat in concert with the anti-Japanese units and thus widely demonstrated the correctness and vitality of the line of joint anti-imperialist front, inspired and encouraged the anti-Japanese units which were very much wavering in the struggle against the Japanese imperialists, and consolidated and developed the joint front with them.

Comrade Kim Il Sung dispatched many political workers to the anti-Japanese units in different areas to induce the class awakening of their rank and file, and, at the same time, organized and conducted numerous large and small triumphant operations in alliance with the anti-Japanese units, thereby boosting their confidence in victory and constantly giving them revolutionary education and training, which led a great many anti-Japanese units to join the anti-Japanese allied forces.

The formation of the joint anti-imperialist front by Comrade Kim Il Sung and its strengthening and development proved a heavy political and military blow to the Japanese imperialist aggressors, and also furnished a trail-blazing example in the international anti-fascist popular front movement.

Comrade Kim Il Sung actively developed the joint anti-imperialist front to deal heavy blows to the Japanese imperialist aggressors and, at the same time, extensively organized and conducted the work of disintegrating the enemy from within by diverse methods by taking advantage of the national and class contradictions within the enemy forces. Thus, thanks to the skilful operations of the Anti-Japanese Guerilla Army for disintegrating the enemy forces, numerous soldiers of the puppet Manchurian army raised mutinies in succession and came over to the Anti-Japanese Guerilla Army, and many units of the puppet Manchurian army refused to fight the Anti-Japanese Guerilla Army.

Comrade Kim Il Sung, fortifying the guerilla bases rock-firm, defended them stoutly against the enemy's invasion, and energetically expanded and developed the anti-Japanese armed struggle by relying on the guerilla bases.

Flurried by the consolidation of the guerilla bases, the operational base of the Korean revolution, and by their growing influence, the Japanese imperialists took frantic military and political offensives, calling the guerilla bases a "cancer of peace in the East."

Having failed in their repeated military attacks on the guerilla bases, the Japanese imperialists set up "concentration hamlets" in the districts under their control, herded the inhabitants into them by force and introduced a mediaeval "collective watch system" in their efforts to cut the ties between the guerillas and the people and carried on vile sabotage manoeuvres to subvert the guerilla bases from within by mobilizing their espionage and hireling organizations and various propaganda means. While carrying on such political and economic blockade and subversive activities against the guerilla bases, the Japanese imperialists mobilized huge forces and resorted to the "scorched earth tactics" to burn all, kill all and loot all in the guerilla bases and to the "siege operations" to encircle and attack them for a long time.

But this frenzied general offensive of the enemy, too, was frustrated at every step by the correct measures and superb tactics adopted by Comrade Kim Il Sung and his wise leadership.

Already in the early days of the establishment of the guerilla bases, Comrade Kim Il Sung foresaw this offensive of the enemy and steadily strengthened the combat capacity of the Anti-Japanese Guerilla Army; at the same time, he set forth the original line of arming the entire people and fortifying the bases and established an all-people defence system.

The all-people defence system established by Comrade Kim Il Sung was a most powerful system of defence making it fully possible to repel the armed attack of any enemy with one's own strength.

Armed with the great revolutionary ideas of Comrade Kim Il Sung, the anti-Japanese guerillas and the people in the bases, who rose united like one man in defence of the bases under this mighty defence system established by him, could heroically beat back, even with meagre arms, the huge attacking forces of the enemy outnumbering them scores of times, sometimes more than hundreds of times, and defend the guerilla bases to the last.

In the early days when the guerilla army was organized and the struggle started, there was neither ready-made tactics of guerilla warfare nor military manual on guerilla activities.

It was simply because Comrade Kim Il Sung worked out new, brilliant strategy and tactics of guerilla warfare and skilfully applied them in the course of practical struggle that the Anti-Japanese Guerilla Army always secured definite ideological and tactical superiority over the enemy and could hold the initiative and win brilliant victories in the defensive battles for the guerilla bases and all other battles.

Regarding it as the basic principle of guerilla warfare to wipe out as many enemies as possible while preserving the guerilla forces, Comrade Kim Il Sung worked out and skilfully applied in actual battle the superb tactics that when the enemy makes a concentrated attack, the guerillas disperse and attack the enemy everywhere from behind to wipe him out, and when the enemy is dispersed, the guerillas attack and annihilate him with concentrated force.

Comrade Kim Il Sung resolutely rejected the reckless argument of military adventurists who insisted on only direct confrontation with the enemy overwhelmingly superior both in number and armament in defending the guerilla bases from the tenacious "siege operations" of the enemy, laid down the superb tactical line of combining active defensive battles with mobile operations to harass the enemy's rear, and dispersion with concentration, and personally set the examples in the practical struggle and had them generalized in all guerilla units. Thus, he administered telling blows to the enemy and could heroically safeguard the vast guerilla bases by thwarting the enemy's large-scale winter offensive against the guerilla bases in 1933-1934 and his "siege operations" that continued subsequently.

Recalling those days Comrade Kim Il Sung said to the following effect:

...Because we used this tactics, we could defend the guerilla bases for 4-5 years despite the enemy's desperate offensives. At that time the Japs only hung about the highways around the towns, and could not go out to the countryside freely. Had we any good arms at that time? Only the guerillas had rifles and matchlocks and other people spears and swords, and some possessed hunting guns at best. Even with such arms, we all armed ourselves, men and women, and fought valiantly according to correct guerilla tactics and thus could maintain the guerilla bases for 4-5 years....

Comrade Kim Il Sung educated the guerillas and the people to an indomitable revolutionary spirit, to firm faith in victory and revolutionary optimism.

He always went down to the companies and platoons where he lived together with the men and personally gave guidance to their political life. And he often organized short military and political training courses to heighten their level of political and military knowledge and practical ability. Always staying among the men and the masses, Comrade Kim Il Sung educated them in an unbending revolutionary idea.

Regarding the joys and sufferings of the people as his own, Comrade Kim Il Sung showed deep concern and solicitude for the life of the people in the bases even in the days when fierce battles were ceaselessly fought to beat back the enemy.

He proceeded almost every day to district and village government offices to get himself acquainted with their work and help them solve knotty problems, and set up schools and educated those children who were living in the guerilla bases, especially those children who came to the guerilla bases after their parents had been killed by the enemy. He looked after all aspects of the life of the people in the bases with paternal care, even seeing to the work of getting clothes and beddings for the children and supplying medicaments to the old and infirm and the sick.

When the people in the bases suffered from hard life owing to the protracted encirclement and attack by the enemy, Comrade Kim Il Sung, while organizing and commanding defensive battles for the bases, personally went out to the enemy-controlled areas in defiance of danger and attacked the enemy's convoys and logistical depots to capture large quantities of vital goods such as provisions, clothes and footwear, which he divided among the people.

Upholding the teachings of Comrade Kim Il Sung, the guerillas and the people in the bases who enjoyed such a profound love and care of the Leader, pounded on the enemy incessantly with redoubled courage even in the midst of manifold difficulties and defended the guerilla bases—the revolutionary gains won at the cost of blood—to the last.

This shining victory which was won in safeguarding the guerilla bases by repelling the enemy who made desperate attacks with huge forces equipped with the latest weapons, was the outcome of the distinguished leadership and ever-victorious brilliant strategy and tactics of Comrade Kim Il Sung, and was the fruit of the mass heroism displayed by the guerillas and the people of the bases who, educated by him and trusting and revering him boundlessly, fought in monolithic unity around the Leader.

The heroic struggle of the anti-Japanese guerillas and the people in the guerilla bases who defended the bases at the cost of their lives enduring the rigorous ordeals for such a long period, is an immortal heroic epic inscribed by the Korean people in their glorious revolutionary history under the leadership of Comrade Kim Il Sung.

In March 1934, Comrade Kim Il Sung organized the Korean People's Revolutionary Army by reforming the organizational system of the Anti-Japanese Guerilla Army in order to further strengthen and develop the anti-Japanese armed struggle.

By conducting numerous battles including Lotzekou battle and other large-scale attacks on towns, ambushes and assaults in command of the People's Revolutionary Army units which had grown and gained in strength, Comrade Kim Il Sung dealt serious blows to the enemy in succession. In the meantime, he strengthened political work among the people in the areas in enemy hands with a view to mobilizing broad segments of the people to the anti-Japanese struggle. In particular, he dispatched many People's Revolutionary Army details and political workers into the homeland to step up the anti-Japanese struggle of the people at home.

The details and political workers sent into the homeland carried out daring combat activities in the northern border areas including Musan, Yuson, Onsong and Kyongwon counties, thus demonstrating the power of the armed struggle. In the meantime, they set up secret camps in the northern parts of Korea and, operating from those camps as their bases, extended the sphere of their activities to the industrial centres, ports, mining districts and rural areas, organized and conducted brisk political work among the vast masses of the people, thus arousing them to the anti-Japanese struggle.

With the growth of the influence of the anti-Japanese armed struggle and the activities of the political workers, the anti-Japanese struggle of the masses of the people including strike struggles of the workers and the tenancy disputes of the peasants took place vehemently in all parts of the country.

In the winter of 1934 Comrade Kim Il Sung, personally leading some units of the People's Revolutionary Army, advanced far up to northern Manchuria to expand the influence of the armed struggle.

The great successes in consolidating the guerilla bases, expanding and developing the anti-Japanese armed struggle and increasing and strengthening the revolutionary forces, were attained in the course of the struggle against the "Minsaengdan," a hireling organization manufactured by the Japanese imperialists and on the other hand, in the course of the serious struggle to smash the subversive manoeuvrings of the great-power chauvinists and factionalists who abused the anti-"Minsaengdan" struggle and to carry out the line of *Juche* with all consistency in the Korean revolution.

The Japanese imperialists who had come to the realization that they could not subdue the fierce flames of the anti-Japanese armed struggle by only armed attacks and blockade policy against the bases, slipped their agents affiliated to the "Minsaengdan," a counter-revolutionary spy organization they had rigged up, into the guerilla bases in an attempt to disorganize the revolutionary ranks from within.

The Japanese imperialist rogues used the "Minsaengdan" in their manoeuvres to make mischief between the Koreans and the Chinese and pit Koreans against Koreans to disorganize the revolutionary forces from within, but their manoeuvres were frustrated in the incipient stage by the struggle of the awakened people in the bases.

But the anti-"Minsaengdan" struggle was conducted in an ultra-Leftist way and entailed grave consequences owing to the reckless Left opportunist moves of the great-power chauvinists and factionalists.

The great-power chauvinists, factionalists and flunkeys who took no account of the interests of the revolution and were blinded by a thirst for power and high positions, conducted the anti-"Minsaengdan" struggle in an ultra-Leftist way, taken in by the crafty estrangement policy of the Japanese imperialists, and thereby hindered the just struggle of the Korean Communists for national liberation and caused a big crack in the unity and cohesion of the revolutionary ranks. Particularly while Comrade Kim Il Sung was away on an expedition to northern Manchuria, the great-power chauvinists, and the factionalists fawning upon and kowtowing to them, took advantage of it and openly perpetrated the villainous acts of wrecking the revolutionary ranks by conducting the anti-"Minsaengdan" struggle in a more ultra-Leftist way.

Those political ignoramuses killed Korean Communists and revolutionary people or expelled them from the revolutionary ranks, pinning to them the label of "Minsaengdan" at random. In particular, the great-power chauvinists branded those who only mentioned the Korean revolution as "Minsaengdan elements," as "national egoists" and persecuted them, identifying the revolutionary slogans of the Korean people for national liberation with the reactionary slogan of "national autonomy" put up by the "Minsaengdan." This gave rise to an ugly situation in which comrades could not trust each other, people in the bases became dispirited and uneasiness grew every day.

The Korean revolution was faced with a really serious crisis.

No one dared to come out in the struggle for saving the situation in the dreadful atmosphere in which dire persecution would ensue if anyone should have merely showed signs of his sympathy with a comrade who was falsely accused of being a member of the "Minsaengdan."

The people in the bases impatiently waited for Comrade Kim Il Sung to return from the expedition at an early date.

This grave situation could be overcome only by Comrade

Kim Il Sung who possessed an unfailing fidelity to revolutionary principle, a lofty spirit of always dedicating his all to the struggle for the interests of the revolution and an indefatigable will and stubborn revolutionary mettle.

In the spring of 1935, soon after his return from the northern Manchurian expedition, Comrade Kim Il Sung convened the Tahongwae and Yoyonggu Conferences and waged a daring struggle to decidedly smash the manoeuvres of the great-power chauvinists and factionalists and to set right the anti-"Minsaengdan" struggle.

Comrade Kim Il Sung scathingly exposed and denounced the wrong views of the great-power chauvinists who disapproved of the national revolutionary duties, identifying the revolutionary slogans of the Korean people for national liberation with the reactionary "Minsaengdan" slogans and opposing the national duties of the Korean Communists to their international duties, and rightfully clarified the line of *Juche* and independent stand on the Korean revolution.

Comrade Kim Il Sung made it clear that it was an inviolable, legitimate right and lofty revolutionary duty of the Korean people that the Korean Communists and the Korean people assumed the responsibility for the revolution of their country and struggled for the Korean revolution. He also elucidated the fact that it was not an act of national egoism but, on the contrary, conformed to the principle of proletarian internationalism and contributed to the development of the international revolutionary movement that the Communists of each country should successfully carry out the revolution of their country.

Comrade Kim Il Sung sharply castigated the intolerable criminal acts of the Left chauvinists and the factionalists who, duped by the cunning policy of the Japanese imperialists for national estrangement, confounded friend with foe and were disrupting the revolutionary ranks, and put up a tenacious

Comrade Kim Il Sung, Commander of the Korean People's Revolutionary Army

struggle in defence of the internal revolutionary forces and the unity and cohesion of the revolutionary ranks.

Comrade Kim Il Sung taught that a revolutionary comrade should be duly judged mainly by his practical struggle, not by any preconception or prejudices, and that comrades should always be trusted and the unity and cohesion of the revolutionary ranks firmly safeguarded. He then taught that an end should be put to such practices as taking a superficial view of the masses and forming a hasty judgment on their doings, and they should always be given careful and scientific consideration, and that, with an eye to the fundamental interests of the revolution, the broad anti-imperialist revolutionary forces should be united and mobilized all-out to wiping out Japanese imperialism, the main enemy.

He also taught that since the "Minsaengdan" was an organization of spies and running dogs of the Japanese imperialists, it was necessary to fight against it, but this struggle should be waged in all cases to foil the crafty tricks of the enemy, further strengthen the unity and cohesion of the revolutionary ranks, destroy the prime movers, embrace, educate and remould the unconscious followers so as to win greater masses over to the side of revolution.

Owing to the fidelity of Comrade Kim Il Sung to revolutionary principle, his correct teachings based on a scientific analysis and his stubborn and resolute struggle, the great-power chauvinists and the factionalists suffered a decisive blow and became crestfallen and, finally, the anti-"Minsaengdan" struggle which had been carried on in an ultra-Leftist way was put on the right path.

In accordance with the wise line set forth by Comrade Kim Il Sung, the consequences of the Left deviation in the anti-"Minsaengdan" struggle were liquidated. Especially, his profound trust in the revolutionary comrades and great tolerance saved many persons who had been falsely stigmatized as members of the "Minsaengdan" and expelled from the revolutionary ranks and subjected to all sorts of maltreatment and persecution

As a result, they fought valiantly in the whole course of the anti-Japanese armed struggle as faithful revolutionary soldiers of Comrade Kim Il Sung, giving full play to their indomitable revolutionary spirit.

The grave crisis of the Korean revolution caused by the great-power chauvinists and the factionalists was thus overcome thanks to the principled and staunch struggle of Comrade Kim Il Sung, the great Leader of revolution, and the Korean revolution was able to continue to advance dynamically along the great revolutionary line of *Juche* originated by him.

Through the struggle for overcoming the Left deviation in the anti-"Minsaengdan" struggle, the manoeuvres of the great-power chauvinists and factionalists who had hindered the implementation of the revolutionary line of *Juche* advanced by Comrade Kim Il Sung were completely shattered and the Left adventurism, dogmatism, flunkeyism and factionalism implanted and encouraged by them were surmounted. As a result, the unity and cohesion of the revolutionary ranks were achieved and the internal revolutionary forces of the Korean people could be built up more solidly.

All those who had suffered from the hard and bitter trials of the anti-"Minsaengdan" struggle trusted and looked up ever more heartily to Comrade Kim Il Sung, the great Leader and outstanding Leader of the Korean revolution, and marched forward vigorously along the road indicated by him in monolithic unity around him.

After the Yoyonggu Conference, Comrade Kim Il Sung, in conformity to the new situation created and to the requirements of the development of the armed struggle, dissolved the fixed guerilla base-liberated areas for further advance and sent out the units of the People's Revolutionary Army to vast areas of Korea and northern and southern Manchuria to switch over to an active offensive against the Japanese imperialists.

In the summer of 1935 Comrade Kim Il Sung advanced to northern Manchuria personally in command of the main force of the Korean People's Revolutionary Army and administered severe blows to the enemy repeatedly by conducting large-scale mobile operations over vast areas around Ningan and Emu districts till January 1936, thus widely demonstrating the great fighting power of the Korean People's Revolutionary Army. Besides, he dispatched excellent commanders and guerillas to the People's Revolutionary Army units in northern Manchuria to firmly build them up politically and militarily, and inspired the masses of the people with confidence in victory, thus making the flames of revolution rage over vast areas.

The course of struggle in the period up to early 1936 after Comrade Kim Il Sung founded the Anti-Japanese Guerilla Army and started the anti-Japanese armed struggle was, externally, a course of a bloody struggle to repulse the frenzied punitive offensives of Japanese imperialism, the formidable enemy, and expand and develop the armed struggle and, internally, was a path of an arduous struggle to shatter all sorts of harmful manoeuvres of the Left opportunists, factionalists and great-power chauvinists within the revolutionary ranks and to establish *Juche* in the Korean revolution, expand the revolutionary ranks and achieve their unity and cohesion.

The Korean revolution rode out all the difficulties and advanced vigorously thanks to the wise leadership and brilliant strategy and tactics of Comrade Kim Il Sung.

In the course of this struggle, the anti-Japanese guerillas and revolutionary masses were equipped more closely with the unitary ideology to acquire the revolutionary trait of arming themselves with the revolutionary ideas of Comrade Kim Il Sung and unconditionally carrying out the lines and policies set forth by him.

All these shining achievements and valuable experiences obtained under the leadership of Comrade Kim Il Sung in the first half of the 1930's became solid assets in leading to a great upsurge the whole revolutionary movement of Korea centering on the anti-Japanese armed struggle.

3

In the latter half of the 1930's Comrade Kim Il Sung set forth a new strategic and tactical line to bring about a great upswing in the general revolutionary movement of Korea centering on the anti-Japanese armed struggle.

In February 1936 Comrade Kim Il Sung convened the Namhodu Conference and put forward a new strategic and tactical line, and further concretized it at the Tonggang Conference in May the same year.

In the mid-1930's the Japanese imperialists busied themselves with expansion of the aggressive war on the continent and further intensified their fascist suppression and economic plunder of the Korean people, while trying frantically to stamp out everything of the Korean people that was national. This led to further aggravation of the national contradictions between the Korean people and the Japanese imperialists and inflamed the anti-Japanese spirit of the Korean people ever higher.

Having made a scientific analysis of the situation, Comrade Kim Il Sung advanced the line of forming a permanent organization of the united anti-Japanese national front embracing all the patriotic forces to expand and develop the united anti-Japanese national front movement rapidly on a nation-wide scale, and of stepping up more vigorously the struggle for founding a Korean Communist Party.

He also elucidated the line of advancing the Korean People's Revolutionary Army to the northern border areas of our country to administer heavier blows to the enemy and setting up bases of a new type around Mt. Paekdu-san and, more, extending the armed struggle deep into the homeland so as to further encourage and inspire the Korean people in their anti-Japanese struggle and strengthen the guidance of the Korean revolution as a whole.

This line advanced by Comrade Kim Il Sung was a sagacious line which he had elaborated on the basis of the combat achievements and valuable experiences gained in the early period of his revolutionary activities and in the subsequent few years of the anti-Japanese armed struggle; it most correctly reflected the objective requirements of the development of the revolution in keeping with the changing situation at home and abroad.

This was the most correct line based on the unshakable position of *Juche* that the Korean people should solve all problems arising in the carrying out of the Korean revolution on their own responsibility and in conformity to the actual conditions of their country, relying on their own strength.

This line marked a great turning-point in the development of the revolutionary movement in our country.

The formulation of the line made it possible to establish *Juche* more thoroughly in the Korean revolution, overcome great-power chauvinism, flunkeyism and dogmatism and bring about a new, great upsurge in the Korean revolution.

Upholding the great line set forth by him and his sagacious leadership and taking a boundless pride in the revolution and firmly convinced of its victory, the Korean Communists rose in high spirits in the struggle for carrying through this line.

Comrade Kim Il Sung worked out a detailed plan and personally took the lead in the struggle for the execution of this great line.

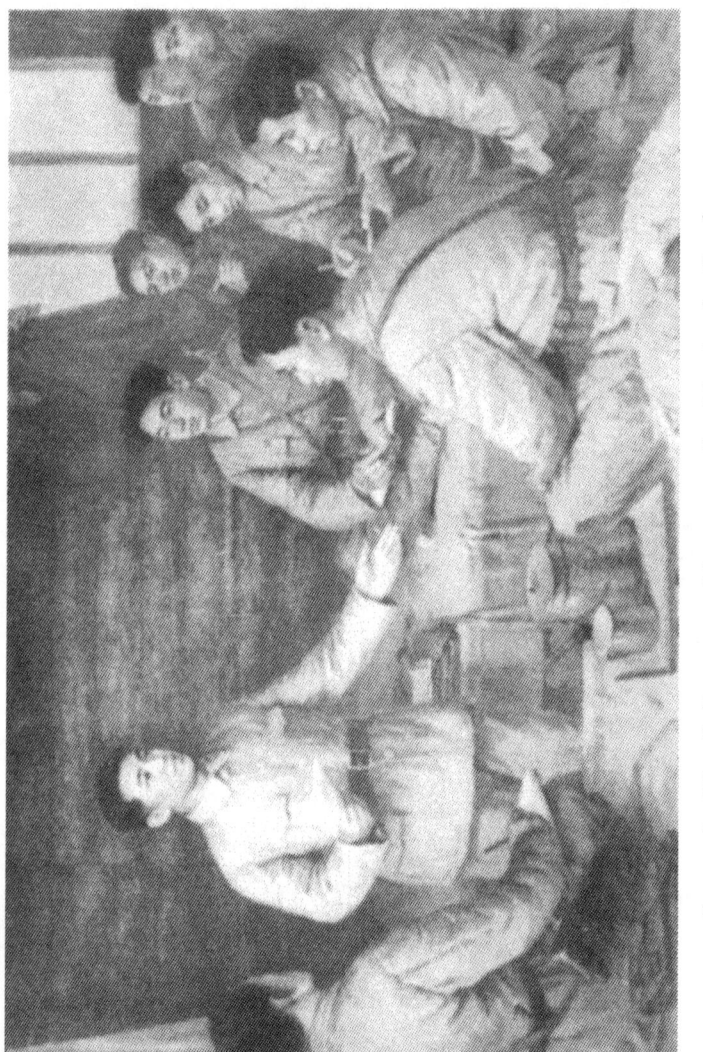

Comrade Kim Il Sung presides over the Namhodu Conference

On May 5, 1936, Comrade Kim Il Sung founded the Association for the Restoration of the Fatherland (ARF), the first organization of the united anti-Japanese national front in our country, on the basis of long preparations and the experiences gained over many years.

Comrade Kim Il Sung was elected Chairman of the Association for the Restoration of the Fatherland.

The ARF was a permanent organization of the united anti-Japanese national front with its unique system and form of organization and, at the same time, a revolutionary organization with the Communists as its core under the personal leadership of Comrade Kim Il Sung.

The foundation of the ARF was a precious fruit of the great plan elaborated by Comrade Kim Il Sung over a long period for the purpose of crushing Japanese imperialism and restoring the fatherland by uniting all the patriotic forces and of the sanguinary struggle for its realization; it was an event marking a turn in the development of the anti-Japanese national-liberation struggle of our people. With the foundation of the ARF the long-cherished desire of the Korean people to achieve the unity of the entire nation in the struggle against foreign imperialist aggressors was splendidly realized and the united anti-Japanese national front movement in our country entered upon a new stage of development.

Founding the Association for the Restoration of the Fatherland, Comrade Kim Il Sung made public the Ten-Point Programme, the Inaugural Declaration and the Rules of the ARF, which were personally worked out by him.

In the Inaugural Declaration of the ARF Comrade Kim Il Sung laid bare and denounced scathingly the exploitation, plunder and brutal suppression by Japanese imperialism, and appealed: All of the 23 million people, irrespective of the distinctions in their classes, sexes, positions, age, religious beliefs, etc., should unite as one and join the anti-Japanese fatherland restoration front in such a way that those who have money donate money, those who have provisions contribute provisions and those who have skill and learnings offer their skill and learnings.

The Ten-Point Programme of the Association for the Restoration of the Fatherland, drawn up personally by Comrade Kim Il Sung, is as follows:

"1. A broad united anti-Japanese front shall be formed through the general mobilization of the Korean nation to overthrow the rule of the bandit Japanese imperialism and to establish a genuine people's government in Korea.

2. Japan and its puppet 'Manchukuo' shall be overthrown by the Koreans resident in Manchuria through a close alliance of the Korean and Chinese nations, and a genuine national autonomy shall be effected by the Koreans resident within Chinese territory.

3. The Japanese army, gendarmerie and police and their lackeys shall be disarmed and a revolutionary army which can fight truly for the independence of Korea shall be formed.

4. All the enterprises, railways, banks, ships, farms and irrigation facilities owned by the Japanese government and Japanese individuals, and all the properties and land of the traitorous pro-Japanese elements shall be confiscated to obtain funds for the independence movement and, partly, for the relief of the poor.

5. The credits and all taxes and the monopoly system imposed by the Japanese and their lackeys on the people shall be abolished; the livelihood of the masses improved; and the national industry, agriculture and trade developed smoothly.

6. Freedom of speech, the press, assembly and association shall be won; pursuance of the terrorist policy and encouragement of feudalistic thoughts by the Japs be rejected; and all political offenders released.

7. Inequality between the nobility and the commonalty and other inequalities shall be removed; human equality irrespective of sex, nationality and religion be ensured; the social status of women elevated and their personality be respected.

8. Slave labour and slave education shall be abolished; forced military service and military education of the youth and children be rejected; education carried on in our speech and letters, and compulsory free education introduced.

9. The eight-hour day shall be introduced; working conditions be improved; wages raised; labour law adopted; a law on various insurances for the workers be enacted by the state organ; and the unemployed working masses be relieved.

10. A close alliance shall be formed with those nations and states that approach the Korean nation on an equal footing; and comradely friendship be maintained with those states and nations that express good will and neutrality towards our national-liberation movement."

The Ten-Point Programme of the ARF was a programme which organically combined and most correctly reflected the fundamental demands of the working class and the interests of various strata of the people in the stage of the anti-imperialist, anti-feudal democratic revolution, and, at the same time, it was an original programme expressing all the fundamental tasks to be fulfilled by the Marxist-Leninist Party in this stage of the revolution.

This was a revolutionary programme which envisaged opening up a favorable phase for the carrying out of the tasks of the socialist revolution by thoroughly fulfilling the tasks of the anti-imperialist, anti-feudal democratic revolution, and which, for the present, aimed at general mobilization of the workers, peasants and all other sections of the masses who were against Japanese imperialism, to the fulfilment of the tasks of anti-imperialist national liberation.

The Ten-Point Programme of the ARF is a splendid embodiment of the great idea of *Juche* of Comrade Kim Il Sung, the brilliant Leader of the Korean revolution and an outstanding Marxist-Leninist, and is an immortal document which is an original development of Marxist-Leninist theory.

Being the most correct revolutionary Marxist-Leninist programme, the first of its kind in the revolutionary history of our people, the Ten-Point Programme of the ARF served the Korean people as a beacon clearly showing them the goal of struggle and vistas of the revolution and as an eternal banner for the Korean revolution.

The Programme became the political and ideological basis for firmly guaranteeing the unity and cohesion of the ranks of the communist and national-liberation movements in Korea by knitting them together with one and the same goal of struggle set by Comrade Kim Il Sung.

The Ten-Point Programme of the ARF had a grip on the masses of the people with a great revolutionary attraction.

In his work **"How to Organize the Anti-Japanese Movement of the Broad Masses in Korea?"** which was written in the spring of 1937, Comrade Kim Il Sung expounded the concrete ways of carrying into effect the Ten-Point Programme of the ARF.

In this work Comrade Kim Il Sung made a scientific analysis of the experiences and lessons gained in the course of the struggle waged by the Korean people against the Japanese imperialist aggressors and clarified the immediate tasks of the Korean people and Communists in their struggle in the prevailing situation of the time.

As a programmatic document giving a scientific elucidation to the practical ways of the struggle which the Korean Communists had to wage for the time being in accordance with the line on the united anti-Japanese national front, the work of

Comrade Kim Il Sung which was pervaded with the idea of *Juche* served as a guide to action in organizing and mobilizing the people of all walks of life vigorously to the anti-Japanese struggle.

Even in the circumstances of the arduous struggle, Comrade Kim Il Sung not only wrote many revolutionary works himself, but also set up publishing organs at secret camps in the depths of backwoods and personally organized and directed the publication of the revolutionary press in order to strengthen the political education of the guerillas and the people.

On December 1, 1936, Comrade Kim Il Sung founded the monthly "Samil Wolgan" (March First), an organ of the Association for the Restoration of the Fatherland.

From the early days of the anti-Japanese armed struggle Comrade Kim Il Sung taught that as weapons were to a revolutionary army in defeating the enemy, so were publications, an incisive and militant ideological weapon, to a revolutionary organization in leading the masses to victory. The "Samil Wolgan" published under the personal guidance of Comrade Kim Il Sung played a really tremendous role as organizer and agitator not only in educating the guerillas but also in rallying the broad sections of the patriotic people including the workers and peasants closely around the united anti-Japanese national front and in organizing and mobilizing them vigorously to the anti-Japanese struggle.

Comrade Kim Il Sung not only organized and directed personally the publication of such newspapers as "Sogwang" (Dawn) and "Chongsori" (The Toll of the Bell) and various booklets as well as the "Samil Wolgan," but also wrote many treatises and articles for educational purpose.

The revolutionary publications issued under the meticulous concern and personal guidance of Comrade Kim Il Sung became mighty means of thoroughly defending the great revolutionary ideas and lines of the Leader and equipping the people closely with his revolutionary ideas and furnished ammunition for crushing the vicious reactionary propaganda of the Japanese imperialists.

After the founding of the Association for the Restoration of the Fatherland Comrade Kim Il Sung personally led the main force of the Korean People's Revolutionary Army to advance to the areas along the River Amnok-gang and guided the building of the Mt. Paekdu-san base.

Leading the Korean People's Revolutionary Army to unfold positive military and political activities, Comrade Kim Il Sung set up secret camps in the forests around Mt. Paekdu-san and formed organizations of the ARF among the revolutionary masses in wide areas by using the secret camps as footholds, thereby establishing the Mt. Paekdu-san base, a new-type base.

The Mt. Paekdu-san base was an invisible citadel which indissolubly linked up the secret camps set up by taking advantage of the favorable geographical features of the vast forests stretching along the Rivers Amnok-gang and Tuman-gang with the revolutionary organizations rooted among the broad sections of people in those areas.

The Mt. Paekdu-san base played an enormous role in enabling the Korean People's Revolutionary Army to crush the enemy's desperate offensives and unfold positive, mobile military activities under the leadership of Comrade Kim Il Sung and in further strengthening his unified and systematic leadership of the Korean revolution as a whole and bringing about a great advancement in the whole Korean revolution which pivoted on the anti-Japanese armed struggle.

After the establishment of the Mt. Paekdu-san base Comrade Kim Il Sung rapidly expanded military activities in the areas southwest of Mt. Paekdu-san with the active support and encouragement of the people and dealt successive crushing blows to the enemy.

Greatly scared at the advance of the Korean People's Revolutionary Army to the northern border areas, the Japanese imperialists made haste to take "emergency measures," and started a large-scale offensive against the Korean People's Revolutionary Army by mobilizing huge forces.

They employed the "combing tactics"—one unit combing the mountain ridge, another the mid-slope, and yet another the bottom of the ravine—so that the Korean People's Revolutionary Army might not get loose.

To cope with the enemy's frantic offensive, Comrade Kim Il Sung employed a new, superb guerilla tactics of curbing the enemy and wiping him out by skilfully combining large-unit and small-unit operations. In accordance with the superb tactics of Comrade Kim Il Sung, the small units threatened and plunged the enemy into confusion everywhere, hampering his freedom of action, while large units, operating quietly, surprised and annihilated big forces of the enemy.

Along with this tactics, Comrade Kim Il Sung masterfully employed really multifarious guerilla tactics everywhere the enemy was entrenched, which consisted in attacking the west while making sounds in the east, in turning up in the west and then striking the south and the north simultaneously, in isolating the enemy at a place and assailing the enemy reinforcements in ambush, in making the enemy forces bump into each other by slipping into and out of their midst agilely, in making believe to move far away but coming back right under the nose of the enemy to hit him, and in changing a majestic formation of march in an instant into open order to smite the enemy in the flank and strike him from behind, thereby administering heavy blows in succession to the enemy, always taking the initiative firmly in keeping the enemy on the defensive and leading him by the nose.

Under the command of Comrade Kim Il Sung the Korean People's Revolutionary Army advanced to the northern border areas of our country and carried out powerful military activities, thus exerting a tremendous revolutionary influence on the Korean people. As a result of the victory won by the Korean People's Revolutionary Army in battle, the northern border areas of our country seethed with revolutionary ardor and the whole land of Korea was swept with revolutionary spirit.

While inflicting blows upon the enemy through powerful military activities and stirring up the revolutionary spirit of the people, Comrade Kim Il Sung organized and guided the work of rapidly expanding the organizational networks of the Association for the Restoration of the Fatherland throughout the country by relying on the Mt. Paekdu-san base.

Comrade Kim Il Sung extended the organizational networks of the ARF throughout the country by dispatching best political workers to all parts of the homeland and, at the same time, personally directing the Communists at home.

In the Changpai areas there was formed the Changpai county committee of the Association for the Restoration of the Fatherland under the personal guidance of Comrade Kim Il Sung, and it had many subordinate organizations under it; and the organizational networks of the ARF penetrated deep into the homeland and were extended rapidly to various localities, one of the examples being the formation of the National Liberation Union of Korea, an organization of the ARF at home.

The organizational networks of the ARF expanded rapidly with a well-regulated system under various names over North and South Hamgyong Provinces, North and South Pyongan Provinces, Kangwon Province, Kyonggi Province, South Kyongsang Province and other parts of the country and vast areas of Manchuria. In only a few months the anti-Japanese masses comprising hundreds of thousands of workers, peasants, youths, students, intellectuals, nationalists, national capitalists and patriotic religious men were rallied under the ARF.

Comrade Kim Il Sung said as follows:

"The fact that in only a few months following its foundation the Association for the Restoration of the Fatherland united under it hundreds of thousands of people of various social strata in our country shows what a great trust the ARF enjoyed among our people.

"The Association for the Restoration of the Fatherland played a great role in explaining the aims and tasks of our national-liberation struggle to the broad masses of the people and enlisting and rallying all the patriotic forces of Korea under the banner of joint struggle for the liberation of the fatherland."

With the successful organization and unfolding of the united anti-Japanese national front movement, powerful internal revolutionary forces of the Korean people were built up and the revolutionary movement in Korea achieved a big advancement with the anti-Japanese armed struggle as the axis.

Comrade Kim Il Sung organized and carried on the united anti-Japanese national front movement in close combination with the anti-Japanese armed struggle in keeping with the requirements of the developing situation, and thus dealt mortal blows militarily and politically to Japanese imperialism, one of the main forces of international fascism, and made a great contribution to developing the united anti-imperialist front movement on an international scale.

The excellent realization of the united anti-Japanese national front and the immortal achievements in the united anti-Japanese national front movement in our country were precisely a result of the wise leadership of Comrade Kim Il Sung, the brilliant Leader of the Korean revolution, and a splendid fruit of his great idea of *Juche*.

With the revolutionary influence of the anti-Japanese armed struggle growing rapidly all over the country and the organizational networks of the ARF extending under the personal leadership of Comrade Kim Il Sung, the support and encouragement of the masses of the people to the Korean People's Revolutionary Army were further strengthened.

The whole-hearted assistance rendered by the revolutionary masses to the anti-Japanese guerilla units in the whole course of the anti-Japanese armed struggle was an expression of their boundless trust in and reverence for Comrade Kim Il Sung, the great Leader of the Korean revolution, which stemmed from their keen realization that the Korean People's Revolutionary Army led by him was precisely an army fighting truly for their freedom and liberation. It was also attributable to the fact that Comrade Kim Il Sung created the revolutionary work method of always going among the people and organizing all work believing in and relying on their strength, and personally set an example in applying it, and that he established the revolutionary trait of unity between the army and the people among the guerillas.

Comrade Kim Il Sung said to the following effect:

...Who is our army fighting for? Ours is an army fighting for the country and the people.

Herein lie the noble aims of our guerilla struggle and the source of its might,...

As fish cannot live without water, so the guerillas cannot live without the people. Only when we trust the people and rely firmly on them in our struggle can we achieve our aims....

Comrade Kim Il Sung always defended the interests of the people thoroughly and, regarding the people's sufferings as his own, exerted all his endeavours to relieve them.

The profound love and solicitude of Comrade Kim Il Sung for the people evoked from them infinite respect for and deep trust in him and brought them to assist the Korean People's Revolutionary Army with all sincerity.

Particularly, Comrade Kim Il Sung, while organizing and guiding the united anti-Japanese national front movement, pushed ahead more energetically with the organizational and ideological preparations for founding a Korean Communist Party on a nation-wide scale.

From the early days of his preparations for the anti-Japanese armed struggle Comrade Kim Il Sung raised it as one of the most important tasks to found a Marxist-Leninist Party, and struggled for its realization. During the whole period of the anti-Japanese armed struggle he successfully carried forward the difficult and complex work of preparing for the foundation of a Party and building up the revolutionary forces in spite of the difficult circumstances in which the tyrannical oppression by the Japanese imperialists was at its height and the subversive activities and sabotage of opportunists and factionalists of all hues ran to the extreme.

In connection with the question of founding the Party Comrade Kim Il Sung grasped the actual conditions of the Communists at home and admonished them against indulging in polemics based on erroneous arguments, and showed them the correct way to its foundation. He assigned them concrete tasks with regard to organizing Communist circles at home and personally guided their work.

Also, Comrade Kim Il Sung, thoroughly repudiating the tendency of flunkeyism to found the Party by relying on foreign forces, clarified the firm position of pushing ahead independently and creatively with the preparations for the foundation of the Party in conformity to the historical conditions and the actual situation in the communist movement of our country, and fought resolutely for its realization.

Comrade Kim Il Sung steadily expanded the ranks of Communists amidst the practical struggle—the anti-Japanese armed struggle and the united anti-Japanese national front movement—and brought them up into staunch Communists through day-to-day education and organizational life. He directed the Party and Young Communist League organizations in the detachments to intensify the education of the guerillas, and personally went down to the detachments quite often to educate the guerillas or to attend Party meetings and teach scrupulously how to strengthen the organizational life. Thanks to the wise leadership of Comrade Kim Il Sung, a new generation of Communists of worker and peasant origins boundlessly loyal to the Leader and the revolution were reared in large numbers in the crucible of the arduous armed struggle, the organizational backbone for the foundation of a Party was firmly built up and the ranks of Communists were organizationally united and their purity ensured.

Comrade Kim Il Sung waged an active struggle to achieve the unity of the Communist ranks in thoughts and purpose based on the revolutionary line of *Juche* laid down in the Ten-Point Programme of the Association for the Restoration of the Fatherland. In the course of the struggle for implementing the revolutionary line and strategy and tactics worked out by Comrade Kim Il Sung, the Communists ensured the complete and unconditional unity of thoughts, purpose and action on the basis of his revolutionary ideas.

Comrade Kim Il Sung also promoted energetically the work of laying the mass foundation for the founding of a Party in the course of the armed struggle and the united anti-Japanese national front movement. Under the personal leadership of Comrade Kim Il Sung, the Communists went among the people at large, smashed the anti-communist propaganda of the enemy and worked devotedly for the people, which brought the people to realize that the Communists were true patriots of Korea and revolutionaries fighting in defence of the interests of the people and to express deep trust in and support for the Communists. Through the struggle for building up the mass foundation for the establishment of the Party, the essential drawbacks of the communist movement of our country in the preceding period were overcome and the Communists won the great confidence of the masses of the people and took deep root in them.

In this way Comrade Kim Il Sung made full organizational and ideological preparations for founding a Korean Communist Party and firmly built up the revolutionary forces for further development of the Korean revolution in the course of the protracted revolutionary struggle

Comrade Kim Il Sung extended the scope of the armed struggle to the depths of the homeland to bring the Korean revolution to a great upsurge.

In those days, the Japanese imperialist aggressors made frantic attempts to strangulate our nation with their story "Japan and Korea is one" or "The Japanese and the Koreans are descended from one and the same ancestor," while perpetrating outrageous fascist suppression and robbery to turn Korea into a "supply base" and "solid rear" for their invasion of the continent.

Comrade Kim Il Sung convened the Sogang Conference in March 1937 where he set forth a strategic line for the sorties of the units of the Korean People's Revolutionary Army deep into the homeland with the aim of dealing heavier blows to the Japanese imperialist aggressors and, at the same time, of instilling confidence in victory and lighting a torch of struggle in every heart of the Korean people who were in a dark plight.

On June 4, 1937 Comrade Kim Il Sung, personally leading the main force of the Korean People's Revolutionary Army, advanced on Pochonbo, a place of strategic importance for the enemy.

Breaking through the frontier guard line loudly advertised by the enemy as an "iron wall," the Korean People's Revolutionary Army units under the direct command of Comrade Kim Il Sung made an assault on Pochonbo and wiped out the ruling apparatuses of the Japanese imperialists, showering a fire of revenge on the enemy.

The furious flames of revolution that flared up into the

nocturnal sky over Pochonbo struck terrors into the brigandish Japanese imperialists and illumined the road to national resurrection for the Korean people who were filled with resentment.

With regard to the great historic significance of the Pochonbo battle, Comrade Kim Il Sung said as follows:

"The significance lies not in the fact that we killed a few Japs but in the fact that the Pochonbo battle threw revolutionary rays of hope inspiring confidence that the Korean people were not dead but were alive and they could beat Japanese imperialism if they fought against it. The Pochonbo battle declared to the whole world: the Korean people resist Japanese imperialism; they do not accept the idea that Korea and Japan is one; the Japs and the Koreans are not of the same ancestry; the Koreans do not join the Japs in invading China; the Koreans will not abandon their mother tongue, nor will they change their surnames into those of the Japs; the Korean people are not dead but are alive; and they can beat the Japs if they fight against them. This is the strategic significance of the Pochonbo battle. Herein lies the historic significance of the Pochonbo battle."

The news of the advance of the Korean People's Revolutionary Army to the homeland under the personal command of Comrade Kim Il Sung and its victory in the Pochonbo battle spread to every nook and corner of the country like a flash of light to fan the flames of fierce struggle among the people.

The triumph in the Pochonbo battle instilled in the Korean people an unshakable confidence in the restoration of the fatherland and gave a powerful impetus to the anti-Japanese national-liberation struggle in our country.

Even in those days when the suppression by Japanese imperialism was at its height, the Korean people entrusted their all to Comrade Kim Il Sung, the sun of the nation, who, bearing the destinies of the fatherland and the nation on his shoulders, always led the people to victory, and forged ahead dynamically

Comrade Kim Il Sung, answering the enthusiastic cheers of the people during the Pochonbo battle, calls upon them to rise as one for the freedom and independence of the country

along the revolutionary road indicated by him. Firmly convinced that the Korean revolution would surely emerge victorious as long as there were the wise leadership of Comrade Kim Il Sung and the heroic struggle of the Korean People's Revolutionary Army led by him, the people further intensified the anti-Japanese struggle throughout the country in response to the anti-Japanese armed struggle.

At last, in July 1937, Japanese imperialism unleashed the Sino-Japanese war after prolonged preparations for the aggression of the continent, and set out to further intensify their harsh suppression and plunder of the Korean people.

To cope with the newly created situation Comrade Kim Il Sung, in accordance with the grand strategy he had already worked out, actively promoted the struggle for dealing heavier blows to the Japanese imperialist aggressors by extending the activities of the Korean People's Revolutionary Army units deep into the homeland and stepping up the armed struggle, combining an all-people resistance war with it.

At the meeting of commanding personnel and soldiers of the Korean People's Revolutionary Army held in August 1937 and in his appeal addressed to the Korean people in September of the same year, Comrade Kim Il Sung set forth a line of more active struggle to cope with the new situation.

Giving a scientific analysis of the political, economic and military vulnerability of Japanese imperialism, Comrade Kim Il Sung said that the extension of war of aggression by Japanese imperialism would meet with a powerful resistance of the broad anti-Japanese revolutionary forces at home and abroad and thus would eventually speed up its own collapse.

More, Comrade Kim Il Sung pointed out that the obtaining situation made it possible to hasten the liberation of the fatherland, and stressed that the Korean People's Revolutionary Army should expand the armed struggle actively behind the enemy line to deliver heavier political and military blows to the Japanese imperialist aggressors. At the same time, he emphasized that more political workers should be sent deep into the homeland to continue to expand the united anti-Japanese national front movement and extensively organize and unfold mass strike and sabotage struggles against Japanese imperialist war of aggression. Particularly, he appealed that preparations should be made for an all-people resistance war so that people might wage a decisive struggle in all parts of our country in combination with the military activities of the Korean People's Revolutionary Army.

The appeal of Comrade Kim Il Sung aroused the Korean People's Revolutionary Army and the entire people to a new struggle.

In accordance with the line advanced by Comrade Kim Il Sung, the units of the Korean People's Revolutionary Army conducted fierce rear-harassing operations such as assaulting towns and destroying the enemy's military installations and thus gave telling blows to the enemy. Quite a number of political workers were also sent out to important military bases, war-industrial districts and various other areas in the depths of the homeland to enlarge the organizational networks of the Association for the Restoration of the Fatherland and organize and mobilize the broad masses to a struggle for the implementation of Comrade Kim Il Sung's appeal.

Thus, in response to the militant appeal of Comrade Kim Il Sung, the workers dislocated the production of war supplies and projects for expansion of military installations by continued and vigorous large-scale strikes and sabotages against the aggressive war of Japanese imperialism, while the peasants fought stubbornly against the Japanese imperialists' policy of forcible expropriation and for tenant-rights and reduction of farm-rents.

The struggles of people from all walks of life at that time were united and organized under the banner of the united anti-

Japanese national front; they were unfolded vigorously in close combination with the struggle against the war policy of Japanese imperialism.

As the anti-Japanese revolutionary struggles of the Korean people centering around the anti-Japanese armed struggle grew fiercer still on a nation-wide scale, the Japanese imperialists were utterly dismayed.

The Japanese imperialists extensively reinforced their guard line along the frontiers and concentrated their forces on "security for national defence," while resorting to a wholesale "punitive operation" against the Korean People's Revolutionary Army with a view to suppressing the anti-Japanese armed struggle waged to make incessant attacks on them in the rear. At the same time the Japanese imperialists were running amuck to destroy the subordinate organizations of the ARF in the border zone and in our country and to arrest and imprison innumerable Communists and revolutionary people.

To cope with the ever intensified vicious offensive of the Japanese imperialists, Comrade Kim Il Sung personally led the main force of the Korean People's Revolutionary Army to give fatal blows to the enemy by surprise attacks everywhere, and took a series of measures for dispatching the details and small groups of the Korean People's Revolutionary Army to the border zone and deep into the homeland to save and regroup the revolutionary organizations and strengthen the guidance of them.

In the winter of 1937, Comrade Kim Il Sung deftly threw the oncoming enemy off the track and arranged and guided intensive winter political and military studies for the units of the Korean People's Revolutionary Army.

Through his work **"The Tasks of the Korean Communists,"** Comrade Kim Il Sung brought the guerillas to have a clear understanding of the character and tasks of the Korean revolution and taught them to fight, firmly maintaining the stand of *Juche*.

Later at the Nampaeja Conference in November 1938, Comrade Kim Il Sung reviewed the activities of the past period and set forth a specific line of combat for establishing *Juche* more firmly in the struggle, actively smashing the malicious, reactionary offensive of the enemy and continuously leading the Korean revolution to an upsurge.

At the conference, Comrade Kim Il Sung laid stress on firmly building up the armed ranks and incessantly annihilating the enemy by means of mobile operations of large units to cope with the manoeuvres of the enemy.

And Comrade Kim Il Sung pointed out that units of the Korean People's Revolutionary Army would have to go again into the zone along the River Amnok-gang and further intensify military and political activities in the border zone and deep in the homeland, restore and expand the revolutionary organizations and call the broad masses of the people vigorously to the anti-Japanese struggle.

In accordance with Comrade Kim Il Sung's line, forces of the units were reorganized and their spheres of action were designated at the conference.

The line set forth by Comrade Kim Il Sung was a sagacious one for solving all problems from the standpoint of *Juche* under all complex and arduous circumstances, for actively breaking through the difficulties on the road of the advancing revolutionary movement, and continuously leading the Korean revolution to an upsurge.

After the conference Comrade Kim Il Sung, personally leading the main force of the Korean People's Revolutionary Army, triumphantly directed the arduous struggle to advance again to the areas contiguous to the northern frontiers of our country from the end of 1938 to the spring of 1939, crushing the desperate attacks of the enemy.

The course of the march was tough and arduous, indeed. The main force of the Korean People's Revolutionary Army had to march through the snow more than a fathom deep in the teeth of the cutting wind. The enemy made attacks without respite, hurling in huge troops, and there were unmitigated hunger and severe cold. In those arduous days, Comrade Kim Il Sung, by dint of his excellent leadership and gifted guerilla tactics, firmly took the initiative and led the Korean People's Revolutionary Army to victory. Under all arduous and complex circumstances he employed varied tactics confidently and skilfully to leave the numerically superior enemy forces in a passive position and give them an annihilating blow.

In those days of fierce battle Comrade Kim Il Sung educated the guerillas in the revolutionary spirit and revolutionary optimism of bearing up in whatever distress and adversity, and personally bore the brunt of the difficulties and broke the repeated deadlocks. Also, he valued and loved his men with paternal care, and this all the more so when in distress. In spite of fatigue, he would personally carry his men's weapons and accouterments on his shoulders to help and encourage them, and portioned out to the men even a bowl of parched-rice powder that was his own share. The love and care shown by Comrade Kim Il Sung for the guerillas were as deep as would spring from the heart of a real father. Such paternal love and scrupulous care shown by Comrade Kim Il Sung for the guerillas from the first days of the anti-Japanese armed struggle were a source of the great strength that closely knit together the ranks of the Korean People's Revolutionary Army into one and enabled them to fight unyieldingly and emerge victorious in face of any difficulty.

The anti-Japanese guerillas fighting under the leadership of Comrade Kim Il Sung, unconditionally carried his orders and instructions through to the end in any adversity, even going through fire and water, and resolutely defended politically, ideologically and with their lives the headquarters of the Korean revolution where he was; against the incessant encirclement and attacks of the enemy.

The course of this struggle recorded as "Arduous March" in the revolutionary history of our people was crowned with great victory thanks to the distinguished leadership, superb tactics, indomitable will and extraordinary revolutionary sweep of Comrade Kim Il Sung.

After finishing the Arduous March triumphantly Comrade Kim Il Sung convened the historic Pukdaejongja Conference in April 1939.

At the conference, Comrade Kim Il Sung summed up the military activities of the winter of 1938 and put forward a line of struggle for the immediate future.

Comrade Kim Il Sung stressed the need to keep advancing deep into the homeland, giving no breathing spell to the enemy who had sustained serious setbacks in the previous winter operations and to further intensify political activities among the masses along with military actions. And he taught that when the enemy concentrated huge forces in the area southwest of Mt. Paekdu-san, the Korean People's Revolutionary Army should quickly move to the area northeast of Mt. Paekdu-san, thereby throwing the enemy into confusion and creating favorable conditions for political and military activities.

This line of Comrade Kim Il Sung represented an active measure taken most correctly on the basis of his intelligent judgment on the situation and extraordinary revolutionary sweep, the wisest measure that guaranteed the continuous development of the Korean revolution.

After the conference Comrade Kim Il Sung himself led the main force of the Korean People's Revolutionary Army to go over to a large-scale offensive and inflicted one blow after another on the enemy in the areas along the frontiers in preparation for a large-scale operation to advance deep into the homeland.

In May 1939, Comrade Kim Il Sung, personally leading the

main force, crossed the River Amnok-gang again and conducted operations to assault the Musan area.

The Korean People's Revolutionary Army units which launched into the Musan area under the personal command of Comrade Kim Il Sung carried on operations in this area as long as a week, dealing stunning blows to the Japanese imperialist aggressors in many battles including the Taehongdan battle, while conducting brisk political work among the people.

The advance of the Korean People's Revolutionary Army commanded personally by Comrade Kim Il Sung on the Musan area and its victory in the battle there infused fresh strength into the people who had been dispirited temporarily at the enemy's suppression and the wreck of the revolutionary organizations.

The advance of the Korean People's Revolutionary Army units upon the Musan area, like the Pochonbo battle, was a historic operation that aroused the Korean people with greater force to the anti-Japanese struggle.

The massive offensive of the Korean People's Revolutionary Army and its victory in the assaulting operations on the Musan area following the Pukdaejongja Conference shattered the deceptive demagogy of the Japanese imperialists against the Korean People's Revolutionary Army, imbued the people with firm confidence in victory of the revolution and called them to a positive struggle against Japanese imperialism.

After the triumphant battle in the Musan area, Comrade Kim Il Sung, in accordance with the line he had already advanced, led the main force of the Korean People's Revolutionary Army into the area northeast of Mt. Paekdu-san and pounded hard on the enemy in succession, firmly taking the initiative. The quick change of the theatre of military activity was the wisest measure commensurate with the changing revolutionary situation at the time and the development of the guerilla struggle itself.

When Comrade Kim Il Sung had suddenly moved to the

area northeast of Mt. Paekdu-san, personally commanding the Korean People's Revolutionary Army units, and conducted brisk political and military activities, the enemy, thrown into great confusion, ran helter-skelter and set up the "Punitive Command" in a hurry and, under the name of "clean-up campaign for security in the southeastern area," made a desperate attack on the units of the Korean People's Revolutionary Army by means of "blockade" and "encircling operations," mobilizing large troops numbering hundreds of thousands.

To cope with the enemy's offensive, Comrade Kim Il Sung employed new guerilla tactics.

Having seen through the insidious scheme of the enemy, Comrade Kim Il Sung prearranged the course of the units' movement, and then conducted large-unit circuit operations, constantly on the move not within the limits of a definite area but over the vast expanses around Mt. Paekdu-san to foil the enemy's scheme in good time, thereby leaving the enemy forces entirely in a passive position and annihilating them.

Thanks to this brilliant guerilla tactics of Comrade Kim Il Sung, the units of the Korean People's Revolutionary Army administered heavy blows one after another to the enemy, sending him atremble at all times with uneasiness and fear.

While carrying on military activities to wipe out the enemy forces by his superb tactics, Comrade Kim Il Sung sent small units of political workers to the border areas and deep into the homeland and guided the work of continuously developing the united anti-Japanese national front movement and of restoring and expanding the revolutionary organizations.

Despite the strict watch of the enemy, the small units of political workers waged a tenacious struggle at all risks to thoroughly implement Comrade Kim Il Sung's line on the united anti-Japanese national front, and rebuilt and expanded the revolutionary organizations in various parts of the country including the Musan area and in the vast areas northeast of Mt. Paekdu-san, rallying numerous people.

Over the whole period of the anti-Japanese armed struggle Comrade Kim Il Sung, taking into account the constantly changing and developing situation and the requirements of the revolutionary tasks, newly put forward and solved in a unique manner the strategic and tactical problems of the armed struggle such as the selection of areas for military activities, establishment of various forms of guerilla bases, choice of the forms of guerilla struggle, and strengthening and development of the guerilla ranks, thereby perfecting the theory of guerilla warfare splendidly.

Even in the circumstances of such fierce battles during the anti-Japanese armed struggle, Comrade Kim Il Sung showed deep concern for the political and military studies of the guerillas in order to strengthen the revolutionary ranks.

Comrade Kim Il Sung taught to the following effect:

... Without firmly arming the guerillas with communist ideas it is impossible to win victory in the protracted, arduous anti-Japanese armed struggle. Therefore, the military training of the guerillas should be intensified and, at the same time, their ideological education be strengthened....

Putting up the militant slogan "Study is the first and foremost task for the revolutionaries," Comrade Kim Il Sung armed the guerillas firmly with the revolutionary idea of *Juche* and the Marxist-Leninist theory to establish revolutionary world outlook thoroughly, and strove heart and soul to educate and rear them into indomitable revolutionary soldiers, into ardent Communists prepared politically and ideologically and in military techniques by closely combining practical struggle with political and military studies. Comrade Kim Il Sung himself delivered lectures to help the guerillas in their studies and guided their studies collectively or individually till late at night. And he personally wrote many books and teaching materials for the education of the guerillas.

Bearing in mind the teachings of Comrade Kim Il Sung, the guerillas studied in a militant way to arm themselves thoroughly with his revolutionary ideas and lines, strategy and tactics, utilizing all conditions and possibilities in the intervals of battles. The anti-Japanese guerillas were thus equipped thoroughly with the revolutionary ideas of Comrade Kim Il Sung and were fully prepared politically and militarily, so that they could triumphantly wage a stubborn struggle along the road of revolution indicated by him without the slightest vacillation in any adversity, convinced firmly of victory in the revolution and united closely around him.

Comrade Kim Il Sung always remained true to proletarian internationalism from the first days of his revolutionary activities.

When the Japanese imperialists launched an armed invasion on Nomonhan in the summer of 1939, too, Comrade Kim Il Sung held aloft the banner of proletarian internationalism against it and hit the enemy forces successively in the rear to keep their military activities in check.

Comrade Kim Il Sung further strengthened proletarian internationalist solidarity and defended the Soviet Union with arms, actively supported the Chinese people in their revolutionary struggle and gave powerful encouragement and impetus to the struggle of the peoples in colonial and dependent countries, thereby greatly contributing to the development of the world revolution.

By conducting such intensified political and military activities in the area northeast of Mt. Paekdu-san in personal command of the Korean People's Revolutionary Army, Comrade Kim Il Sung led the anti-Japanese revolutionary movement of the Korean people centering around the anti-Japanese armed struggle right along the path of victory.

Entering the 1940's, Comrade Kim Il Sung set forth the line for the fatherland's liberation and the final victory of the anti-

Japanese armed struggle, and fought for its implementation.

The aggressive war ignited by the fascist countries had now been extended into World War II. At the time, the Japanese imperialists openly revealed their sinister aggressive designs against the Soviet Union and Southeast Asia, while manoeuvring to bring the Sino-Japanese war to an early conclusion. To fulfil this wild ambition, the Japanese imperialists resorted to every possible means and method in their attempt to convert Korea and Manchuria into their "solid rear." The Japanese imperialists concentrated all their strength first of all on the "complete destruction" of the Korean People's Revolutionary Army which gave them grave menace from behind. The enemy hurled into the "punitive operations" the main force of the Kanto army one million strong and the Japanese imperialist aggressor army's divisions stationed in Korea.

What line of struggle was to be adopted in the newly created situation presented itself as a serious question on which depended the destinies of the anti-Japanese armed struggle and the whole Korean revolution.

Comrade Kim Il Sung convened the Sohalbaryong Conference in August 1940 and, on the basis of a scientific analysis of the obtaining situation and the balance of forces between the enemy and us, expounded a new strategic line for the decisive victory in the anti-Japanese armed struggle.

Comrade Kim Il Sung, having gained a deep grasp on the trends and prospects of the situation at home and abroad, elucidated scientifically the fact that the fascist countries including Japanese imperialism would fall and the Korean revolution would certainly emerge victorious before long.

In the light of the development of the situation, Comrade Kim Il Sung foresaw the future of the revolution and taught that many political and military cadres should be trained and the large-unit activities be turned into small-unit ones and the underground struggle be intensified to deal heavy blows in succession to the Japanese imperialist aggressors and, at the same time, a nation-wide uprising should be prepared.

The new line advanced by Comrade Kim Il Sung, which reflected the requirements of the development of the situation most correctly, was the most positive, *Juche*-motivated line intended to deal blows in succession to the enemy by maintaining the political, ideological and tactical superiority in the guerilla warfare and, at the same time, to actively ride out the difficult situation of the moment by firmly building up the revolutionary forces of the Korean people and ensure the final victory for the Korean revolution centering around the anti-Japanese armed struggle.

The correctness of the strategic line mapped out by Comrade Kim Il Sung was confirmed clearly by the subsequent revolutionary practice.

Comrade Kim Il Sung taught that the Korean People's Revolutionary Army should conduct its military activities more quietly and carry on organizational and political work among the masses in strict secrecy, and suggested that temporary secret bases be set up as bases for its military and political activities.

After the conference Comrade Kim Il Sung divided the units of the Korean People's Revolutionary Army into scores of details and small groups, dispatched them to different areas and commanded their activities.

In the spring of 1941, Comrade Kim Il Sung advanced to the area of Antu and Yenchi counties in personal command of a detail and directed the activities of other details sent out to various places, while showing examples himself for the details in military activities.

Under the direction of Comrade Kim Il Sung, the details of the Korean People's Revolutionary Army dispatched to different places set up temporary secret bases in all areas where military activity was being conducted and, relying on

Comrade Kim Il Sung in the days of the anti-Japanese armed struggle

these bases, carried out combat actions to attack by surprise and wipe out the enemy and conducted brisk political work among the masses of the people.

In his speech before the commanders and soldiers of the Korean People's Revolutionary Army in June 1941, Comrade Kim Il Sung clarified again the line of action for the immediate future to cope with the fast-changing situation at home and abroad.

In his speech Comrade Kim Il Sung made an analysis of the prevailing internal and external situation and then taught that the more complex and difficult the situation became, the firmer confidence one should have in the victory of the revolution, thoroughly establishing *Juche* in all activities, and that the military and political activities should be further intensified to actively meet the great event of the country's liberation and the revolutionary forces of the Korean people be built up more solidly.

Upholding the teachings of Comrade Kim Il Sung, the members of the details carried on brisk military and political activities on a nation-wide scale with firm faith in victory.

Under the guidance of Comrade Kim Il Sung guerilla details intensified their military operations. A large number of small groups conducted their activities more actively than ever before in Unggi, Rajin, Chongjin, Hamhung, Pyongyang, Wonsan, Seoul, Inchon, Pusan and many other places of our country.

The details and small groups of the Korean People's Revolutionary Army, braving it out in the face of the close watch of the Japanese imperialists, gave fierce battles to assault the enemy and destroy railways, bridges and arms depots in various places, further stepped up military reconnaissance activities in anticipation of the forthcoming showdown battle.

In the meantime, they rebuilt the wrecked revolutionary organizations, formed and expanded new organizations, and explained and brought home to the broad sections of the people including the workers and peasants the great revolutionary ideas and revolutionary lines of Comrade Kim Il Sung, thus instilling in them a firm conviction of victory in the revolution and arousing the people to the anti-Japanese, anti-war struggle.

Thanks to the positive activities of the details and political workers of the Korean People's Revolutionary Army, the reputation of the ever-victorious iron-willed brilliant commander Comrade Kim Il Sung, coupled with the news about brilliant war results in the anti-Japanese armed struggle, spread widely to every nook and corner of the country, from the foot of Mt. Paekdu-san to Cheju-do Island.

In the darkest days of Japanese imperialist rule, the Korean people vigorously waged the anti-Japanese struggle in various forms, including strike and sabotage, against the Japanese imperialists' plunder, forced military service and compulsory manpower draft, placing all hopes and expectation on the great Leader Comrade Kim Il Sung. In those days, the move to join in the anti-Japanese armed struggle rapidly gained ground in a mass form among the people.

Particularly, the working class and youths and students formed clandestine organizations and stepped up preparations for armed uprisings to join up with the Korean People's Revolutionary Army under the leadership of Comrade Kim Il Sung at the decisive hour.

All this anti-Japanese struggle waged by people of all strata in our country had deep roots in their boundless trust in and hope on Comrade Kim Il Sung, the great Leader of the Korean people, and was a struggle in which they rose with a firm confidence that independence of Korea was soon to come as far as the Korean revolution was guided by the great Leader Comrade Kim Il Sung.

Thus, the revolutionary spirit of the Korean people rose still higher to expedite the ruin of Japanese imperialism and achieve the liberation of the fatherland under the leadership of Comrade Kim Il Sung, and all preparations were being made to hasten the great revolutionary event actively.

The Japanese imperialists facing their doom at the time made every desperate attempt to check the great force of the anti-Japanese armed struggle, but with no efforts could they check it, and with no frantic attempts could they break the revolutionary fighting will of the people.

Comrade Kim Il Sung devoted his energies to guiding the military and political training of the main force of the Korean People's Revolutionary Army, while directing the details in their operations.

While closely equipping all the Korean People's Revolutionary Army personnel with the unshakable idea of *Juche* in view of the trend of developments, Comrade Kim Il Sung educated and trained them into reliable pillars for the building of the Party and the state in anticipation of the new struggle ahead.

Comrade Kim Il Sung said in the following vein:

... On no account should we hope to rely upon others in carrying out our revolution. Our revolution should be carried out in any case by our own efforts.

Herein lies the great significance of our anti-Japanese armed struggle.

Only by so doing can we meet the forthcoming great event with pride and carry out democratic construction on our own in the liberated fatherland....

Upholding the teachings of Comrade Kim Il Sung, the entire commanding officers and men of the Korean People's Revolutionary Army devoted all their energies to arming themselves thoroughly with his great idea of *Juche* and intensifying the studies in Marxism-Leninism to prepare themselves firmer politically and ideologically.

And Comrade Kim Il Sung led his men to master military

techniques and further intensified their military training to cope with modern warfare and thus brought them up into competent military commanding personnel capable of skilfully commanding battles in a large-scale modern warfare.

In his speech made before the entire members of the Korean People's Revolutionary Army in September 1944 Comrade Kim Il Sung summed up the military and political activities following the Sohalbaryong Conference and clarified the fighting tasks for the Korean Communists to carry out immediately in the prevailing situation.

In those days the Japanese imperialists were put entirely on the defensive on the main fronts of their aggressive war, and the hour of their doom was gradually approaching.

Comrade Kim Il Sung saw through the obtaining situation with a foresight and further intensified the activities of the details and military and political training of the main force to cope with the situation. In the meantime, he taught that preparations should be completed to attain the liberation of the fatherland through the general mobilization of the anti-Japanese forces of the Korean people and all thorough-going preparations be made to found the Party, establish a government and carry out democratic construction successfully in the liberated country in the future.

The historic speech of Comrade Kim Il Sung was of tremendous significance in strengthening the internal forces of the revolution and ensuring the final victory for the anti-Japanese armed struggle, making political and ideological preparations for the building of the country after liberation and firmly building up the backbone force of the revolution.

With the final victory of the anti-Japanese armed struggle within sight, Comrade Kim Il Sung devoted all his energies to the preparations for it.

Under the leadership of Comrade Kim Il Sung the detail operations of the Korean People's Revolutionary Army became active, military and political training was conducted for all the ordinary and special arms and the final battle preparations such as the formulation of operational plans and the formation of forces were completed. In the meantime, the anti-Japanese struggle of the people forged ahead vigorously and arrangements were made actively for a nation-wide uprising to join in the military actions of the Korean People's Revolutionary Army.

On August 9, 1945 Comrade Kim Il Sung issued an order for the general mobilization of the Korean People's Revolutionary Army units to the sacred war to liberate the country.

According to the operational plans of Comrade Kim Il Sung, the Korean People's Revolutionary Army units took part in the final, decisive battle to defeat Japanese imperialism side by side with the Soviet troops.

Units of the Korean People's Revolutionary Army advanced to Rajin, Chongjin, Namyang and Unggi respectively and liberated many areas, and in concert with the struggle of the people crushed and wiped out everywhere the Kanto army of Japanese imperialism and its troops stationed in Korea that offered resistance.

The glorious anti-Japanese armed struggle organized and waged under the leadership of Comrade Kim Il Sung for 15 long years was crowned with a historic victory and our country was liberated from the yoke of nearly 40 years of Japanese imperialist rule.

The anti-Japanese armed struggle organized and waged under the leadership of Comrade Kim Il Sung was a proud struggle in which the revolutionary mettle of the Korean people was demonstrated and the honour of the nation was defended, a great revolutionary struggle in which the independence of the country and the liberation of the people were achieved, and the most glorious revolutionary struggle in the course of which were scored the immortal achievements that are and will be the source of strength for the victory of our revolution.

The brilliant victory of the anti-Japanese armed struggle is the outcome of the sagacious leadership of the great Leader of revolution Comrade Kim Il Sung who is an outstanding Marxist-Leninist and peerless patriot.

Thoroughly establishing *Juche* for the first time in the history of the anti-Japanese national-liberation struggle and the communist movement in our country, Comrade Kim Il Sung developed Marxism-Leninism through its creative application to the actual conditions of the Korean revolution, set forth the revolutionary line, strategy and tactics in an original way and correctly organized and led the struggle for putting them into effect.

For the first time, by Comrade Kim Il Sung, Marxism-Leninism was applied to suit the realities of Korea and the communist movement was closely linked with the revolutionary struggle of the Korean people for national liberation and social emancipation to develop in a single current.

By organizing and leading the anti-Japanese armed struggle to victory, Comrade Kim Il Sung defeated the Japanese imperialists once for all, changed the balance of class forces in our country decisively in favour of the revolution, and solidly built up the internal revolutionary forces of the Korean revolution.

Through the anti-Japanese armed struggle Comrade Kim Il Sung substantiated that the armed struggle is the only right path to the final victory in the anti-imperialist national-liberation struggle against the counter-revolutionary forces armed to the teeth.

In the crucible of the anti-Japanese armed struggle

Comrade Kim Il Sung established the glorious revolutionary traditions, the historical roots of the socialist and communist revolution in our country.

The revolutionary traditions established by Comrade Kim Il Sung embody his great revolutionary ideas and sagacity of his leadership, his superb strategy and tactics and lofty virtues, his strong will and fidelity to the revolutionary principle, and his revolutionary method and popular style of work.

The brilliant revolutionary traditions whose main contents consist in the ideological system, fighting spirit, method and style of work, experiences and achievements of the struggle attained by Comrade Kim Il Sung in the years of the anti-Japanese armed struggle, constitute the most valuable revolutionary wealth and the solid assets and roots of the Korean revolution, that should be carried forward from generation to generation in an all-round way by our Party and people.

It was thanks to the glorious revolutionary traditions established by Comrade Kim Il Sung that the Korean people could found the Party and the people's government without delay even under such complex circumstances after liberation and carry out all the democratic reforms successfully, found the Korean People's Army with the anti-Japanese revolutionary fighters as its backbone and consolidate the revolutionary democratic base rock-firm politically, economically and militarily in a short span of time, win a great victory in the Fatherland Liberation War by defeating U.S. imperialism, the chieftain of world imperialism, and push ahead vigorously with the socialist revolution and building of socialism.

For his distinguished leadership and brilliant strategy and tactics which brought the anti-Japanese armed struggle to a victorious conclusion and for his boundless devotion to the people and lofty virtues, Comrade Kim Il Sung earned unquestioned prestige and profound confidence among the people, and commanded the unbounded trust and respect of the entire Korean people as their great Leader.

From the time when Comrade Kim Il Sung undertook preparations for the organization of the anti-Japanese armed struggle, the Korean people fought in close unity around the Leader, looking up to him as the sun of the nation and firmly convinced that the revolution would certainly triumph so long as they had his sagacious leadership.

4

Having defeated the Japanese imperialists, Comrade Kim Il Sung returned home from his victories.

The Korean people fervently welcomed the triumphal return home of the respected and beloved Leader Comrade Kim Il Sung, for whom they had long been entertaining a high regard.

Amidst seething enthusiasm and joy with which the whole country was greeting him, over 100,000 working people held a grand mass rally in Pyongyang to welcome Comrade Kim Il Sung's triumphal return to the homeland.

In his speech before the welcoming crowd, Comrade Kim Il Sung made the following appeal:

"Our nation has got rid of the 36-year long dark life and won liberation and freedom, and our country, the land of three thousand *ri*, now beams with hope like the shining morning sun.

"The time has now come for us Korean nation to unite our strength and march ahead to build a new, democratic country. This great mission cannot be fulfilled by any party or individual alone. The entire people who really love the country, the nation and democracy should fully unite and build our country into a democratic, sovereign and independent state, contributing labour, knowledge, or money according to what they have."

With emotion and excitement at the national liberation,

the Korean people upheld the call of the respected and beloved Leader Comrade Kim Il Sung and set out to create a new history of the country, crushing the colonial ruling machine of Japanese imperialism and exposing and denouncing the pro-Japanese elements and traitors to the nation.

Immediately after the liberation an extremely complex situation prevailed in our country, and our people were confronted with new, grave difficulties. After the surrender of the Japanese imperialists, the U.S. imperialists who had long since been extending their crooked hands of aggression to our country, occupied South Korea unlawfully and made desperate efforts to turn the whole of Korea into their colony, into a military base for their Asian aggression, while suppressing the patriotic democratic forces and lining up the reactionary forces to consolidate their foothold. The reactionaries at home and abroad gathered in South Korea, and the previous lackeys of Japanese imperialism, having now become agents of U.S. imperialism, manoeuvred insidiously against the Korean people. At such a time, the factionalists, the Right and Left opportunists crawled out and disguised themselves as a "patriot" or a "revolutionary" each, and engaged themselves in machinations to split the revolutionary forces and drive the people who rose in the building of a new country into confusion, saying that a bourgeois republic had to be set up, or that a socialist revolution had to be carried out.

Which way to go? The people were quite at a loss. It was an urgent problem for the future of the revolution to show them a correct line of struggle and organize and mobilize the patriotic democratic forces for the implementation of the line.

Comrade Kim Il Sung made a scientific analysis of this very situation and taught that the communist ranks should be reorganized rapidly and broad masses of the people united and, on this basis, a struggle should be waged to thoroughly carry

A Pyongyang city mass rally held in welcome of the triumphal return to the homeland of Comrade Kim Il Sung

out the democratic revolution against the remnant forces of imperialism and the feudal forces and build a unified, independent democratic state. Above all, he taught that the way to the unification of the country and the nation-wide victory of the revolution could be successfully opened up only when a powerful revolutionary base was built in the northern half in view of the aggressive policy of the U.S. imperialists.

This revolutionary line elucidated by Comrade Kim Il Sung was a most sagacious one for achieving the victory of the Korean revolution on a country-wide scale, being a development, in conformity to the new situation, of the Ten-Point Programme of the Association for the Restoration of the Fatherland and of the line of establishing the revolutionary base set forth by him back in the years of the anti-Japanese armed struggle.

Especially, the line of creating a democratic base set forth by him was a firm revolutionary line of *Juche* and thoroughgoing anti-imperialist, anti-U.S. line to build up the northern half of the country into a powerful revolutionary base in view of the U.S. imperialist aggressive policy, and to drive out the U.S. imperialists and achieve the unification of the country and win the nation-wide victory of the revolution by the Korean people themselves by relying on the revolutionary base.

The Korean people saw in the revolutionary line elucidated by Comrade Kim Il Sung a clear direction for the foundation of a new country, and vigorously turned out in a struggle to carry it out.

Having put forward the revolutionary line, Comrade Kim Il Sung set out to tackle, first of all, the work of founding a Marxist-Leninist Party in order to save the complex situation speedily and lead the revolution victoriously.

Only by founding the Party, the General Staff of the revolution, could the broad popular masses including the working class be united and the powerful revolutionary forces be built up for the unification of the country and the nation-wide victory of the revolution, and a powerful revolutionary democratic base be established in the northern half at the earliest date. The issue of founding the Party was really the key problem deciding the destiny of the Korean revolution.

There were many difficulties to tide over in founding the Party.

The U.S. imperialists in South Korea ran amuck to line up the reactionaries at home and from abroad to produce pro-U.S. reactionary political parties and suppress the revolutionary forces. On the other hand, the factionalists in South Korea who had wormed into the communist ranks, put up the signboard of a "Communist Party" each by deceptive and intriguing means with no foothold whatever among the masses, and dispatched their agents to different areas and were engrossed in whipping together forces for their respective factions. At the same time, the factionalists and provincialists in North Korea were busy trying to build up the foothold of their own factions and take hold of the "hegemony."

The issue of founding the Party under such complex and confused circumstances could be successfully settled only by Comrade Kim Il Sung who had laid the organizational and ideological groundwork for founding the Party amidst the flames of the protracted revolution and enjoyed absolute authority and prestige among the Korean Communists and people.

Comrade Kim Il Sung put forth, and strove for the implementation of, the line of founding a united Party with the Communists steeled and seasoned in the protracted anti-Japanese armed struggle as its core and by embracing the communist groups active in various localities, strictly according to the Marxist-Leninist principle of Party building.

While administering a decisive blow to the subversive manoeuvres of the U.S. imperialists and the reactionaries and the schismatic activities of the factionalists, he sent to various regions those revolutionary fighters whom he had personally brought up in the course of the anti-Japanese armed struggle to enlist Communists with generosity, and he himself went to various localities and explained the line of the revolution and the policy of founding the Party, and thus scrupulously guided the preparatory work for founding the Party.

Comrade Kim Il Sung, on the basis of this preparatory work, formed the Central Organizing Committee of the Communist Party of North Korea in Pyongyang on October 10, 1945, and proclaimed to the world the foundation of our Party which inherited the glorious revolutionary traditions of the anti-Japanese armed struggle.

At the Inaugural Party Congress Comrade Kim Il Sung elucidated the political line of the Party, which was an embodiment of the Ten-Point Programme of the Association for the Restoration of the Fatherland suited to the new situation after the liberation.

In the political line Comrade Kim Il Sung raised it as the fundamental task to struggle for the foundation of a Democratic People's Republic and put forth the following four-point immediate tasks to carry it out:

"1) To rally the broad patriotic, democratic forces by forming a united democratic national front embracing all patriotic and democratic political parties and groups and, on this basis, to work for the establishment of a Democratic People's Republic which will ensure our complete national independence and sovereignty;

2) To liquidate thoroughly the remnant forces of Japanese imperialism, the running dogs of international reaction and all other reactionary elements, which constitute the biggest obstacle to the building of a democratic state, thereby facilitating the development of our nation along democratic lines;

3) To lay the groundwork of an independent democratic state with a view to establishing a unified all-Korea democratic

provisional government, by organizing, first of all, people's committees, the organs of genuine people's power, in all localities, by carrying out all democratic reforms, restoring the factories and enterprises and the national economy as a whole, which were destroyed by the Japanese imperialists, and by raising the material and cultural standards of the people;

4) To further expand and strengthen the Party and energetically push forward the work of the public organizations for organizing and rallying the masses of all walks of life around the Party to fulfil all these tasks."

Comrade Kim Il Sung prescribed it to be the political line of the Party to create a powerful revolutionary democratic base in the northern half of the country in view of the aggressive policy of the U.S. imperialists.

Comrade Kim Il Sung said as follows:

"Right after the liberation our Party prescribed it to be the fundamental political line to create a firm democratic base in North Korea with a view to fully liberating the Korean nation and making Korea a rich and powerful sovereign independent state in the future by thoroughly carrying out the democratic reforms and stepping up democratic construction in North Korea."

At the Inaugural Party Congress, Comrade Kim Il Sung also formulated the correct organizational line of strengthening the Party organizationally and ideologically, of ensuring the unity of the ideology and will of the Party and rapidly expanding the Party ranks.

The Party's political and organizational lines set by Comrade Kim Il Sung constituted the basis for the political, ideological and organizational unity of the Party and served as the guiding pointer for the activities of our Party.

The establishment of our Party was the priceless fruit of the untiring struggle of Comrade Kim Il Sung who had put forth all his energy for the foundation of a revolutionary Party since the days of the anti-Japanese armed struggle, and was a brilliant victory in the long-drawn struggle of the Korean Communists and working class under his leadership.

The foundation of our Party, a genuine Marxist-Leninist Party, was a great event that marked a historic turning-point in the development of the communist movement in our country and the Korean revolution as a whole. Moreover, the foundation of our Party was of tremendous significance in the development of the international communist movement and the world revolution.

From that time onward the Korean working class and people were able to victoriously pave the glorious way of the revolution under the leadership of a Marxist-Leninist Party, their vanguard detachment, the General Staff of the Korean revolution, headed by Comrade Kim Il Sung.

Following the foundation of the Party, Comrade Kim Il Sung exerted efforts to strengthen the Party organizationally and ideologically and rally the broad toiling masses around it.

Comrade Kim Il Sung said as follows:

"It is the decisive guarantee of victory both in the revolutionary struggle and the constructive work to build up the revolutionary forces, that is, to fortify the Party, the General Staff of the revolution, and rally the broad masses around it. In building up the revolutionary forces, it is the consistent line of our Party to consolidate the Party organizationally and ideologically through the practical struggle for revolution and construction, awaken the masses and win them over to the side of the revolution, to bring up all the Party members into revolutionaries through the nuclear role of the Communists tested in the long years of revolutionary struggle and to arm all the people with the revolutionary spirit through the nuclear role of the Party members."

In order to strengthen the Party Comrade Kim Il Sung,

first of all, dealt a decisive blow to the factionalists and provincialists in the Party who had been in the way of carrying through the political and organizational lines of the Party, and gave guidance to strengthen the unity of the whole Party in thought and will on the basis of the unitary ideology of the Party, to strengthen the organizational discipline of the Party based upon the principle of democratic centralism, to improve the composition of the Party, to rapidly extend the Party ranks, and, at the same time, to strengthen the ties between the Party and the masses.

The Second and Third Enlarged Sessions of the Executive Committee of our Party held in November and December 1945 under the guidance of Comrade Kim Il Sung were of epoch-making significance in crushing the manoeuvres of the factionalists who hampered the carrying out of the political and organizational lines of the Party, in defending the Party's political line, establishing the system of the Party's organizational leadership, putting Party work on the right track, and boosting the fighting efficiency of the Party. Above all, the Third Enlarged Session of the Executive Committee took resolute measures for overcoming wrong organizational, political and ideological tendencies in the Party in accordance with the line set by Comrade Kim Il Sung. This brought about a great innovation in Party work and Party life, and the Party could develop as a really sound and powerful one.

Through the struggle for the fulfilment of the instructions given by Comrade Kim Il Sung at the Third Enlarged Session of the Executive Committee, the schismatic and provincialist manoeuvres and all liberalistic actions of the factionalists were hard hit, a well-regulated Party organizational system was set up from the centre of the Party down to the cells, the principle of democratic centralism was established, unity of the Party was strengthened, and the Party could find root deeper among the masses.

Comrade Kim Il Sung, while strengthening the Party organizationally and ideologically, strove energetically to rally the broad masses around it.

In his speech **"On Building Up a New Korea and on the United National Front,"** delivered to the responsible provincial Party workers on October 13, 1945, Comrade Kim Il Sung extensively elucidated the united front policy of the Party.

In this speech Comrade Kim Il Sung, scientifically prescribing the character and tasks of the Korean revolution, taught that with a view to building a Democratic People's Republic a united front should be formed with the participation of not only the working class and the peasantry but also all the other patriotic democratic forces including national capitalists and definitely clarified the fundamental principles to be observed by our Party in the united front movement.

He taught that within the united front the Communist Party should firmly maintain its independence and definitely play the leading role, and that the united front should in any case be based on the worker-peasant alliance led by the working class and rally the broadest possible patriotic democratic forces including even the national capitalists, and yet the principle of combining unity and struggle should be observed in forming an alliance with the national capitalists. And he emphasized that the united front had to be formed on all accounts according to the principle of uncompromising fight with the reactionary forces.

Clarifying the tasks arising in the united front movement, Comrade Kim Il Sung said as follows:

"The issue of building a new democratic Korea depends entirely upon whether we succeed or not in strengthening the Communist Party, forming a united national front, and rallying the broad masses around the Communist Party. Every member of the Communist Party must actively struggle to extend and strengthen the Party ranks continuously, to co-op-

erate sincerely with associate parties, and to win over the broad masses."

Comrade Kim Il Sung's speech **"On Building Up a New Korea and on the United National Front"** represented a classical Marxist-Leninist document which gave perfect answers to the questions of principle arising in the work of winning over the masses, particularly to the strategic and tactical problems posed in the united front movement; it served as a programmatic guide, a powerful theoretical and practical weapon of the Party for winning over the broad masses.

With a view to rallying the broad masses around the Party, Comrade Kim Il Sung personally directed the work of founding such organizations surrounding the Party as the Trade Union, the Peasants' Union, the Democratic Youth League, and the Democratic Women's Union, and rallied millions of toiling people in organizations within a short length of time.

Particularly, it was of great significance for the strengthening of the revolutionary forces to rally the broad sections of the youth firmly around the Party by reorganizing the Young Communist League into the Democratic Youth League.

Right after the liberation, the youth movement was very complex. The reactionaries at home resorted to every possible manoeuvre to split and disrupt the youth movement by forming all sorts of reactionary youth organizations, and each of the various political parties was striving to draw over young people under it. But the Young Communist League organizations embraced a very small number of young people within limited circles.

If such a state of affairs was left alone, a large number of young people could possibly be drawn away by the reactionaries, not to mention the fact that the youth movement could be split.

Comrade Kim Il Sung, having seen through this grave situation, clearly explained the position and role of the youth in the revolution, and put forward the sagacious line of reorganizing the Young Communist League into the Democratic Youth League under the slogan: "Patriotic youth, unite under the banner of democracy!"

This line set forth by him was a most correct and original one mapped out on the basis of the rich experiences he had accumulated in personally organizing and directing the youth movement from his early years of revolutionary activities and on the basis of a scientific analysis of the character and tasks of our revolution and the class positions of the youth from various walks of life after the liberation, and the peculiarities of the development of the youth movement in our country. Nevertheless, the factionalists and dogmatists, who did not have even the elementary understanding of and experience in the youth movement, hampered the realization of the line, bluntly calling it a "Right deviation of the Party" or a "retrogression of the youth movement."

Even the persistent obstructive manoeuvres of the anti-Party factionalists could not impede the onward movement of the masses of the youth who had risen in pursuance of the correct line of Comrade Kim Il Sung. Under the personal guidance of Comrade Kim Il Sung, the work of reorganizing the Young Communist League into the Democratic Youth League made headway successfully, frustrating all manner of obstructive manoeuvres of the anti-Party factionalists and dogmatists.

The Korean Democratic Youth League was founded on January 17, 1946, guided by the great revolutionary ideas of Comrade Kim Il Sung and carrying forward the brilliant revolutionary traditions of the youth movement established by him. In this way, broad sections of the patriotic youth, rallied still firmer around the respected and beloved Leader Comrade Kim Il Sung, could participate more actively in the struggle to build up a new country.

In accordance with the united front policy of the Party set

forth by Comrade Kim Il Sung, the work of strengthening the unity in action with the democratic political parties was also pushed forward actively.

Thus, the United Democratic National Front, which embraced the masses of all walks of life on the basis of the worker-peasant alliance led by the working class, was successfully realized.

Comrade Kim Il Sung, while founding the Party and building up the revolutionary forces, organized and directed the work of setting up, consolidating and developing the people's government, the powerful weapon of the revolution.

It was indispensable to smash the old ruling machine of Japanese imperialism and establish a new people's government in order to suppress the resistance of the enemy, successfully carry out the socio-economic reforms for ensuring welfare and democratic freedom and rights to the entire people, build up the northern half into a powerful base for the Korean revolution and continue to drive the revolution forward.

Immediately after the liberation, however, the work of establishing the people's government, too, did not proceed smoothly. The Right and Left opportunists threw obstacles in the way of establishment of a genuine people's government, clamouring for a bourgeois republic or a government of the proletarian dictatorship.

Comrade Kim Il Sung crushed these manoeuvres of the Right and Left opportunists and creatively solved the question of setting up a people's government on the basis of the original line on the people's revolutionary government he had set forth and the wealth of experiences he had accumulated in the struggle for the materialization of it back in the days of the anti-Japanese armed struggle, and on the basis of a scientific analysis of the situation in our country immediately after the liberation.

Comrade Kim Il Sung led our people to thoroughly demolish the old colonial ruling machine of Japanese imperialism and to set up people's committees in every nook and corner of the country and, on this basis, established the North Korean Provisional People's Committee, a new form of government, in February 1946.

Comrade Kim Il Sung was elected Chairman of the North Korean Provisional People's Committee.

The North Korean Provisional People's Committee was a government which had inherited the brilliant revolutionary traditions of the glorious anti-Japanese armed struggle, a genuine people's government relying upon the United Democratic National Front which embraced the broad anti-imperialist, anti-feudal democratic forces on the basis of the worker-peasant alliance under the leadership of the working class, a government which carried out the functions of the people's democratic dictatorship. It was the basic task of this government to fulfil the tasks of the anti-imperialist, anti-feudal democratic revolution and create a revolutionary democratic base in the northern half.

As a result of the establishment of the North Korean Provisional People's Committee as a new form of government by Comrade Kim Il Sung the question of power, the fundamental question of the revolution, was brilliantly solved in our country, and our people became proud masters of power, who came to hold a powerful weapon of revolution and construction firmly in their hands.

The establishment of the North Korean Provisional People's Committee was of great significance in fulfilling the tasks of the anti-imperialist, anti-feudal democratic revolution and creating the revolutionary democratic base of the northern half and, on this basis, setting up later a unified all-Korea government and winning the nation-wide victory of the revolution.

Comrade Kim Il Sung published the Eleven-Point Immediate Tasks and the Twenty-Point Platform, which embodied the Party's political line and specified the tasks of the people's government.

In those tasks and platform he put forward the tasks of cleaning up the remnants of Japanese imperialism and feudal customs and assuring democratic liberties and rights in all fields of social life, building up the government bodies more solidly through democratic elections, carrying out the democratic reforms including the land reform and the nationalization of industries, introducing universal compulsory education and establishing the public educational system, and of assuring by the state the development of science, culture, arts, health services, etc.

The Twenty-Point Platform was a platform of a thoroughgoing anti-imperialist, anti-feudal democratic revolution, a further embodiment and development of the Ten-Point Programme of the Association for the Restoration of the Fatherland, which he himself had drawn up in the days of the anti-Japanese armed struggle, and became the banner of struggle to the entire people in North and South Korea for the unification, independence and democratization of the country.

Guiding the Party and the people's government, Comrade Kim Il Sung victoriously carried out the historic democratic reforms. It was a lawful demand of the socio-economic development of our country to carry out the democratic reforms.

Comrade Kim Il Sung taught that the economic basis of the reactionary classes including the landowners and comprador capitalists could be eliminated, a broad way could be opened for social progress, the socio-economic foundations of the people's power could be cemented and the northern half could be turned into a powerful revolutionary democratic base only when the democratic reforms were carried out.

Comrade Kim Il Sung raised the solution of the land

problem as the prime task in carrying out the democratic reforms.

Comrade Kim Il Sung said as follows:

"The question of land is a burning question to be solved before anything else in the stage of democratic revolution. The solution of the land question is indispensable for wiping out the economic foothold of the reactionary forces rooted in the rural areas, for emancipating the peasants from the shackles of feudalistic exploitation to raise their political zeal to a great degree and fortifying the socio-political foundations for the democratization of all political, economic and cultural life in the country. And only by carrying out land reform is it possible to free the agricultural productive forces from the feudal fetters, develop them quickly and promote forcefully the rehabilitation and development of the national industry and the whole of the national economy. The solution of the land question acquired a particularly important meaning in our country which was a backward colonial agrarian country, the overwhelming majority of its population being peasants."

For a correct solution of the land problem, Comrade Kim Il Sung, despite the claims of busy work right after liberation, personally went out to many farm villages, had heart-to-heart talks with peasants to acquaint himself concretely with how matters stood there and what they needed, and, taking into full consideration the balance of class forces and the relations of landownership in the countryside of our country, the age-old aspirations of our peasants for the land and even the question of the socialist transformation of agriculture to be carried out later, prescribed whom the land was to be confiscated from and decided on the most thoroughgoing line of land reform based on the principle of confiscating the lands of the landowners and giving them gratis to the landless and land-poor peasants.

Prior to the enforcement of the land reform, Comrade

Kim Il Sung heightened the revolutionary enthusiasm and political awakening of the peasants through political work among them and through the struggle for the enforcement of the three-to-seven system, and, on this basis, put forth the slogan "Land to the tillers!" and aroused the peasants to the materialization of the land reform.

On the basis of these preparations Comrade Kim Il Sung proclaimed the historic Law of Land Reform on March 5, 1946.

The peasants of the whole country enthusiastically supported the Law of Land Reform which mirrored their centuries-old aspirations and earnest desire.

For the successful fulfilment of the land reform Comrade Kim Il Sung organized and mobilized the whole Party and the entire people. He personally dispatched Party members and best contingents of the working class to the countryside, and organized the Rural Committees with the hired and poor peasants, and let them undertake and carry out the land reform themselves with the support of the working class.

The land reform was carried out amidst an acute class struggle. The U.S. imperialists who occupied South Korea and their lackeys infiltrated numerous spies, terrorists, wreckers and saboteurs into the northern half to ruin the land reform, and the landowners and the reactionaries viciously came out against the land reform.

Comrade Kim Il Sung guided the Party and the people's government to frustrate the enemy's subversive manoeuvres at every step, rectified Right and Left deviations revealed in the course of the land reform, and led this great reform to a splendid victory.

Under Comrade Kim Il Sung's sagacious guidance, the land reform was carried out most thoroughly and victoriously in a very short span of time—some twenty-odd days. Thus, in the northern half the feudal relations of landownership and exploitation system were liquidated and the peasants became masters of land which they had been longing for over centuries. As a result of the land reform, the agricultural productive forces were freed from the feudal fetters, and the rehabilitation and development of the national industry and the national economy as a whole could be forcefully driven forward by rapidly developing agriculture. Further, the economic foundations of the reactionary forces rooted in the countryside were liquidated, political enthusiasm of the peasants was highly elevated and the socio-political foundations for the democratization of the country's political, economic and cultural life as a whole were consolidated. Through the land reform, the worker-peasant alliance was further strengthened and the class positions of the Party were fortified further in the countryside.

Indeed, the land reform in our country carried out for the first time in the East and in a most thoroughgoing way under the wise leadership of Comrade Kim Il Sung, was a bright beacon that illumined the way ahead of the peoples of the countries who were suffering from colonial and feudal exploitation, and immensely inspired and stimulated their struggle against imperialism and the feudal forces at home.

Following the land reform, Comrade Kim Il Sung proclaimed the Law on the Nationalization of Industries on August 10, 1946.

This was a historic measure which rendered it possible to eliminate the political and economic footholds of the imperialists and the domestic reactionaries, make use of the country's major means of production for independent development of the national economy and for promotion of welfare of the entire people, and lay the basis of the socialist economy.

As a result of the nationalization of industries, all industrial establishments which had belonged to the Japanese imperialists and the comprador capitalists were nationalized and the roots of all social miseries were eliminated in the main from industrial fields, socialist production relations came into being, the basis was provided for a planned development of the national economy, the working class became master of the means of production and its leading position grew firmer

Besides the economic reforms, Comrade Kim Il Sung promulgated the Labour Law, Law on the Equality of the Sexes, etc., to guarantee full democratic freedom and rights of the working people, and took a series of measures for the democratization of the judicial administration and education.

Right after the liberation Comrade Kim Il Sung raised the issue of training national cadres as one of the fundamental questions for the upbuilding of a new country, as a key problem on which depended the success of the revolution and constructive work, and he always directed deep concern to it and gave scrupulous guidance in the work.

Comrade Kim Il Sung taught as follows:

"For the regeneration of our nation and the building of our country into an independent democratic state, we should have our own men of culture and arts, scientists and technicians. In other words, we need national cadres fully capable of building and developing our country in every field of politics, economy and culture."

Comrade Kim Il Sung set forth the policy of training national cadres, a policy of boldly embracing old intellectuals, educating and remoulding them and actively drawing them into building up a new society, while training new national cadres of working people origin in a big way.

Even under the difficult conditions immediately after the liberation, he established numerous schools of all levels everywhere in the country including colleges and specialized schools to rear new intellectuals of worker and peasant origins; and he took positive measures for training more national cadres at a faster rate by establishing the educational system which combined study with work, besides the regular educational system.

Right after the liberation, on the direct initiative of Comrade Kim Il Sung and thanks to his concern, Party schools of all levels including the Central Party School were established, many higher and common educational institutions and various training centres were set up, including the Kim Il Sung University, and a large number of talent were trained. Besides, numerous cadres were trained in the course of practical revolutionary work.

Especially, Comrade Kim Il Sung personally established the Mangyongdae Revolution School to bring up into pillars of the revolution the bereaved children of those revolutionaries who had fallen in battle for freedom and independence of the country in the days of the anti-Japanese armed struggle, and showed deep concern and solicitude for their education.

Thanks to the parental love and concern of Comrade Kim Il Sung, the bereaved children of the revolutionaries were brought up as reliable successors to our revolution.

Comrade Kim Il Sung paid particular attention to the upbuilding of democratic national culture, and organized and directed this work.

With a view to liquidating the aftermaths of the Japanese imperialist policy of keeping the Korean people in ignorance and obliterating the national culture of Korea, Comrade Kim Il Sung democratized education and saw to it that upwards of 8,000 adult schools were established and run immediately after the liberation and thus made it possible to wipe out the illiteracy from this land for ever.

He also indicated a clear course of developing science. literature, arts and physical culture and took various measures for their advancement.

Comrade Kim Il Sung energetically aroused the political enthusiasm of the people, which had been keyed up through the democratic reforms, for the upbuilding of a new country, and he himself led the van of it.

In May 1946 he suggested riparian works on the River Potong-gang as the first step in the materialization of the far-reaching plan of remaking the nature of the country; he himself attended the ceremony for starting the works and took up the first spade to dig earth. This first spade taken up personally by Comrade Kim Il Sung, this scintilla immensely stirred up the hearts of the liberated people and forcefully aroused them to the construction of a new country.

The citizens of Pyongyang, boundlessly encouraged by the initiative of the respected and beloved Leader Comrade Kim Il Sung, by the example shown by him, wrought the miracle of winding up this difficult riparian project in no more than 55 days, which the Japanese imperialists could not accomplish even in ten years.

Upholding the appeal of the respected and beloved Leader Comrade Kim Il Sung for coming out in the upbuilding of a new country, the workers displayed the revolutionary spirit of self-reliance and devoted all their wisdom and stamina to the work of rehabilitating the factories and enterprises severely destroyed by the Japanese imperialists. And in the year of 1946 alone 822 factories and enterprises including the Hungnam Fertilizer Factory and the Hwanghae Iron Works were rehabilitated and put into operation. Holding aloft the appeal of the Leader "Let us greet the first spring of the liberated Korea with increased production and let us not leave even an inch of land in furlough!" the peasants successfully ensured the spring tilling and sowing in 1946, and started the irrigation and reclamation works including river-dyke projects in an all-people movement.

While victoriously guiding the democratic reforms and democratic construction in the northern half, Comrade Kim Il Sung organized and directed the work of further strengthening and developing the Party.

At the time, the U.S. imperialists and the domestic reactionaries were frightened at the fact that the people in the northern half, united firmly around the Leader, scored revolutionary successes in carrying out epoch-making changes and the people in South Korea, inspired by those successes, rose resolutely in a revolutionary advance, and made all possible manoeuvres to split the democratic forces and frustrate the united action of the toiling masses.

Comrade Kim Il Sung comprehended such a political situation and the requirements of the development of the revolution with a quick insight and set forth the sagacious line of merging the Communist Party with other parties of toiling people and developing it into the Workers' Party, a powerful mass political party, which would be able to give unified guidance to the entire toiling masses.

His line of founding the Workers' Party was the only correct one laid down on the basis of a concrete calculation of the political situation prevailing in the country, the objective requirements of development of the revolution, the lawful requirements of development of the Party itself, and the positions of the toiling people which underwent changes in the course of the democratic reforms. Above all, it was a sagacious line which made it possible to frustrate the manoeuvres of the enemy to split the revolutionary forces, and rally the broader toiling masses around the Party and energetically organize and mobilize them to the revolutionary struggle. Also, this was an original line which was a new development of the Marxist-Leninist theory on Party building in conformity to the actual conditions of our country.

Particularly, Comrade Kim Il Sung set forth the line of bringing up core Party members and expanding their ranks in connection with the building of a mass party.

His line for rearing and increasing core Party members was a most sagacious measure to consolidate the Party ranks qualitatively in a short space of time in view of our Party being developed into a mass party, and was an original organizational line which most correctly expressed the lawful requirements of the building of a mass party.

Thus, in August 1946 the Communist Party merged with the New Democratic Party and developed into the Workers' Party under the direct guidance of Comrade Kim Il Sung.

The development of our Party into the Workers' Party, a unified political party of the toiling masses, was an epoch-making event in extending and strengthening our revolutionary forces.

Comrade Kim Il Sung said as follows:

"The merger of the Communist Party with the New Democratic Party made it possible to strengthen the Party forces, to further increase the ranks of the revolutionaries and make the Party strike roots deeper among the broad masses. It also eliminated the danger of dividing the revolutionary forces of the toiling people by leaving the two political parties of the toiling people to exist further, strengthened the alliance of the workers, peasants and toiling intellectuals under the leadership of the working class, and it further consolidated the united front of the democratic forces of all walks of life."

The development of the Communist Party into the Workers' Party, a mass political party, under the sagacious guidance of Comrade Kim Il Sung, made it possible to rally the working masses firmer around our Party, further enhance the fighting efficiency and leading role of the Party and drive forward the revolution and construction successfully.

Thanks to the wise leadership of Comrade Kim Il Sung, the tasks of the anti-imperialist, anti-feudal democratic revolution were thus triumphantly carried out in the northern half in no more than 1-2 short years. As a result of the successful fulfilment of the tasks of the anti-imperialist, anti-feudal democratic revolution, in the northern half of our country new socio-economic relations came into being, a system of people's democracy was firmly established, and a revolutionary democratic base, a reliable guarantee for the unification of the country, was created.

Comrade Kim Il Sung said as follows:

"The successful fulfilment of the tasks of the democratic revolution completely rid the socio-economic system of its colonial and semi-feudal character and fundamentally changed the socio-economic relations in the northern half. In the national economy of the northern half of the Republic the socialist form of economy composed of state and co-operative economies came to hold the leading place, and, besides, there remained the small-commodity economic form consisting of individual peasant and urban handicraft economies and the insignificant capitalist form of economy confined to private capitalist trade and industry in towns and to the rich farmer economy in the countryside.

"On the basis of such new economic relations a radical change took place in class relations in our society. Landlords, comprador capitalists, pro-Japanese elements and traitors to the nation were liquidated, the working people became masters of the country, the leading role of the working class was enhanced and the worker-peasant alliance further strengthened in the northern half.

"As a result, there was firmly established in the northern half the people's democratic system and laid the powerful revolutionary democratic base, a reliable guarantee of national unification."

With the carrying out of the tasks of the anti-imperialist, anti-feudal democratic revolution in the northern half, Comrade Kim Il Sung organized and mobilized the masses of the people continuously to fulfilling the tasks of the period of transition to socialism.

To go over to the period of transition to socialism in the

northern half where the tasks of the democratic revolution were accomplished, was a lawful requirement of its socio-economic development.

Comrade Kim Il Sung taught that the important tasks to be solved in the transition period were to reorganize the old production relations along socialist lines and to achieve the complete victory of socialism by carrying on the revolution even after the establishment of the socialist system and thereby putting down all the hostile elements thoroughly while educating and remoulding the entire working people to revolutionize and *working-classize* the whole society and obliterating the distinctions between towns and the countryside, the class distinctions between the working class and the peasantry, and laying the material and technical basis of socialism through development of the productive forces.

For the successful fulfilment of the tasks of the transition period, Comrade Kim Il Sung solved in an original way, first of all, the question of setting up the government of the proletarian dictatorship by the method of further developing the existing people's government to fit in with the carrying out of the tasks of the socialist revolution.

Comrade Kim Il Sung taught that all-people democratic election would have to be held as a means of further strengthening and developing the people's government.

The first historic democratic election held in North Korea under his personal guidance was concluded with a great victory. On the basis of this historic election, the North Korean People's Committee was set up in February 1947

Comrade Kim Il Sung was elected Chairman of the North Korean People's Committee.

The North Korean People's Committee was the first government of the proletarian dictatorship in our country.

Comrade Kim Il Sung said as follows:

"**...Our Party put forward the task of further developing**

Comrade Kim Il Sung plants rice seedlings with peasants

the people's government, the weapon of our revolution, to suit the carrying out of the tasks of the socialist revolution. Thus, the first historic democratic election was held and the North Korean People's Committee was set up. This was the first government of the dictatorship of the proletariat in our country. As a powerful weapon of the socialist revolution and socialist construction, the North Korean People's Committee strove to fulfil the tasks of the period of transition gradually to go over to socialism and develop the national economy in a planned way."

Comrade Kim Il Sung concentrated his energies first of all on strengthening the new-born government of the proletarian dictatorship and on enhancing its functions and role.

The speech of Comrade Kim Il Sung made in November 1946 "**Results of the Democratic Election and the Immediate Tasks of the People's Committee,**" became a programmatic pointer not only in enhancing the functions and role of the people's government at the time but also in strengthening the government of the proletarian dictatorship to be newly born.

In this speech he taught us to put down thoroughly the resistance of all class enemies, saying that the greater our victory would become, the more viciously the reactionaries would act.

While raising the functions and role of the government of the proletarian dictatorship, Comrade Kim Il Sung vigorously drove forward the ideological revolution to remould the thought and consciousness of the working people for the successful accomplishment of the tasks of the early stage of the transition period.

Here, the general ideological mobilization movement for national construction initiated by him in November 1946, was of great significance.

Proposing to unfold the general ideological mobilization movement for national construction, Comrade Kim Il Sung taught as follows:

"...We must carry out an ideological revolution to foster the spirit, traits, morality and militancy worthy of functionaries of a new, democratic Korea. We must carry out a great ideological remoulding work to do away with all survivals of degenerated and corrupt customs and attitude to life, left over by Japanese imperialism in the bygone days, and create national traits of an animated and vibrant, new democratic Korea."

While leading the entire Party members and working people to wage an energetic ideological struggle for doing away with the survivals of old ideology and habits of life, Comrade Kim Il Sung guided them to conduct the general ideological mobilization movement for national construction in close connection with economic construction.

He taught that this movement should be carried on in close combination with a mass struggle to care for and economize the state property, strengthen labour discipline, raise labour productivity, lower production costs and to acquire techniques. And he gave instructions to acquire, through this movement, the revolutionary traits of conscientiously carrying out all the assigned tasks, of helping and uniting with each other and courageously overcoming all the difficulties in building a new society.

Upholding his instructions, the entire Party members and working people unrolled this movement in close combination with the practical struggle for the fulfilment of the revolutionary tasks, while waging a vigorous ideological struggle to do away with the remnants of old ideology and arm themselves with new ideology. In this course, selfishness, tendency towards corruption and indolence, bureaucratism, irresponsibility for work, and menial spirit were criticized and overcome, and hostile elements, alien elements, position seekers and loafers who had wormed into the revolutionary ranks were detected and purged, and the national and class consciousness of the masses was enhanced extraordinarily. And the activity and creative initiative of the masses were displayed to a high degree in the revolution and construction.

Indeed, the general ideological mobilization movement for national construction organized and conducted on the personal suggestion of Comrade Kim Il Sung was a great ideological remoulding movement for building a new country and a new society and, at the same time, it was a patriotic movement of the masses as a whole closely linked with economic construction.

While suppressing the resistance of the overthrown exploiting classes by strengthening the proletarian dictatorship and forcefully driving forward the ideological revolution among the working people in this way, Comrade Kim Il Sung energetically propelled economic construction.

Under the circumstances where the democratic reforms were carried out and the socio-economic foundations for the independent development of the national economy were laid in the northern half, it was for more solidly building up the democratic base and for firmly guaranteeing the independence of the country to vigorously carry on economic construction.

Comrade Kim Il Sung clearly expounded the Party's economic policy in the early stage of the transition period.

He taught that it was the fundamentals of the Party's economic policy in the early stage of the transition period to assure the direct planned management by the state of the major industrial branches, railway transport, communications, foreign trade and the banking organs, and to properly combine the state, co-operative and private economic sectors on the basis of steady enhancement of the leading role of the state sector in the development of the national economy. He instructed that while this fundamental principle was strictly observed, the socialist transformation of production relations had to be carried out partially and, at the same time, thorough preparations had to be made for the extensive promotion of the socialist transformation.

Comrade Kim Il Sung clearly indicated the basic direction of economic construction, too.

He taught us to restore rapidly the destroyed economy, to pay great attention, above all, to the production of articles of daily use and to the solution of the food problem and make stable and improve the livelihood of the people, to get rid of the backwardness and colonial lopsidedness of the economy, and to lay the foundations of an independent national economy.

In the early days of economic construction, Comrade Kim Il Sung, on the basis of the economic programme set forth in the Ten-Point Programme of the Association for the Restoration of the Fatherland during the anti-Japanese armed struggle, advanced the great line of building an independent national economy for the first time in history.

In his concluding speech delivered on February 20, 1947 at the Congress of the Provincial, City and County People's Committees of North Korea, Comrade Kim Il Sung taught as follows:

"To build an independent democratic state, the basis of an independent economy of one's own nation should be laid firmly without fail, and to lay the firm basis of an independent economy the national economy should be developed rapidly. Without the basis of an independent economy we can neither achieve independence nor can build the state nor can maintain our existence."

Later, Comrade Kim Il Sung said as follows as to what is meant by the building of an independent national economy:

"The building of an independent national economy means developing the economy in a diversified way, equipping it with up-to-date techniques and creating our own firm raw material bases, thus building up a comprehensive economic system in which all branches are organically interlinked with each other, so as to turn out domestically, in the main, the heavy and light industrial products and agricultural produce needed for making the country rich and strong and improving the people's livelihood."

The line of building an independent national economy, an embodiment of Comrade Kim Il Sung's great idea of *Juche,* is an original line which nobody had ever presented in history; it is a most correct line of economic construction, which makes it possible to ensure the political independence, prosperity and development of the country, eliminate inequality between nations, achieve national prosperity and to successfully build socialism and communism.

Indeed, the line of building an independent national economy mapped out by Comrade Kim Il Sung is a revolutionary line of economic construction which most correctly expresses the lawful requirements of national independence and socialist and communist construction.

Based upon the Party's economic policy for the early stage of the transition period and the line of building an independent national economy set forth by Comrade Kim Il Sung, a national economic plan was drawn up for the first time in the history of our country.

Comrade Kim Il Sung called the whole Party and the entire people to the fulfilment of the national economic plan for 1947 and that for 1948 for laying the foundation of an independent national economy.

In response to the call of the Leader, the entire working people came out as one in the struggle for the pre-schedule fulfilment of the national economic plans.

There were many difficulties, however, on the way of fulfilling the national economic plans.

Owing to the evil colonial rule of the Japanese imperialists, the industry of our country had suffered from colonial lopsidedness and distortion in the past, and even that was severely destroyed by the Japanese imperialists.

We lacked also the economic and technical workers and administrative cadres.

The U.S. imperialists and the reactionaries at home resorted to all possible manoeuvres to impede the fulfilment of our first national economic plan and the factionalists carped at the execution of the planned economy in every possible way, calling it "fantastic" or "absolutely infeasible."

But Comrade Kim Il Sung, tiding over all the difficulties and hardships with a firm conviction that the national economic plans could be fulfilled without fail, and with an indomitable fighting spirit and extraordinary revolutionary sweep, actively organized and mobilized the whole Party and the entire people to the fulfilment of the national economic plans.

Comrade Kim Il Sung taught that for the successful accomplishment of the tasks confronting the Party, it was necessary, first of all, to raise the leading role of the Party and improve and strengthen Party work.

The Sixth Session of the Party Central Committee held in March 1947 under his direction discussed the question of improving and strengthening Party work in conformity to the new circumstances and took specific measures for the intensification of the Party's direction in carrying out the national economic plans.

The treatise **"The North Korean Workers' Party Greeting Its First Anniversary"** by Comrade Kim Il Sung and his speech **"On the Tasks of Our Party Organizations"** delivered at a conference of the North Korean Workers' Party organization of Sunchon county, South Pyongan Province, were of special importance for strengthening the Party organizationally and ideologically and raising the vanguard role of the Party members.

Besides the work of raising the leading role of the Party in economic construction, Comrade Kim Il Sung saw to it that the functions of the new-born government of the proletarian dictatorship were strengthened and its role as the economic organizer was raised, and he propelled more energetically the general ideological mobilization movement for national construction to arouse the masses to the struggle for building a new country.

Through the general ideological mobilization movement for national construction, Comrade Kim Il Sung, while remoulding the thinking and consciousness of the masses and arousing their patriotic zeal, appealed to the entire people to display the revolutionary spirit of self-reliance to successfully carry out economic construction, breaking through the manifold difficulties and hardships.

Comrade Kim Il Sung taught as follows:

"...Destroyed factories, dislocated transport facilities, ruined agriculture, the treasury with nothing but account-books—this was all that we took over from Japanese imperialism. With us, many things are lacking and difficulties are great. At present we are struggling to build a new country under very hard circumstances, bearing the destiny of the whole nation on our shoulders. We must therefore turn out what we do not have, and put up with the shortage, and break through all the hardships with clenched teeth."

The principle of self-reliance, being a revolutionary principle which he had been firmly adhering to since the early days of his revolutionary struggle, was a source of great strength and priceless spiritual wealth, which made it possible to surmount all the difficulties and trials and guarantee the victory of our revolution.

Later, Comrade Kim Il Sung taught as follows:

"**Self-reliance is a thoroughly revolutionary stand for a people to accomplish the revolution in their country basically by relying on their own internal forces. It is an independent stand to construct their country by their own labour and with their domestic natural resources.**"

He taught that only when the revolutionary position of self-reliance was abided by, was it possible to continue the struggle without losing the revolutionary constancy in any complex situation, to assure victory in the revolutionary struggle by valiantly tiding over all difficulties and bottlenecks, and enlist the strength of one's people and the internal resources of one's country to the maximum.

In wholehearted response to the appeal of the Leader, the entire working people devoted all their wisdom and stamina to the struggle for the rehabilitation and development of the national economy.

Comrade Kim Il Sung actively organized and mobilized the keyed-up patriotic enthusiasm and creative ability of the masses to the fulfilment of the national economic plans.

Comrade Kim Il Sung personally guided the Hwanghae Iron Works, Kangson Steel Plant and other major factories and enterprises on the spot, and taught the methods of work to the functionaries, consulted the workers on practical measures and settled knotty problems, and saw to it that emulation drives for increased production were organized and unfolded extensively among the working masses.

Immensely inspired by the appeal of Comrade Kim Il Sung and his on-the-spot guidance, the entire working people achieved such brilliant successes as fulfilling both annual plans (for 1947 and 1948) ahead of schedule and, then, carrying out the two-year national economic plan for 1949-1950 by the first half of 1950 in the main. As a result, the national economy in the northern half of the Republic was restored on the whole and the pre-liberation level was surpassed in a number of branches of production.

Of industry the state sector accounted for over 90 per cent, and the building of the engineering industry and light industry was started. As agricultural production increased, the northern half turned from a food-short zone into a zone self-sufficient in provisions. Farm-machine hire stations and state agro-stock farms were set up in some areas, and thus more favorable conditions were created for further developing the productive forces of agriculture in future. In this way, big successes were made in laying the foundations of an independent national economy, and the livelihood of the people was also improved markedly.

While building up firmly the revolutionary democratic base of the northern half politically and economically, Comrade Kim Il Sung organized and directed the building of the people's armed forces to safeguard the people's democratic system and to guarantee with arms the victory of the revolution.

Comrade Kim Il Sung, on the basis of his personal experiences of building up revolutionary armed forces in the days of the anti-Japanese armed struggle, exerted himself to found the people's armed forces from immediately after liberation, perspicaciously looking ahead through the vistas of the development of the revolution, under the circumstances in which our country was faced with the U.S. imperialists, the chieftain of world reaction, and, particularly, the U.S. imperialists were manoeuvring to turn the whole of Korea into their colony.

Resolutely beating back the slanders of the anti-Party elements who were loudly bandying about, "What is the use of having armed forces when the country is not yet unified?" and all their obstructive manoeuvres, he established the Pyongyang Institute, the Central Security Cadres' School and security cadres' training centres right after the liberation, and trained military and political cadres.

On the basis of such preparations, Comrade Kim Il Sung founded the Korean People's Army in February 1948 with those revolutionary fighters whom he himself had brought up amidst the flames of the anti-Japanese armed struggle as its backbone and with best sons and daughters of the workers and the peasants.

With the foundation of the Korean People's Army, a modern

regular armed force, which is the direct continuer of the brilliant revolutionary traditions of the glorious anti-Japanese armed struggle, the Korean people came to have their own revolutionary armed forces which would reliably defend the revolutionary gains from the encroachment of the enemy and guarantee the final victory of the Korean revolution.

This was a splendid embodiment of Comrade Kim Il Sung's line of self-defence and a great victory won by the Korean people in building a new country.

After the founding of the people's armed forces Comrade Kim Il Sung, with a view to reinforcing them politically and ideologically and in military techniques and strengthening and developing them into an a-match-for-a-hundred revolutionary army, sent numerous fine cadres to the army to intensify military and political training and increase combat readiness and, at the same time, organized and directed the campaign of assisting the People's Army in an all-people movement. As a result, the People's Army was strengthened and developed into an invincible revolutionary armed force equipped with the traditional traits of unity between officers and men and between the army and the people, as the army of the Workers' Party of Korea armed firmly with the great revolutionary ideas of Comrade Kim Il Sung, infinitely loyal to the Leader and ablaze with animosity against the enemy.

At the Second Congress of the North Korean Workers' Party convened in March 1948, Comrade Kim Il Sung extensively reviewed the activities of the Party since its Inaugural Congress, set forth the policy of independently unifying the country, and the tasks of further strengthening the revolutionary democratic base of the northern half and of cementing the Party ranks qualitatively, thereby clearly indicating the road to be followed by our Party and people.

In his report to the Congress Comrade Kim Il Sung advanced, above all, the line of unifying the country on an independent, democratic principle to cope with the situation where the danger of national split was increased by the U.S. imperialists.

Comrade Kim Il Sung also set the task of further strengthening the revolutionary democratic base of the northern half, the material guarantee for the unification of the country, and stressed the need to concentrate all the efforts of the Party on economic construction.

Comrade Kim Il Sung said as follows:

"The present situation in our country demands not only that our Party should become a party capable of organizing and politically leading the masses, but also that it should become a party of builders able to build the economy and manage enterprises and possessing knowledge of economics and technology."

Also, Comrade Kim Il Sung taught that for the qualitative consolidation of the Party ranks it was necessary to strengthen the cells of the Party, its basic organizations, and properly bring up the cores of the cells, improve the work of personnel administration, intensify the ideological education of the Party members, and, particularly, to keep waging the struggle against factionalism energetically.

The report of Comrade Kim Il Sung delivered at the Second Congress of the North Korean Workers' Party became a combat programme for the entire Party membership and people in the work of unifying the country independently, strengthening the revolutionary democratic base of the northern half of the Republic, and of cementing the Party qualitatively.

While firmly building up the revolutionary democratic base of the northern half politically, economically and militarily, Comrade Kim Il Sung guided the struggle of the Korean people for the accomplishment of the South Korean revolution, a major component of the Korean revolution, and the unification of the country.

He set it as the immediate supreme task of the nation to drive the U.S. imperialists out of South Korea, accomplish the national-liberation democratic revolution on a nation-wide scale and achieve the unification of the country, and organized and mobilized the entire Korean people to the struggle for carrying out the task.

At that time, some people thought that the question of the unification of Korea could be solved only by relying on outside forces.

Comrade Kim Il Sung gave a resolute rebuff to such erroneous views, and elucidated the line of unifying the country in an independent way.

Comrade Kim Il Sung taught as follows:

"**Today the question of Korea can be solved only by the Koreans themselves; no one other than the Korean people has the ability or right to solve it.... Only the Korean people should settle the Korean question by themselves. We alone are fully capable of solving it.**"

Comrade Kim Il Sung also clearly set forth the strategic and tactical line for the revolutionary struggle of the South Korean people.

He taught that the people in the southern half should wage a vigorous mass struggle against the U.S. imperialists and their accomplices—the landowners, comprador capitalists and reactionary bureaucrats, avoid foolhardy, hazardous struggles under the circumstances of intensified suppression by the enemy, preserve and expand the revolutionary forces by properly combining various forms of struggle, and form and strengthen a united front by all means which widely unites patriotic people from all walks of life with the working class and the peasantry as the core. He also taught that the aggressive nature of the U.S. imperialists should be thoroughly exposed and all illusions about U.S. imperialism be completely dispelled among the people in the southern half, and political work should be strengthened for extensively explaining and bringing home to them the successes of the revolution in the northern half.

In spite of the intense subversive and sabotaging activities of the hired spies of the U.S. imperialists and the factionalists who had wormed into the revolutionary ranks, the people in the southern half, looking up to Comrade Kim Il Sung, the great Leader of the nation, and encouraged by the results of all the democratic reforms achieved in the northern half under his guidance, rose in the surging anti-U.S., national-salvation struggle, including the September General Strike and the October Popular Resistance in 1946, and dealt a heavy blow to the enemy.

The U.S. imperialists unlawfully placed the Korean question on the agenda of the United Nations in October 1947 and, usurping its signboard, manoeuvred to rig up a separate puppet "government" in South Korea. In doing so, they were pursuing the heinous aims of justifying their occupation of South Korea and of perpetuating the national split in Korea.

Comrade Kim Il Sung took measures for striking blows at the U.S. imperialist manoeuvres to split our nation and, then, for carrying into effect without delay the Party's political line of founding a Democratic People's Republic.

In his New Year message of 1948 and in his speech at the 25th Session of the Central Committee of the United Democratic National Front held in March the same year, Comrade Kim Il Sung appealed to the entire people in North and South Korea to elect a supreme legislative body of Korea representing the will of the Korean people and establish a unified, all-Korea central government to remove the danger of national split.

He drafted the Constitution of the Democratic People's Republic of Korea and brought it up for the nation-wide discussion.

Comrade Kim Il Sung's line for the formation of the unified central government and the draft Constitution of the D.P.R.K. were unanimously supported by the entire people of Korea.

The Joint Conference of Representatives of the North and South Korean Political Parties and Public Organizations held in April 1948 on the personal suggestion of Comrade Kim Il Sung fully supported and approved his line of foiling the separate election in South Korea and of setting up a unified central government on an independent and democratic principle, and the participants in the conference unanimously resolved to fight for its materialization.

Even the die-hard nationalists and leaders of the Rightwing political parties of South Korea who were present at the conference, unanimously resolved to struggle under the guidance of Comrade Kim Il Sung, moved by the correctness of the line set forth by him, by all the achievements scored in the northern half under his guidance, his ardent love for the country and the people, and his lofty virtue.

The success of this historic conference was ascribable entirely to the correctness of the line set forth by Comrade Kim Il Sung, the sagacity of his leadership and his high prestige and lofty virtue.

The realization of the line of Comrade Kim Il Sung for founding the Democratic People's Republic of Korea was the greatest national task of the entire people of North and South Korea. Only by founding the D.P.R.K. was it possible to establish a unified central government representing the interests and will of the entire people in North and South Korea, thoroughly expose the illegal and reactionary nature of the South Korean puppet "government" hammered out by the U.S. imperialists, and to bring the struggle of the entire Korean people for the unification of the country onto a higher plane under the banner of the Republic.

Moreover, the establishment of the D.P.R.K. alone could

provide favorable conditions for the struggle to drive out the U.S. imperialist troops of aggression from South Korea and achieve the independent unification of the country, and for the external activities, and could further strengthen our solidarity with the international revolutionary forces.

In August 1948, the elections of the deputies to the Supreme People's Assembly were victoriously held throughout North and South Korea amidst high political zeal of the entire Korean people.

Comrade Kim Il Sung was elected deputy to the Supreme People's Assembly with the absolute support of the entire people.

The Supreme People's Assembly, convened in September 1948 on the basis of the North and South Korean general elections, adopted the Constitution of the D.P.R.K., formed the Government of the D.P.R.K., and appointed Comrade Kim Il Sung, the respected and beloved Leader of the Korean people, as Premier of the Cabinet.

The founding of the D.P.R.K. with Comrade Kim Il Sung as the head was the embodiment of the unanimous desire of our nation for the attainment of freedom and independence of the country, a brilliant victory of the Korean people in their struggle for the building of a sovereign, independent state, a historic event of epochal significance in the revolutionary struggle of our people marching forward for the bright future of socialism and communism.

Comrade Kim Il Sung said as follows:

"**With the foundation of the Democratic People's Republic of Korea, our people turned from a nation who had been deprived of their country by foreign imperialists and suffered all sorts of humiliation and insult, into a mighty and dignified nation whom no one would dare to flout, into a resourceful people of a sovereign independent state who build their country with their own efforts, firmly holding power in their hands.**

The establishment of the Republic enabled the Korean people to shed the bitter fate of a ruined nation once and for all and enter a new arena of history under the banner of a full-fledged independent state, it enabled our country, which had long suffered an eclipse on the world map, to enter the international arena on a par with big and small countries of the world."

The D.P.R.K. has become the banner of freedom and independence for the Korean people and the powerful weapon for the building of socialism and communism.

As a result of the founding of the D.P.R.K., a powerful citadel of socialism rose and shone brilliantly in the East which had long been kept in imperialist bondage. The founding of the Republic forcefully stimulated and propelled the revolutionary struggle of the peoples of the world for national independence, democracy and socialism, and dealt a heavy blow at the U.S. imperialist policy of colonial enslavement.

At that time the U.S. imperialists became more open in their manoeuvres of military provocation against the northern half and ran amuck further to unleash another war. In the meantime, the U.S. imperialists made frantic efforts to suppress and ruin the revolutionary forces, perpetrating the atrocity of slaughtering South Korean people in masses. Further, the spy clique, who had cunningly covered up their cloven hoofs and wormed their way into our revolutionary ranks, nefariously manoeuvred to split and destroy the revolutionary forces under the manipulation of the U.S. imperialists.

While further building up the defence power of the country to cope with these manoeuvres of the enemy, Comrade Kim Il Sung took the epochal measures of merging the North and South Korean Workers' Parties into the Workers' Party of Korea in June 1949 with the object of setting right the Party work in South Korea which was on the point of bankruptcy and strengthening the united leadership of the North and South Korean Workers' Parties.

To rally the broad revolutionary forces around the Party, Comrade Kim Il Sung also amalgamated the United Democratic National Fronts of North and South Korea, which had embraced over 70 political parties and public organizations, to form a single Democratic Front for the Unification of the Fatherland.

In June 1950, under the circumstances in which the manoeuvres of the U.S. imperialists to provoke a war had reached a grave stage, Comrade Kim Il Sung made a series of new, reasonable proposals to prevent the outbreak of war in Korea by all means and realize the peaceful unification of the country.

The proposals enjoyed unanimous support not only of the Korean people, but also of the progressive peoples of the whole world.

Comrade Kim Il Sung fought energetically to strengthen the international revolutionary forces and hasten the victory of the world revolution, while victoriously leading the Korean revolution.

Comrade Kim Il Sung set it as a consistent policy of the Party and the Government to fight for the advancement of the world revolution as a whole, which is organically coordinated with the Korean revolution, and strove for the realization of the policy.

He led the Party and the people to turn resolutely against the policy of aggression and war pursued by the U.S. imperialists in all parts of the world and render active support and encouragement to the revolutionary struggle of the peoples of other countries, and taught that all the anti-imperialist, anti-U.S. forces should unite and fight against imperialism headed by U.S. imperialism.

He made devoted efforts to render active support and encouragement to the anti-imperialist national-liberation struggle of the oppressed peoples of the world and to ensure the unity of the socialist camp and the international communist movement.

In December 1949 when the U.S. imperialists launched an all-out "anti-communist" campaign while stepping up preparations for a new war and the revisionists, keeping pace with them, openly manoeuvred to split the international revolutionary forces, Comrade Kim Il Sung called the Second Plenary Meeting of the Party Central Committee where he laid bare and condemned the nefarious manoeuvres of the U.S. imperialists, the Tito clique and other revisionists and elucidated the principled stand of the Communists to be maintained in the struggle to prevent war and preserve peace.

Comrade Kim Il Sung taught as follows:

"**Historical experiences show that the weaker the position of the imperialists and the less their hope of getting out of the fix grow, the more desperate their flounce and adventurism become. It is a big mistake, and harmful to the cause of peace, to jump at the conclusion that the danger of war has already lessened, simply because the imperialist camp has been weakened and the democratic camp strengthened.**

"**Peace cannot be safeguarded unless the struggle against the war incendiaries is organized and waged effectively, no matter how strong the force of the democratic camp may be and how sincerely the freedom-loving peoples of the whole world may want peace. To prevent war and win peace, war incendiaries and marauders must be exposed and repudiated, and a vigorous struggle waged against them in all parts of the world.**"

Having elucidated the revolutionary Marxist-Leninist position on war and peace, Comrade Kim Il Sung stressed the need for all the anti-imperialist forces in the world to unite and intensify the anti-imperialist, anti-U.S. struggle.

In the post-liberation period of peaceful construction, Comrade Kim Il Sung guided the Korean people to build the northern half into a revolutionary democratic base and fortify it politically, economically and militarily, and thereby provided a firm guarantee for crushing the armed invasion of the U.S. imperialists, defending the independence of the country and actively driving forward the Korean revolution.

Comrade Kim Il Sung also set forth the correct line and policy for the South Korean revolution and the unification of the country, and led the Korean people in their struggle for the materialization of the line and policy along the rightest path, thus dealing a heavy blow at the colonial enslavement policy pursued by the U.S. imperialists in South Korea and their intrigue for the split of our nation.

Indeed, thanks to the wise leadership and unflagging struggle of Comrade Kim Il Sung the Korean people with their revolutionary Party, people's government and their invincible People's Army could wage a fruitful struggle to create a new life under the people's democratic system in the northern half for the first time in their history, and unfold an energetic struggle for the nation-wide victory of the revolution, relying upon the revolutionary democratic base—the northern half.

Through these historic changes and their actual life, the entire people of Korea realized more deeply the great vitality of Comrade Kim Il Sung's revolutionary ideas and the sagacity of his leadership and marched forward, rallied steel-strong around him with the firm conviction that they would definitely win victory if they advance along the road indicated by him.

5

The U.S. imperialist aggressors and their lackeys, Syngman Rhee puppet clique, rejected the reasonable proposals of the Government of the Republic for the realization of the peaceful unification of the country, and at last started the war of aggression against the Korean people by launching a surprise armed attack on the northern half on June 25, 1950.

The armed invasion of the U.S. imperialists forced our people to suspend their peaceful labour and undergo the severe trials of war.

The war forced upon us by the U.S. imperialists was a life-and-death struggle to decide whether we defend the independence of the fatherland and the honour of the nation or fall into U.S. imperialist colonial slavery.

The struggle of the Korean people against the armed invasion of the U.S. imperialists and their stooges was a just national-liberation war to repulse the aggression of the U.S. imperialists and safeguard the freedom and independence of the country, a fierce class struggle against the U.S. imperialists and their accomplices, the domestic forces of reaction, and a bitter anti-imperialist, anti-U.S. struggle against the allied forces of world reaction headed by U.S. imperialism. At the same time, it was a great revolutionary war for smashing the U.S. imperialist scheme to unleash another world war through expansion of the Korean war, for defending the security of the socialist camp and world peace and further developing the world revolutionary movement.

The Presidium of the Supreme People's Assembly and the Government of the Democratic People's Republic of Korea appointed the respected and beloved Leader Comrade Kim Il Sung, the ever-victorious iron-willed brilliant commander and military strategic genius, as Chairman of the Military Commission and Supreme Commander of the Korean People's Army.

Taking upon his shoulders all the Party, Government and military affairs, all work at the front and in the rear, Comrade Kim Il Sung organized and mobilized the entire Korean people to the struggle for victory in the war.

In his historic radio address **"Every Effort for Victory in the War"** made on June 26, 1950, Comrade Kim Il Sung set forth militant tasks for victory in the war and called upon the entire Korean people and the men and officers of the People's Army to rise as one in the sacred struggle for wiping out the U.S. imperialist armed invaders and their stooges from the territory of our country.

Comrade Kim Il Sung taught in the address that in the Fatherland Liberation War against the U.S. imperialists and Syngman Rhee gang the Korean people must defend with their lives the Democratic People's Republic of Korea and its Constitution, overthrow the traitorous puppet regime in the southern half and liberate the southern half of our country from the colonial rule of the U.S. imperialists, restore in the southern half the people's committees—the organs of genuine people's power—and accomplish the cause of national unification under the banner of the Democratic People's Republic of Korea.

Comrade Kim Il Sung raised the slogan "Everything for victory in the war!" and turned the front and the rear into a formidable combat formation.

Comrade Kim Il Sung took emergency measures to strengthen the People's Army, place the country's economy on a war footing and consolidate the rear.

The war forced upon the Korean people by the U.S. imperialists was a severe trial to them.

Our Republic was then still young. Our people were liberated only five years before from the Japanese imperialist yoke and it was only two years after the birth of the People's Army. Our economic power was still weak, too.

Under these circumstances, the Korean people had to fight against the U.S. imperialists who had the strongest military and economic power in the capitalist world and a long history of aggressive wars, and the armed invaders of 16 countries headed by them and the stooge of the U.S. imperialists, the traitorous Syngman Rhee clique.

This really could not but be a hard strain for our people.

But as leading their van was Comrade Kim Il Sung, the ever-victorious iron-willed brilliant commander, military strategic genius and the great Leader of the revolution, who had beaten the strong Japanese imperialists even in the worst conditions without any help except the support of the revolutionary masses during the anti-Japanese armed struggle and led the anti-Japanese armed struggle to victory, our people were filled with the firm conviction that they could surely defeat the U.S. imperialists.

Comrade Kim Il Sung made a subtle analysis of the unjust character of the aggressive war by the U.S. imperialist aggressors, their vulnerability, the adventuristic nature of their strategy, the instability of imperialist alliance, etc. He also fully analyzed all factors of victory in the war— the just character of the war the Korean people were waging, the political and moral superiority of our People's Army inheriting the revolutionary traditions of the anti-Japanese armed struggle, inexhaustible might of the people united closely around the Party and the Leader, indestructible vitality of the people's democratic system and the international support and encouragement of the peoples of the whole world. Then he laid down brilliant strategic and tactical lines in each period and stage of the war and guided the entire people and People's Army to victory in the war.

At the first stage of the war, Comrade Kim Il Sung set forth the strategic line of frustrating the enemy's armed invasion and going over swiftly to the counter-offensive to smite and wipe out the main forces of the enemy with a high degree of manoeuvre and successive blows before the U.S. imperialist aggressors could bring in large troops in reinforcement, and thereby liberating the people of the southern half.

The People's Army which, thanks to Comrade Kim Il Sung's superb strategy and tactics and commanding art, repulsed the surprise attack of the enemy and went over to the counter-offensive, continued to advance southward, administering a crushing blow to the enemy.

Already at the beginning of the counter-offensive, Comrade Kim Il Sung made a scientific analysis of the enemy's designs, his deployment and so on, and, on this basis, set forth the detailed operational lines and skilfully commanded the People's Army units in their combat actions.

This enabled the People's Army firmly to take the initiative from the outset of the war and keep striking at the enemy, allowing him no breathing space to strengthen his defences in new sectors.

Advancing southward like surging waves, the People's Army liberated the Seoul area, where the main enemy forces were concentrated, three days after the outbreak of the war and continued to advance in the direction of Taejon breaking through the enemy sectors of defence.

The U.S. imperialists tried madly to check the advance of our People's Army by reinforcing their forces of aggression in a big way.

In this connection, Comrade Kim Il Sung, in his radio address on July 8, 1950, emphasized that the entire Korean people and men and officers of the People's Army should decisively rout and drive out the armed invaders from our land and achieve the final victory in the Fatherland Liberation War, appealing to them as follows:

"Let us march forward to drive out the U.S. imperialists to the last man from the soil of the country where generation after generation of our ancestors lie buried and where our beloved younger generation is growing up. Let us carry our righteous liberation struggle to a victorious conclusion so that the glorious flag of the Democratic People's Republic of Korea will wave high over Pusan, Mokpo and Mt. Halla-san on Cheju-do Island."

In response to the militant call of the Leader, the People's Army continued to advance southward, dealing a crushing blow at the enemy.

Even with their large military reinforcements the U.S. imperialist aggressors could not alter the situation on the front.

The combined People's Army units that had closed in upon Taejon, a point of strategic and operational importance for the enemy, applied various tactics—frontal attack, annihilation through encirclement, swift manoeuvre and detour, ambush and assault—and won a shining victory in completely wiping out the 24th Division of the U.S. imperialist aggression army which the U.S. imperialist aggressors had boasted as an "ever-victorious division" and in routing and finishing off large numbers of puppet army troops, thereby liberating Taejon.

The operation for liberating Taejon conducted under the personal command of Comrade Kim Il Sung inflicted a mortal defeat upon the U.S. imperialist aggression forces; it again showed clearly the invincible force of his outstanding strategy and tactics.

In those days of fierce battles, Supreme Commander

Comrade Kim Il Sung went to the front under a rain of shells to plan and direct operations personally, and inspired and encouraged the fighting men and officers in the trenches.

Under the superb leadership of the respected and beloved Leader, the People's Army men and officers, displaying matchless bravery and mass heroism, routed the U.S. imperialist aggressors and liberated more than 90 per cent of the whole territory of the southern half and over 92 per cent of its population in one month and a half and drove the enemy into a corner, the narrow area of North and South Kyongsang Provinces, thus registering brilliant war results.

While commanding the People's Army units at the front, Comrade Kim Il Sung made every effort to organize and enlist the entire people in the rear for victory in the war.

In wholehearted response to the militant call of the Leader, the people in the rear came out as one in the sacred war to annihilate the enemy. About 850,000 youths and students volunteered for the front in only a few weeks after the war started.

Our working class formed workers' regiments everywhere to go to the front and, at the same time, voluntarily prolonged the working hours, organized and unfolded a "front shock brigade movement," a "youth workteam movement" and various other types of emulation drives for increased production to aid the front. The peasants put all their patriotic zeal into the wartime production of food. And our transport fighters ensured wartime transportation, improving every minute.

Comrade Kim Il Sung directed the work of forming Party and government bodies and public organizations and carrying out a land reform and other democratic reforms in those areas of the southern half liberated by the People's Army, and thus ensured democratic freedom and rights for the people there. The political and economic footholds of the U.S. imperialists and their stooges were eliminated in vast areas of the southern half, and a new democratic system and order was established in all spheres of social life.

The liberated people of the southern half, full of joy at the new life, rallied firmly around the great Leader Comrade Kim Il Sung and did all they could to aid the People's Army advancing southward.

Large numbers of patriotic youths and students in the southern half voluntarily joined the Volunteers' Corps and took part in the sacred war for the annihilation of the enemy. Their number reached more than 400,000 in a few weeks after the liberation by the People's Army.

Faced with defeat, the U.S. imperialist aggressors made frenzied efforts. The U.S. imperialists mobilized all their Pacific forces, ground, naval and air, and part of their Mediterranean fleet and even brought the armed forces of their satellite countries to the Korean front by abusing the signboard of the "United Nations" in a vain attempt to seize our country at a rush.

In September 1950 they conducted a large-scale landing operation on the Inchon area by mobilizing over 300 war vessels, more than 1,000 planes and upwards of 50,000 troops, while rushing hundreds of thousands of fresh troops to the front.

In view of the new military and political situation, Comrade Kim Il Sung set forth the strategic line of ensuring the strategic retreat of the main forces of the People's Army by retarding the enemy's advance and gaining time on the one hand and, on the other, of organizing new reserve units to form strong counter-offensive groups in order to prepare for a fresh, decisive blow at the enemy and turn the general war situation in our favour.

The strategic line set forth by Comrade Kim Il Sung was a most positive and wise line aimed to weaken and defeat the enemy who had secured temporary superiority, and preserve and strengthen the forces of our army, reorganizing them swiftly to deal a decisive blow at the enemy.

In his radio address on October 11, 1950, Comrade Kim Il Sung called upon the entire people and men and officers of the People's Army to defend every inch of soil of the country with blood, prepare all forces for delivering a new decisive blow to the enemy and smite and wipe out the U.S. imperialists and their stooges to the last man from our land.

In wholehearted response to the call of Comrade Kim Il Sung, the entire people fought heroically even in the difficult period of temporary retreat, with the firm conviction that they could surely win the final victory if only they fought bravely, rallied firmly around him.

Comrade Kim Il Sung resolutely organized battles for defending the Seoul-Inchon area where the enemy staged large-scale landing operations, and foiled the enemy's scheme and ensured the operations for the organized retreat of the main units from the front. The main People's Army units completed their retreat successfully in a short span of time, dealing a heavy blow at the enemy everywhere.

Comrade Kim Il Sung saw to it that the second front was formed behind the enemy line with some of the main units in retreat so as to inflict tremendous losses upon the enemy's manpower and materiel, liberate many enemy-occupied areas and prepare themselves to join in the new offensive operations of the People's Army later. Thanks to this measure, the enemy was put on the defensive and hit hard both in front and rear.

In response to the appeal of the Leader to organize guerilla units to strike at the U.S. imperialist aggressors, give the enemy not a gram of rice and resist and fight him in every way, the Party members and people behind the enemy line formed the people's guerilla units and attacked by surprise and wiped out the enemy in many places. Even young boys organized guerilla units and beat the enemy, thereby making him shudder with uneasiness and fear.

From the first days of the war the U.S. imperialists resorted to all sorts of most barbarous methods of warfare unprecedented in the war history. The U.S. imperialists killed peaceable inhabitants savagely by their indiscriminate bombing of schools and hospitals, cultural establishments and populated areas and, particularly during our temporary retreat, committed thrice-cursed massacres and atrocities in all parts of the country.

Referring to such brutal atrocities of the U.S. imperialist aggressors, Comrade Kim Il Sung pointed out as follows:

"Engels once called the British army the most brutal army. During the Second World War, the German fascist army outdid the British army in its savagery. No human brains could ever imagine more diabolical and more horrible barbarities than those committed by the Hitlerite villains at that time.

"But in Korea, the Yankees surpassed by far the Hitlerites."

No amount of bestiality on the part of the U.S. imperialist aggressors, however, could ever bring the Korean people to their knees.

Even in the hard days of retreat, our people remained true to the call of the Leader to the end and fought heroically, following the example of the anti-Japanese guerillas who had thought and acted according to his ideas and will in any adversity and had not even hesitated to lay down their lives in carrying out his orders and instructions.

The enemy's plan to occupy the whole territory of our country at a breath fizzled out completely.

In late October 1950, the strategic retreat of the People's Army ended under the superb leadership of Comrade Kim Il Sung, and the war entered the third stage.

Comrade Kim Il Sung made it clear that the strategic line at the new stage where a counter-offensive would be taken was to drive away the enemy, who had made an inroad into the northern half, to the south of the 38th parallel and weaken his strength through a constant warfare of attrition while making all preparations well for victory in the war.

Conducting bold combat actions in accordance with the strategic line laid down by Comrade Kim Il Sung, the People's Army units completely liberated the enemy-held areas in the northern half of the Republic by the end of December 1950 and foiled the enemy's much-vaunted "Christmas general offensive." Meanwhile, the units operating on the second front behind the enemy line according to the foresighted and positive strategic plan mapped out by Comrade Kim Il Sung, struck hard at the back of the enemy in concert with the frontline units on the counter-offensive, wiping out numerous effectives of the enemy including the U.S. imperialists' 8th Field Army commander and capturing quantities of combat materiel and technical equipment.

In order to recover from their defeat, the U.S. imperialists brought up huge military reinforcements and set out on a new military adventure. The war thus came to assume a protracted nature.

In connection with the protraction of the war Comrade Kim Il Sung convened the Third Plenary Meeting of the Central Committee of the Party in December 1950 in order to further consolidate the front and the rear and take a decisive offensive against the enemy, clear away the temporary confusion caused during the retreat and improve and strengthen the work of the Party and state organs and the army.

Comrade Kim Il Sung delivered the report **"The Present Situation and the Immediate Tasks"** at the plenary meeting.

In the report, Comrade Kim Il Sung criticized some undisciplined practices revealed during the temporary retreat and set it forth as the first and foremost task to strengthen revolutionary discipline in the Party and state organs and in the army

Comrade Kim Il Sung taught that the more difficulties cropped up before the Party and the revolution, the more the Party discipline had to be strengthened and the unity and cohesion of the Party ranks be maintained and only in this way could the ultimate victory be achieved in the war.

Comrade Kim Il Sung taught as follows:

"**One of the essential conditions for defeating the ferocious enemy and winning a glorious victory is that our Party strengthens discipline more than ever and unites its ranks more steel-like around the Party Central Committee.... It should be seen that the firm work style prevails in the whole Party of carrying out the orders of the Party promptly and accurately through fire and water.**"

Touching upon the necessity of rejecting dogmatism and establishing *Juche* thoroughly in military activities, he also taught that the technical equipment of the army had to be improved and reinforced to suit the geographical features of our country which is mountainous and to meet the requirements of modern warfare and that a complete mastery of mountain and night warfares had to be acquired.

In the report, Comrade Kim Il Sung set forth the task of healing the wounds caused during the temporary retreat and firmly building up the rear. He put forward the measures to restore and readjust the Party and government bodies at the shortest possible date, rehabilitate the ravaged national economy and stabilize the people's livelihood in the liberated areas. And he pointed out that those who had joined reactionary organizations during the enemy's temporary occupation should be dealt with correctly, and an all-out offensive be taken against counter-revolutionaries.

Underscoring the question of displaying the revolutionary spirit of self-reliance in the war to a high degree, Comrade Kim Il Sung taught as follows:

"Our problems should be solved by ourselves, no matter who may help us and how. The masters are us, the Korean people. The masters should make more efforts. The inspirer and organizer of our people is our Workers' Party. The member of the Workers' Party is the core, active vanguard and initiator of the working people.

"Whether our nation can work out its own salvation or not depends upon how our Party works and how our People's Army fights."

In accordance with the teachings given by Comrade Kim Il Sung at the plenary meeting, the Party unfolded a vigorous struggle to strengthen revolutionary discipline in all fields and organized and mobilized the entire people and People's Armymen for the ultimate victory in the war.

The Third Plenary Meeting of the Party Central Committee held in the grimmest days of the war had an enormous significance in arming all the Party members with the spirit of strengthening revolutionary discipline to uphold and carry out the orders and instructions of the Leader unconditionally, thereby thoroughly establishing the unitary ideological system in the whole Party, further increasing the combat power of the Party, overcoming dogmatism in military affairs, further enhancing the fighting capacity of the People's Army, consolidating the rear and achieving fresh victories at the front.

From June 1951 on, the front was fixed in the main along the 38th parallel and the war entered a new stage.

Comrade Kim Il Sung, in view of the new situation, set forth the strategic line of building strong defence positions and launching active position defence battles, holding out the areas in our hands and incessantly knocking the enemy out of action and, on the other hand, gaining time to further increase the fighting capacity of the People's Army and consolidate the rear all the more so as to create every condition for the final victory in the war.

Wholeheartedly upholding the line advanced by the Leader, the People's Army men and officers excavated tunnels and, relying on them, switched over to the active position defence battle, thus inflicting heavy blows in succession on the enemy through close co-operation between the infantry and artillery units

The enemy, having suffered reverse after reverse, was compelled to propose to our side to hold armistice negotiations.

The enemy tried to get a breathing space behind the smoke-screen of the armistice negotiations and retrieve his military defeat by crafty diplomatic devices.

Having seen through the enemy's attempt in advance, Comrade Kim Il Sung clarified our stand and attitude to cope with it. Pointing out that no one should harbour any illusion about the U.S. imperialist aggressors, he taught that our forces should be further strengthened, the enemy be dealt military blows without respite, and the insidious attempt of the U.S. imperialists behind the smoke-screen of the armistice negotiations be thoroughly foiled.

The armistice negotiations started on July 10, 1951. The enemy used every conceivable absurd argument and crafty trick in the armistice negotiations. But the foolish, sinister intrigues of the enemy were frustrated each time by the resolute and uncompromising stand of our side.

When they failed to attain their ends in the armistice negotiations, the U.S. imperialists made an attempt to launch a large-scale offensive in combination with landing operations on the coasts, while largely reinforcing their armed forces on the front, and went so far as to threaten us with atomic weapons.

But no military offensive or threat of the enemy could ever frighten the Korean people united rock-firm around the Leader.

Comrade Kim Il Sung said as follows:

"**No matter how desperately the U.S. imperialists may try to threaten the people with atomic weapons and to subdue them** on the strength of their military technique, their wild ambition will inevitably come to grief....

"The valiant struggle of the Korean people has proved to the freedom-loving people of the whole world that atomic blackmail could not have any effect on their struggle for the independence and freedom of the country. The war we are waging will, therefore, give a practical lesson to the imperialist marauders and an immense encouragement to the peoples in colonies and dependent countries and will become the banner of liberation movement for the oppressed nations."

In the period from mid-August 1951 to early November, the enemy launched the "summer and autumn offensives" by mobilizing huge forces in a vain attempt to seize areas of the northern half once again and, politically, to achieve the so-called "honorable armistice" by bringing military pressure to bear upon our side.

While pretending to launch a big offensive in the western sector of the front, the enemy, who had sustained a heavy defeat in the first large-scale "summer offensive" owing to the distinguished strategy and tactics of Comrade Kim Il Sung, concentrated huge forces in the eastern sector of the front and again launched an "autumn offensive" viciously to seize the northern half of the Republic at a stretch in co-operation with his units to be landed on the east coast.

Having seen through the crafty scheme of the enemy in good time, Comrade Kim Il Sung taught that the enemy's offensive had to be crushed by moving some of our defence units from the west coast quickly to the eastern sector of the front and forming, in the meantime, an impregnable zone of defence in the area of Height 1211 where the enemy's large-scale attack was expected, and then by conducting a big annihilation operation there.

While personally commanding the defensive battle for Height 1211, Comrade Kim Il Sung saw that strong reserve units were formed and the defences on the east coast further strengthened to counter the enemy's attempt for landing.

The defenders of Height 1211 who were boundlessly loyal to Supreme Commander Comrade Kim Il Sung fought bloody fights giving a wholesale death to the enemy who made attacks scores of times every day on the grim battlefield where a daily average of 30,000-40,000 enemy shells and bombs were showered and rocks were crushed into powder and the earth scorched. On Height 1211 fierce battles went on day in, day out. Through the heroic struggle the People's Army turned the height into a "Heartbreak Ridge" and the ravine below into a "Punch Bowl" for the enemy and defended the height of the country with honour.

Comrade Kim Il Sung, directing the operations for defending the height, showed paternal love for the fighting People's Army men and officers. When the defence battle for the height was going on fiercely, he told the Army Commander there that each combatant was an invaluable revolutionary comrade-in-arms and priceless asset, and earnestly instructed him to see that as it was getting chilly all of them were served with warm rice meals and hot soup and they were provided with warm beds lest they should catch cold. Encouraged by the deep love of the Leader, the defenders of the height displayed mass heroism with redoubled courage in the battles for annihilating the enemy.

Throughout the whole period of the war, Comrade Kim Il Sung showed warm fatherly concern for every aspect of the life of the People's Army men and officers as he had done for the guerillas in the days of the anti-Japanese armed struggle. All the commanding personnel followed his teachings and examples and fully displayed the traditional traits of revolutionary comradeship and unity between men and officers. Thus, the men and officers of the People's Army performed brilliant exploits in repulsing and thwarting at every step the large-scale offensives conducted by the enemy by employing all barbarous methods of war.

Thanks to the superiority of the military art created by Comrade Kim Il Sung, the "summer and autumn offensives" of the enemy ended in failure and the enemy sustained severe defeats. It demonstrated once again to the whole world that our People's Army equipped with the revolutionary ideas of the great Leader Comrade Kim Il Sung, the ever-victorious iron-willed brilliant commander, and led by him, is invincible in fights against any enemy.

The U.S. imperialists, having suffered decisive setbacks in their "summer and autumn offensives," were compelled to come out again to the conference table for armistice negotiations, which they had unilaterally broken off, and to accept the proposals of our side.

The victories of the heroic People's Army at the front were closely linked with the correct and scrupulous guidance given by Comrade Kim Il Sung to steadily strengthen and develop its combat capacity.

Comrade Kim Il Sung attached a decisive significance to Party political work in strengthening and augmenting the combat capacity of the army.

Comrade Kim Il Sung taught as follows:

"**For an army to win a battle it should, of course, have good weapons, but should have a high degree of fighting spirit, ideological consciousness and a high level of technique. In particular, ideological consciousness has a decisive significance.**"

At the outbreak of the war, he assigned a great number of competent political cadres to the army, reorganized the previous Cultural Department into the Political Department to further strengthen Party political work in the army, and gave concrete teachings on the system and method of its work.

On the personal initiative of Comrade Kim Il Sung, Party

organizations and political organs were set up in the People's Army in October 1950.

The establishment of Party organizations and political organs in the People's Army was a most sagacious measure for arming the People's Armymen more firmly politically and ideologically and an epochal event in strengthening Party political work in the People's Army and enhancing its combat capacity.

The Party organizations and political organs in the army explained and brought home to the entire servicemen the instructions and orders of Supreme Commander Comrade Kim Il Sung in good time, and organized and conducted Party political work energetically for their thorough implementation, thereby uniting all the armymen rock-firm around Comrade Kim Il Sung.

Comrade Kim Il Sung organized and directed the work of training and re-educating large numbers of commanding officers and political cadres of all services and arms in order to expand the ranks of the People's Army in compliance with the increasing requirements of the front, and to strengthen the ranks qualitatively and especially to elevate the ability of the commanding personnel and the staff as organizers. Thus, even under the war conditions, officers' schools at various levels and different training centres were newly set up or expanded, and many new commanding officers and political cadres were trained.

Also, Comrade Kim Il Sung directed deep attention to improving and reinforcing the armament and equipment of the units of every service and arm to suit all the characteristics of modern warfare and the natural-economic and military-geographical conditions of our country. Consequently, the fighting capacity of the People's Army increased constantly even in the conditions of the fierce war, and our People's Army was equipped better with modern military technique.

The model company movement conducted on the initiative of Supreme Commander Comrade Kim Il Sung in 1952 to increase the combat capacity of the People's Army acquired an important significance in strengthening and developing the entire units of the People's Army politically, ideologically and in military technique, and in leading the armymen to display mass heroism on the front.

In particular, the historic speech of Comrade Kim Il Sung, **"Let Us Strengthen the People's Army"** made in December 1952 was of tremendous significance in creatively developing the Marxist-Leninist theory concerning the question of the character of war and the permanent factors of victory in the war and other military affairs, in equipping all the men and officers of the People's Army and the masses of the people with scientific knowledge to ensure victory in the war, and in training the People's Army into a cadre army and modernizing it.

While organizing and directing the operations in every section of the front to assure victory, Comrade Kim Il Sung energetically organized and guided in the rear the work of strengthening the Party and government bodies and enhancing their leading role and organizing and mobilizing the people to victory in the war.

He taught that in the complex and difficult circumstances of the war, no time should be lost to spot and remedy defects in Party work, however trifling they might be, so as to steadily strengthen the Party organizationally and ideologically.

Comrade Kim Il Sung convened the Fourth Plenary Meeting of the Party Central Committee in November 1951, at which he took measures to overcome the Left deviations in Party work, expand and consolidate the Party ranks and strengthen the ties between the Party and the masses.

He severely criticized the close-doorist and penalty-imposing errors committed by the liquidationists for subverting the Party, and advanced the concrete tasks for expanding the Party ranks rapidly and consolidating them qualitatively. He then taught that in order to tighten the bonds between the Party and the masses, the united front work should be improved and strengthened and, especially, bureaucracy be rejected and the method and style of work of the functionaries improved.

The whole Party was mobilized for the struggle to implement the tasks set forth by Comrade Kim Il Sung.

Thus, the Left deviations in Party work were rectified, and in a short span of time hundreds of thousands of advanced elements of workers, peasants, armymen and working intellectuals who had fought devotedly at the front and in the rear were admitted to the Party, whose ranks grew into a big force one million strong. More, the Party organizations at all levels improved their level of guidance and overcame bureaucratic errors, thereby bringing into full play the activity and vanguard role of the Party members.

As a result, our Party was rapidly expanded and strengthened and its fighting power further enhanced, and the ties between the Party and the masses grew stronger.

After the fourth plenary meeting, Comrade Kim Il Sung waged a vigorous struggle against bureaucracy. The historic speech **"The Tasks and Role of the Local Power Organs at the Present Stage"** delivered by Comrade Kim Il Sung in February 1952 was of particular importance in opposing bureaucracy, establishing the popular method and style of work among the functionaries and rallying the masses around the Party.

In the speech, Comrade Kim Il Sung, urging the functionaries to wage an energetic struggle against the bureaucratic style of work, said as follows:

"The functionaries of people's power organs should become true servants of the people, who rely on the people in work, respect their interests, persuade and educate them instead of shouting commands to them, learn from them at all times and serve them wholeheartedly."

The speech of Comrade Kim Il Sung served as a programmatic guide to improving the method and style of work of the functionaries of the Party and government bodies and strengthening their ties with the masses. Through the struggle for implementing the tasks set in the speech, criticisms were made on the bureaucratic style of work manifested among some functionaries of the Party and government bodies who regarded it quite natural to perform their work by dictates and administrative methods in wartime conditions, and all practices detrimental to the Party and the state were thoroughly exposed, criticized and remedied, with the result that the bonds of kinship between the Party and government bodies and the people were further strengthened and the creative zeal of the masses rose greatly.

The Fifth Plenary Meeting of the Party Central Committee held in December 1952 under the guidance of Comrade Kim Il Sung was a great event in strengthening and developing our Party.

At the plenary meeting, Comrade Kim Il Sung delivered the historic report **"The Organizational and Ideological Strengthening of the Party Is the Basis of Our Victory."**

In the report, Comrade Kim Il Sung put forward the programmatic task of tempering the Party spirit of the Party members, cementing the unity and cohesion of the Party ranks and overcoming dogmatism and formalism in ideological work to reinforce the Party organizationally and ideologically.

He raised it as one of the fundamental questions in Party building to steel the Party spirit of the Party members and gave a scientific definition of Party spirit.

Comrade Kim Il Sung said as follows:

"The heightening of Party spirit means for each member of the Workers' Party to be boundlessly loyal to the Party and active in Party work, regard the interests of the revolution and the Party as his life and soul and subordinate his

personal interests to them, defend the interests and principles of the Party when and where and in whatever conditions, fight uncompromisingly against all hues of anti-Party, counter-revolutionary ideas, lead his Party organizational life conscientiously and observe Party discipline strictly and to strengthen the bonds between the Party and the masses at all times."

Also, Comrade Kim Il Sung called upon the entire Party membership to unfold a resolute struggle against factionalist and liberalistic tendencies that hampered the Party's unity and cohesion.

Comrade Kim Il Sung taught in the report that it should be made the central task in the Party's ideological work to thoroughly overcome dogmatism, formalism and national nihilism existing in the Party's ideological work and solve the practical problems of our revolution from the unshaken position of *Juche*.

Stressing in the last part of the report that, first of all, our Party should be further consolidated in order to rout and wipe out the U.S. imperialists and their lackeys and win the freedom, unification and independence of the country, Comrade Kim Il Sung taught as follows:

"What does it mean to consolidate our Party?

"It means that our Party should be equipped with Marxism-Leninism, the all-conquering revolutionary theory that indicates the way to the overthrow of capitalism and emancipation of the working people.

"Consolidation of the Party means that iron discipline should be established in the Party, the unity of its ranks defended, the slightest factionalist tendency not tolerated, and the Party should be firmly protected from the infiltration of bourgeois ideas and tempered politically and ideologically.

"Strengthening of the Party also means educating the Party members in the spirit of serving the Party, the country and the people with all loyalty, of devoting themselves to the cause of emancipation of the labouring masses, remaining faithful to the principle of proletarian internationalism, hating the class enemies, sharpening revolutionary vigilance and of waging an uncompromising struggle against the slightest expression of bourgeois ideas.

"Consolidation of the Party means strengthening the bonds between the Party and the masses of the people, fighting stubbornly against the bureaucratic and formalistic style of work that divorces the Party from the masses and establishing the revolutionary style of work within the Party.

"Consolidation of the Party means permitting no conservatism, stagnation and indolence within the Party and cultivating the Party members in the indomitable fighting spirit of winning victory through a devoted struggle by overcoming all difficulties and in vivacious creative spirit."

The report of Comrade Kim Il Sung furnished a programmatic guide to strengthening our Party organizationally and ideologically and made a great contribution to advancing and enriching the Marxist-Leninist theory on Party building.

The fifth plenary meeting of our Party held under the leadership of Comrade Kim Il Sung was of great significance in reinforcing our Party organizationally and ideologically and hastening victory for the Fatherland Liberation War, as it roused the entire Party to the struggle to consolidate the Party's unity and cohesion, elevate the Party spirit of the Party members and their vanguard role, and establish *Juche* thoroughly against dogmatism and formalism in Party work.

Through the discussions on the documents adopted at the fifth plenary meeting, the Party spirit of the members was heightened markedly and the Party's fighting power increased further. Also in the course of the discussions of the documents, an anti-Party, counter-revolutionary spy clique that had been lurking in the Party for a long time was exposed and expelled, and a struggle started for rooting up factionalism that had been a historical malady in the communist movement in our country.

Even in the difficult conditions of the war, Comrade Kim Il Sung exerted tireless efforts to ensure wartime production adequately and stabilize the people's livelihood and to promote the arrangements for carrying out the far-sighted plans he worked out for the postwar rehabilitation and the country's eternal prosperity and progress.

Even though he was so busy organizing and directing all activities for victory in the war, shouldering the destinies of the country and the nation, he visited factories and rural villages in many parts of the country to lead Party-cell meetings and consult directly with workers and peasants about state affairs, inspiring them with firm confidence in victory in the war and encouraging them.

Indeed, the Leader was always with the people and shared sweets and bitters with them at any time and at any place in the raging flames of the war.

When the people were tackling an arduous job for increasing wartime production, he himself went out to the fields and assisted the peasants in sowing. Moreover, he personally grew vegetables and fruit trees. Besides, he took all possible steps in good time for stabilizing the livelihood of the people such as providing free medical care for war sufferers and exempting the peasants from returning loan grain and paying the tax in kind so that they had no worries about life even during that fierce war.

Comrade Kim Il Sung saw that nursery schools and educational institutes were set up in various places for the bereaved children of the men and officers of the People's Army and the patriotic martyrs who had fallen in the heroic fight against U.S. imperialism, and looked after their management and the study and life of the bereaved children with profound care

Besides, he had primary institutes established in various

places to take care of those orphans who had lost their homes and parents in the enemy's barbarous bombing and massacre and all arrangements made for their education and training at the safe areas.

Moreover, he saw that honoured wounded soldiers' schools were set up in many places for the men and officers of the People's Army and patriots who had been disabled while heroically fighting at the front and in the rear, so that they could study science and technology to their hearts' content according to their hopes and physical conditions.

Comrade Kim Il Sung also saw to it that the benefits of social maintenance were provided preferentially to the honoured wounded soldiers and the special courses for them set up in higher educational institutions and political schools so as to train them into competent national cadres.

Inspired by such meticulous guidance and warm care of the Leader, the workers, peasants and all other people of our country displayed fiery patriotic devotion to ensure wartime production and support the front.

While carrying on the work of consolidating the rear, Comrade Kim Il Sung boldly pushed ahead with the preparations for postwar rehabilitation and construction and socialist construction. Even in the crucible of the fierce war, he took a perspective view of the country's future and actively drove forward the work of creating the powerful base of machine industry. In the meantime, he shaped a plan for postwar rehabilitation and construction, pushed forward the surveys of the actual conditions of the demolished factories and enterprises, and personally directed the work of drafting the plans for the reconstruction of towns and factories and of drawing up their blueprints. And he saw to it that numerous large state agro-stock farms and farm-machine hire stations were set up, which would be of great help in transforming the countryside along socialist lines and, along with this, he organized and guided the work of exploring the country's natural resources and surveying the sites of nature-remaking projects. With a view to rearing the cadres urgently needed in the postwar rehabilitation and construction and socialist construction, he gave instructions to open all institutes of higher learning and call back combatants from the front for study at the institutes Moreover, he himself crossed rugged mountains to visit the university and other higher educational institutions and the Party school, and gave the faculty members and students specific orientations in their instruction and education as well as scientific researches. In April 1952, he convened a conference of scientists and gave them the orientation of scientific development. After that he not only founded the Academy of Sciences but also paid scrupulous attention, and rendered assistance, to individual scientists in their research work.

All this acquired a great significance not only in fortifying the rear reliably and equipping the army and the people with revolutionary optimism to make them fight more valiantly, but also in speedily healing the war wounds and carrying on victoriously the socialist revolution and socialist construction after the war.

Entering 1952, the enemy launched tenacious "offensives," while continuously increasing military forces on the Korean front and using bacteriological and chemical weapons in large quantities at the front and in the rear. But each time he suffered huge losses on his manpower and materiel due to the stubborn defence battles and tactical counterattacks of the People's Army units.

As the people were united firmly around the Leader, the front and the rear were built up impregnably and the combat actions of the People's Army stepped up, the enemy sank deeper into a bog with each passing day. Upset by this, at the outset of 1953 the U.S. imperialist aggressors hurried to stage a massive operation in their last desperation

Eisenhower, the warlike boss of the U.S. imperialists, who personally came to the Korean front at the end of 1952, prattled that "action is better than negotiations," and became more impetuous to accelerate preparations for a large-scale "new offensive" in a wild dream to cut off the front from the rear by conducting landing operations on the east and west coasts and thus "encircle and annihilate" our main units in conjunction with attack at the main front.

But in accordance with the distinguished strategy and tactics of Comrade Kim Il Sung, the ever-victorious iron-willed brilliant commander, and under his personal direction, the People's Army and people built up impregnable positions on the east and west coasts and at the front and waged a heroic struggle with a towering determination to annihilate the enemy and completely frustrated what the enemy called "new offensive."

Meanwhile, in mid-May 1953 the People's Army units at the main sectors of the front launched powerful counter-offensive battles against the enemy in succession and thus gave an annihilating blow to the enemy and liberated a vast area.

The longer the war dragged on, the more irretrievable military and political reverses the U.S. imperialists suffered in succession.

During the three years of the Korean war the enemy lost more than 1,093,800 men including over 397,000 U.S. imperialist aggressor troops, over 12,200 planes, 250-odd war vessels of different types and a huge amount of other combat and technical equipment.

The losses the U.S. imperialists suffered during the three-year Korean war reached nearly 2.3 times as much as the losses they had sustained in the four years of the Pacific War at the time of World War II both in manpower and combat and technical equipment.

Having sustained irretrievable military, political and moral setbacks, the U.S. imperialists found themselves unable to go on with the war any longer, and were compelled to kneel down before the Korean people and sign the Armistice Agreement.

On July 27, 1953, the just Fatherland Liberation War of the Korean people ended in a great victory for them thanks to the distinguished strategy and tactics and wise leadership of Comrade Kim Il Sung.

The shining victory of the Korean people in the Fatherland Liberation War was a splendid victory for Comrade Kim Il Sung's great military thought and brilliant military art Through his many immortal writings and practical activities of the wartime, Comrade Kim Il Sung liquidated dogmatism, established *Juche* more thoroughly in military and all other domains and creatively developed the Marxist-Leninist military science anew.

In many writings, speeches and orders, Comrade Kim Il Sung fully exposed the reactionary nature of bourgeois military theory and gave a unique answer to the question of correlation between man and military technique in the armed struggle.

Comrade Kim Il Sung said that it is man, not technique, that plays the decisive role in war, and technique becomes powerful only when the people master it and wage a just struggle, and taught that what is basic to enhancing the might of the People's Army, a revolutionary army, is to arm it politically and ideologically.

In the whole course of the war, Comrade Kim Il Sung equipped our People's Army and people with the ideology of our Party and the indomitable revolutionary spirit. The People's Army and our people who had been educated by the Leader exhibited matchless mass heroism for the cause of justice under his leadership and defeated the U.S. imperialist aggressors and won the great victory despite the numerical and technical superiority of the latter.

Comrade Kim Il Sung answering the rousing cheers of the men and officers of the heroic People's Army and the people who emerged victorious from the great Fatherland Liberation War

Comrade Kim Il Sung said as follows:

"**In this great struggle, our people fought determinedly as one in mind and body under the correct leadership of the Party and the Government of the Republic, and thereby withstood the harsh trials of war honorably and won a historic victory, inflicting an ignominious defeat on U.S. imperialism and its running dogs.**"

Comrade Kim Il Sung taught that only when its political and ideological superiority was combined with modern military technique, could a revolutionary army put out really great power. Even in the arduous conditions of the war he ensured the steady improvement of the technical equipment of the People's Army and directed its men and officers to be fully versed in military science and technique.

As a result, during the war our People's Army was further strengthened politically, ideologically and in military technique, and grew into a revolutionary army, each of its members being a match for a hundred.

During the Fatherland Liberation War, Comrade Kim Il Sung, not only gave new theoretical expositions to many important military problems such as the decisive role of the political and moral factor in modern warfare and the co-ordinated development of all the services and arms to suit the actual conditions of the country and the combination of regular and guerilla battles in war, but also substantiated their correctness in practice. Moreover, he created various new military arts such as immediate counter-attack action against the enemy's surprise attack, successive striking actions, formation of a second front behind the enemy line, tunnel warfare, building of field positions mainly in the form of tunnels and varied forms of active position-defence battle and assault based on them, snipers' movement, intensive utilization of artillery fire and strengthened activity of mobile artillery in mountain areas, aircraft hunters' team movement and tank hunters' team movement.

Indeed, Comrade Kim Il Sung led the Fatherland Liberation War to victory by overpowering the enemy's numerical and technical superiority with political and ideological, strategical and tactical superiority.

Our victory in the three-year Fatherland Liberation War demonstrated to the whole world that our people and People's Army led by the great Leader of revolution Comrade Kim Il Sung were invincible, and showed clearly that a people who rise with arms in their hands for the freedom and independence of their country can certainly defeat any enemy.

Guided by Comrade Kim Il Sung, the Korean people crushed the armed invaders of U.S. imperialism and thus not only defended the freedom and independence of the country and the honour of the nation firmly but frustrated the U.S. imperialist scheme for war expansion, and safeguarded the security of the socialist camp and peace in Asia and the rest of the world.

Also, our people smashed to atoms the myth about the "mightiness" of U.S. imperialism, thereby greatly inspiring the struggle of hundreds of millions of people the world over who were fighting for national independence and freedom, and brought about the beginning of decline for the U.S. imperialist aggressors, thus opening up a new phase in the anti-imperialist, anti-U.S. struggle.

The victory won by the Korean people in the life-and-death struggle against more than two million strong invasion forces of 16 countries including the U.S. imperialist aggression army which had boasted of being the "strongest" in the world and the South Korean puppet troops, is inconceivable apart from the sagacious leadership of Comrade Kim Il Sung and his brilliant strategy and tactics.

The Korean people could defeat the U.S. imperialist aggressors and win a great victory entirely thanks to the all-conquering, sagacious leadership of the great Leader Comrade Kim Il Sung who had accumulated rich experiences in the crucible of the prolonged anti-Japanese armed struggle and who possessed great revolutionary ideas and profound revolutionary theory, distinguished power of leadership and brilliant military strategy, indomitable will, extraordinary revolutionary sweep and high virtues.

The Presidium of the Supreme People's Assembly of the Democratic People's Republic of Korea, expressing the unanimous will of the entire people, awarded the title of Marshal of the D.P.R.K. on February 7, 1953 and the title of Hero of the D.P.R.K. on July 28, 1953 to Comrade Kim Il Sung, the ever-victorious iron-willed brilliant commander, military strategic genius and the respected and beloved Leader of the Korean people, who performed immortal feats by leading the Fatherland Liberation War to a great victory.

By leading the great Fatherland Liberation War of the Korean people to victory, Comrade Kim Il Sung performed really immortal exploits in the development of our revolution and the world revolution.

6

When the war was over, Comrade Kim Il Sung lost no time to organize and mobilize the whole Party and the entire people to the struggle for the postwar rehabilitation and construction of the national economy.

With the armistice our Party and people had new, tremendous tasks before them.

The armistice did not mean complete peace. Without drawing due lessons from their ignominious defeat in the war, the U.S. imperialists watched for a chance to resume invasion on the northern half. There still remained before our people the supreme national task of driving out the U.S. imperialists from South Korea and achieving the cause of national unification.

Maintaining a stand-by posture against the underhand manoeuvres of the U.S. imperialist aggressors, our Party and people had, above all, to rehabilitate the national economy totally ravaged in the war, stabilize and improve the extremely deteriorated people's livelihood, and more firmly build up the revolutionary base of the northern half politically, economically and militarily in order to achieve the nation-wide victory of the revolution.

It was very difficult to solve these tasks simultaneously under the postwar conditions of our country where everything was destroyed and reduced to ashes.

The enemy, U.S. imperialists, prattled that Korea would

not be able to rise to its feet again even in 100 years time Not a few of our friends who sympathized with us, too, expressed concern over the difficulties in the postwar rehabilitation and construction, for the destruction was so severe.

There was so much work to do and the situation was so difficult that we were quite at a loss what to begin with and how to rehabilitate and build.

But our people were neither discouraged nor wavered in the least in the face of the serious difficulties. The people trusted in the Leader and the Leader reposed faith in the people.

Fully convinced that no matter how serious the damage and how difficult the situation might be, a new life could be built again so long as there were the people, the territory, the Party and the people's government, Comrade Kim Il Sung roused the whole Party and the entire people to the grandiose struggle for the postwar rehabilitation and construction.

Comrade Kim Il Sung called the Sixth Plenary Meeting of the Party Central Committee on August 5, 1953, only a few days after the ceasefire, and clearly indicated the orientation of the postwar rehabilitation and construction, thereby illumining the road for our people to follow. He had a deep insight into the postwar situation in the country and the prospect of our revolution and, on this basis, set forth an original line of economic construction, the basic line of postwar economic construction on giving priority to the growth of heavy industry with simultaneous development of light industry and agriculture, which no one had ever tried his hand at.

Comrade Kim Il Sung taught as follows:

"In postwar economic construction we must follow the line of giving priority to the rehabilitation and development of heavy industry with simultaneous development of light industry and agriculture. This alone will enable us to consolidate the economic foundations of our country and improve the people's living conditions in a short period of time."

The basic line of postwar economic construction laid down by Comrade Kim Il Sung was the most sagacious line which made it possible to properly determine the orientation and order of priority in the rehabilitation and construction of the national economy and to correctly grasp the main link in the chain of work and concentrate efforts on it.

Without the priority development of heavy industry in our country following the war, it was impossible either to successfully rehabilitate and develop the severely war-ravaged light industry and agriculture or to lay the economic basis strong enough to improve the people's livelihood. The solution of the question of abolishing the colonial lopsidedness and technical lag of the national economy and laying the firm foundation of an independent national economy, too, hinged entirely on the priority development of heavy industry.

Yet, the development of light industry and agriculture could not be delayed.

It was necessary to rapidly advance light industry and agriculture, too, in order to quickly improve the people's livelihood which had been deteriorated in the war. And light industry and agriculture, together with heavy industry, had to be developed rapidly for building an independent national economy in our country where agriculture and light industry had been very backward originally.

As Comrade Kim Il Sung taught, this basic line of economic construction is the only correct line based on the proper calculation of the lawful requirements of economic development and actual possibilities in our country, a creative line based on the proper application of the Marxist-Leninist theory on extended reproduction to the specific realities of our country, and a revolutionary line which expresses the unshaken position of the Party for speedily building an independent national economy in the revolutionary spirit of self-reliance. This line represented the only path that afforded the possibility of firmly guaranteeing the independence and sovereignty of the country and building socialism most quickly and in a better way under backward economic conditions.

Indeed, this revolutionary line which embodied Comrade Kim Il Sung's idea of *Juche* in the field of socialist economic construction constitutes a brilliant example of creative application and development of Marxism-Leninism in socialist construction.

Under the postwar conditions in our country where everything was destroyed and in short supply, it was a very complicated and difficult task to ensure the priority growth of heavy industry with simultaneous development of light industry and agriculture.

The anti-Party factionalists infected with flunkeyism towards great powers and dogmatism slandered this line; they alleged that "Machines do not give us food," or that "Too much stress is put on the building of heavy industry while the people are leading a hard life."

Comrade Kim Il Sung resolutely brushed aside the ravings and obstructive manoeuvrings of the anti-Party factionalists and vigorously organized and mobilized the whole Party and the entire people to implementing the line

For the successful implementation of the huge tasks for postwar rehabilitation and construction, Comrade Kim Il Sung set forth the line of carrying out the postwar rehabilitation and construction of the national economy in **three basic stages**— the stage of preparations for overall rehabilitation and construction covering six months to one year, the stage of fulfilment of a three-year plan for regaining the prewar level in all fields of the national economy, and the stage of carrying out a five-year plan for laying the foundations of socialist industrialization.

The entire working people, upholding the line of economic construction advanced by Comrade Kim Il Sung, waged a vigorous struggle to successfully carry out the national economic plan for the postwar rehabilitation and development in the teeth of all hardships.

Our people could build a powerful independent national economy on the debris and radically improve their livelihood in a brief span of time after the war solely because Comrade Kim Il Sung set forth the original line of economic construction which fully accorded not only with the immediate interests of the country and the people but with their vital interests of future, and steadfastly led the Party and the people to carry it through.

Comrade Kim Il Sung energetically drove forward the work of transforming the relations of production on socialist lines in town and country side by side with the postwar economic construction work.

The most important thing in the socialist transformation of the old relations of production is the co-operativization of agriculture. This presented itself as an urgent requirement matured in our country in the postwar period.

In the conditions of our rural economy having been severely devastated in the war and manpower and draught animals being very short, it would have been impossible, if individual farming had been left alone, either to rapidly restore the ruined productive forces of agriculture, or speedily improve the life of the impoverished peasants and solve the problem of the poor peasants whose number had increased during the war. There was a danger that the contradictions between socialist state industry and individual peasant farming would give rise to a disparity between industry which was being rapidly rehabilitated and developed after the war and agriculture which was being rehabilitated very slowly.

On the basis of a concrete analysis of the actual requirements of the development of revolution and all the conditions created in our country, Comrade Kim Il Sung put forward a new, original line of carrying out the socialist reorganization of the form of economy, that is, agricultural co-operativization, prior to the technical reconstruction of agriculture, strictly in keeping with the actual conditions of our country, without sticking to any ready-made formulas or foreign experiences.

Until then it was considered as a law to carry out the socialist transformation of agriculture on the basis of industrialization.

In our country, too, the dogmatists and factionalists only turned to foreigners, and either opposed or hampered in this or that way the socialist transformation of agriculture, alleging that "transformation of production relations is impossible unless socialist industrialization is realized," or that "how can co-operativization be carried out when the North and the South have not yet been unified?"

Comrade Kim Il Sung categorically rejected such anti-Marxist-Leninist allegations alien to the realities and actively pushed forward the agricultural co-operativization.

Comrade Kim Il Sung taught as follows:

"...**Socialist transformation cannot be retarded when life itself demands an immediate reorganization of the outdated relations of production and there are the revolutionary forces prepared to carry it out, even though the level of development of the productive forces and technology is relatively low.**"

The line laid down by Comrade Kim Il Sung was a most active and revolutionary line designed to open up a broad avenue for the technical revolution by transforming, first of all, the relations of production on socialist lines to ensure the rapid advancement of the productive forces in accordance with the urgent requirements of the socio-economic development in the northern half and, by building up the revolutionary forces solidly, reinforce the revolutionary base of the northern half and hasten the nation-wide victory in the revolution.

Already during the war, Comrade Kim Il Sung had fostered

the new buds of co-operative economy in the countryside and, immediately after the ceasefire, organized agricultural co-operatives on an experimental basis by relying, above all, on the poor peasants and the rural Party nuclei and actively promoted this movement as the enthusiasm of the peasants increased.

In carrying out the agricultural co-operativization Comrade Kim Il Sung determined correctly the principles which the Party and the state had to observe, the stages and tempo of development of agricultural co-operativization, the forms and sizes of the co-operatives and so on in conformity with the actual conditions of our country, and gave guidance in promoting this complex and far-reaching socio-economic change rapidly and successfully.

In carrying out agricultural co-operativization, he worked out the correct class policy of relying firmly on the poor peasants, strengthening alliance with the middle peasants and restricting and gradually remoulding the rich farmers. And he saw to it that the peasants were educated by practical examples while the voluntary principle was strictly adhered to in the agricultural co-operative movement and that the guidance and assistance from the Party and the state were strengthened.

The concluding speech of Comrade Kim Il Sung "**On Our Party's Policy for the Future Development of Agriculture**" made at a Plenary Meeting of the Party Central Committee in November 1954 was of great historic significance in successfully accelerating the agricultural co-operative movement.

In the speech Comrade Kim Il Sung summed up the achievements scored in the experimental stage of the agricultural co-operative movement, pointed out the need to guard against all possible Right and Left deviations in the course of this movement and set forth the task of unfolding the agricultural co-operative movement extensively on a mass scale

Following the teaching of Comrade Kim Il Sung, agricultural co-operativization forged ahead apace in a mass movement.

While co-operativizing agriculture, Comrade Kim Il Sung also pushed ahead vigorously with the work of socialist transformation of urban handicrafts and capitalist trade and industry.

Already in 1947 when the transition period started, he set forth the line of reorganizing the individual economy of the handicraftsmen into the socialist co-operative economy by organizing producers' co-operatives with them. As a result, initial success was achieved and some experiences were accumulated in the socialist transformation of handicrafts already before the war.

As to the capitalist trade and industry in our country, too, Comrade Kim Il Sung, on the basis of an all-round analysis of their specific features, pursued the policy of reorganizing them gradually along socialist lines in the transition period while turning to account their good aspects and restricting their evil aspects.

In the postwar years the socialist reorganization of the capitalist trade and industry presented itself as an urgent demand.

The originally insignificant capitalist trade and industry of our country were reduced to almost nonexistence owing to the war, and if there were left any, they were as fragmented as the handicrafts. So, it was impossible for the entrepreneurs and tradesmen of our country either to restore their economy or improve their livelihood in the postwar years without turning to the state for active assistance and without pooling their labour power and funds.

Comrade Kim Il Sung who unerringly grasped such specific conditions, set forth the creative line of reorganizing the capitalist tradesmen and industrialists, together with the handicraftsmen, on socialist lines through various forms of co-operative economy.

This line advanced by Comrade Kim Il Sung for socialist transformation, and not expropriation, of the capitalist elements, was mapped out on the basis of a scientific analysis of the specific realities of our country, and it was the most correct line not only in full accord with the requirements of socialist construction but also in keeping with the interests of the entrepreneurs and tradesmen themselves.

Thanks to the correct line indicated by C o m r a d e Kim Il Sung and his wise leadership, the work of reorganizing urban handicrafts and capitalist trade and industry along socialist lines proceeded very smoothly and rapidly in our country.

With the socialist revolution and socialist construction forging ahead apace in the northern half, Comrade Kim Il Sung clearly explained the character and tasks of the revolution in our country and the ways for its accomplishment, taking into account the new changed situation and the different specific conditions created in the North and the South in the development of the revolution, educated the Party members and working people to have a thorough understanding of the prospects for development of the revolution and dynamically organized and unfolded the work of enhancing their class awakening to further reinforce the revolutionary forces politically and ideologically.

This was posed as a very pressing question in the circumstances where the dogmatists and flunkeys towards great powers were out to impede the onward movement of the revolution; they prattled as they pleased about the Korean revolution and its prospects, declaring that the socialist revolution was not to be advanced farther in the northern half till the North and the South were unified and that the socialist revolution in the northern half was premature.

In April 1955, Comrade Kim Il Sung issued theses on the character and tasks of our revolution "**Every Effort for the Country's Unification and Independence and for Socialist Con-**

struction in the Northern Half of the Republic," thereby lucidly indicating the path to be followed by our revolution.

In this historic work he gave a scientific analysis of the situation and the complex social and class relations created in the North and the South at that time and, on this basis, clearly defined the character and tasks of our revolution and our Party's strategic and tactical lines originating therefrom.

Comrade Kim Il Sung taught in the theses as follows:

"...The basic tasks of our revolution at the present stage are to smite the aggressive forces of U.S. imperialism and their ushers and allies—the landlords, comprador capitalists, pro-Japanese and pro-American elements, and traitors to the nation in the southern half—and to free the people there from imperialist and feudal oppression and exploitation, thereby achieving the country's unification along democratic lines and attaining complete national independence."

And in his theses Comrade Kim Il Sung, incisively exposing and criticizing the reactionary allegations of the anti-Party factionalists and dogmatists that the revolution in the northern half should not be advanced farther till the North and the South were unified and the anti-imperialist, anti-feudal democratic revolution completed on a nation-wide scale, proved in a scientific manner that the socialist revolution and socialist construction in the northern half were by no means contradictory to the nation-wide revolution and the cause of the country's unification, but would rather accelerate them still further, and clarified the general tasks for the building of the foundations of socialism in the northern half of the Republic.

Comrade Kim Il Sung taught as follows:

"Socialist construction in the northern half will be a great incentive to the people in the southern half, especially to the workers, peasants and the broad strata of small propertied classes, and conducive to the formation of a united front even with some of the national capitalists in the southern half.

"The successes gained in socialist construction in the northern half will not only be a decisive force in achieving the unification of the country, but also a strong material guarantee for speedily rehabilitating and developing the economy in the southern half and ensuring socialist construction on a nation-wide scale after the country is unified."

Comrade Kim Il Sung also taught as follows:

"The basic task confronting our Party at the present stage of transition to socialism is to lay the foundations of socialism on the basis of the achievements gained in the struggle for the postwar rehabilitation and development of the national economy, further consolidating the worker-peasant alliance.

"We should further expand and strengthen the predominant position of the socialist form of economy in all spheres of the national economy by gradually transforming the small-commodity and capitalist forms of economy along socialist lines, and should further develop the productive forces to lay the material and technical foundations of socialism."

The tasks of building the foundations of socialism set by Comrade Kim Il Sung were: to transform the small commodity economy and capitalist economy on socialist lines and make the socialist economic form hold undivided sway in all domains of the national economy and to lay the solid foundations of socialist industrialization by further developing the productive forces.

He taught that for the triumph of the revolution the Party should be strengthened and broad patriotic forces be rallied around it to fight against U.S. imperialism and its stooges, and the tasks of building the foundations of socialism should be thoroughly carried out by advancing the revolution in the northern half in order to turn the northern half into a decisive force for winning the unification and independence of our country.

Manuscript of the work of Comrade Kim Il Sung "Every Effort for the Country's Unification and Independence and for Socialist Construction in the Northern Half of the Republic"

The theses constituted a firm programmatic guide for our people in their struggle for the unification and independence of the fatherland and for socialist construction in the northern half of the Republic and became a militant banner that gave a strong impetus to our revolution and construction which entered on a new stage of development after the war.

Comrade Kim Il Sung set forth the line of further intensifying the work of class education to further increase the class awakening of the Party members and the working people and organize and mobilize them actively to the revolution and construction in view of the fact that our revolution assumed a protracted, arduous and complicated nature owing to the occupation of South Korea by U.S. imperialism and, particularly, that the socialist revolution and building of socialism in the northern half were accompanied by an acute class struggle.

In his report **"On Further Intensifying the Class Education of Party Members"** delivered at the April 1955 Plenary Meeting of the Party Central Committee, he gave a full clarification of the need to intensify the work of class education, of its significance, its concrete orientation and principles.

Pointing out that only by arming the Party members and the working people firmly with the ideas of the working class and its class consciousness could they wage an uncompromising struggle against the class enemy and resolutely fight for the triumph of the cause of socialism and communism with a firm confidence in the victory of revolution, Comrade Kim Il Sung taught as follows:

"We must give all Party members a clear understanding of the reactionary nature of our hostile classes, by teaching them which classes oppressed and exploited the Korean people in our country in the past and are doing so at present, why these classes betray the country and the people and how craftily they deceive the workers and peasants. Also we must give the Party members a correct understanding of the problems concerning the main motive force and its allies in the revolution by teaching them who is capable of fighting in the most revolutionary way for the country's freedom and independence, what are the classes and strata with which we can co-operate, and for what grounds."

In the report Comrade Kim Il Sung laid great emphasis on the need to conduct the class education work in proper combination with the concrete realities of our country and the practical struggle for the revolution and construction in our country.

The teachings of Comrade Kim Il Sung on strengthening class education furnished an important historic occasion which brought about a new switchover in the Party's ideological work and became a powerful driving force to firmly build up the forces of revolution politically and ideologically and propel the revolution and construction further still.

Comrade Kim Il Sung set forth the line of thoroughly establishing *Juche* against flunkeyism towards great powers and dogmatism in all domains of the revolution and construction and particularly in the Party's ideological work and saw that a powerful struggle was waged by the whole Party for its implementation to bring about great changes in the ideological life of the Party members and the working people and in the fulfilment of the revolution of the country.

From the first days of his leadership of the Korean revolution, Comrade Kim Il Sung had firmly maintained the revolutionary Marxist-Leninist position that the decisive factor in the triumph of the revolution is the internal revolutionary forces, and set forth a clear-cut line for establishing *Juche* and energetically directed the struggle for its implementation with all consistency, thereby pushing ahead successfully with the revolution and construction.

However, the obstinate flunkeys and dogmatists and factionalists were swallowing foreign things whole and copying them mechanically and would not desist from hampering the implementation of the creative lines and policies of our Party. The accelerated socialist revolution and construction could no longer tolerate such acts.

Without getting rid of flunkeyism and dogmatism it was impossible to thoroughly carry out the lines and policies of the Party that furnished original answers to many questions arising in the socialist revolution and socialist construction in our country, and to tackle the problems arising in the difficult conditions of the postwar rehabilitation period.

At the time it was an essential problem to establish *Juche* also for checking the infiltration of modern revisionism that had appeared in the international communist movement and for upholding the revolutionary principle of Marxism-Leninism.

Comrade Kim Il Sung raised the thorough establishment of *Juche* as the key problem on which depended the destinies of the revolution and construction, as the most pressing task confronting the Party, and put forward a determined policy for establishing *Juche*.

Comrade Kim Il Sung made a historic speech **"On Eliminating Dogmatism and Formalism and Establishing** *Juche* **in Ideological Work"** before the Party propagandists and agitators in December 1955.

He again expounded in an all-round way the revolutionary essence of the idea of *Juche*, its justness and the tremendous significance of its establishment, on the basis of profound analysis of the requirements of development of our revolution and the state of Party ideological work in those days. And he clearly indicated the programmatic task of thoroughly establishing *Juche* in all spheres of revolution and construction, particularly in Party ideological work.

Comrade Kim Il Sung clarified that establishment of *Juche* was not merely a question of theory and practical work, but a question of Communists' attitude and fundamental position in relation to our Party and to the conduct of the Korean revolution as a whole.

In the speech Comrade Kim Il Sung, giving instructions to establish *Juche* in ideological work, said as follows:

"What is *Juche* in the ideological work of our Party? What are we doing? We are engaged not in the revolution of any other country but precisely in the Korean revolution. This, the Korean revolution, constitutes the very *Juche* in the ideological work of our Party. Therefore, all ideological work must be subordinated to the interests of the Korean revolution."

As regards what was meant by establishment of *Juche*, Comrade Kim Il Sung subsequently taught as follows:

"The establishment of *Juche* means holding fast to the principle of solving for oneself all the problems of the revolution and construction in conformity with the actual conditions of one's country, and mainly by one's own efforts. This is the realistic and creative stand opposed to dogmatism and applying the universal truth of Marxism-Leninism and the experiences of the international revolutionary movement to one's country in conformity with its historical conditions and national peculiarities. This is an independent stand of discarding dependence on others, displaying the spirit of self-reliance and solving one's own affairs on one's own responsibility under all circumstances."

Comrade Kim Il Sung's idea of *Juche* is a thoroughly revolutionary idea which emanates from the lawful requirements of the revolution itself and from the principle of Marxism-Leninism and a most correct Marxist-Leninist guiding idea aimed at successfully carrying out the revolution and construction. And it is a genuinely internationalist idea of actively contributing to the international revolutionary movement by thoroughgoingly carrying out the revolution of one's own country.

Comrade Kim Il Sung emphasized that to firmly establish

Juche is a question of special importance for our country in the light of its geographical situation and environments, of the peculiarities of its historical development, and the complex and arduous nature of our revolution.

And he, teaching that the thorough establishment of *Juche* in the ideological domain is prerequisite for the establishment of *Juche* in the political, economic, military and all other fields, instructed that ideological work be conducted in the direction of inducing our people to know well the specific realities of our country and our own things and hold them dear.

Teaching in particular that the keystone in establishing *Juche* among the Party members and the working people is to arm them closely with the lines and policies of our Party and bring them to take guidance from those lines and policies in carrying out all work, he laid great stress on the need to intensify the education in the Party's policies.

He also taught that the Party members and the working people should be brought to have national pride and self-confidence by giving them a correct understanding of the glorious revolutionary traditions of our Party and our revolution and acquainting them well with the politico-economic relations and class relations in our country and its nature, geography, culture, customs, and so on.

The programmatic teaching of Comrade Kim Il Sung on opposing dogmatism, flunkeyism and formalism and thoroughly establishing *Juche* in ideological work opened up the path for a fundamental change in getting rid of the evil ideological aftereffects of flunkeyism and dogmatism which had been handed down through history in our country, in firmly establishing *Juche* in all spheres and in embodying the revolutionary principle of independence, self-sustenance and self-defence to the full. It also provided a solid guarantee for defending and creatively developing the revolutionary principles of Marxism-Leninism in the acute struggle against revisionism and Left opportunism that had appeared within the international communist movement.

Comrade Kim Il Sung said as follows:

"...Our Party in 1955 set forth the definite policy of establishing *Juche* and ever since then it has conducted a vigorous ideological struggle to carry it through. The year 1955 marked a turning-point in our Party's consistent struggle against dogmatism. In fact, our struggle against modern revisionism that had emerged within the socialist camp began at that time. Our struggle against dogmatism was thus linked up with the struggle against modern revisionism."

Through the struggle to thoroughly establish *Juche* against flunkeyism and dogmatism, our Party grew stronger organizationally and ideologically and the internal forces of the revolution were built up solidly.

In particular, the establishment of *Juche* freed our Party members and working people from the ideological fetters of dogmatism and flunkeyism, markedly increased their creative initiative, and brought about a great change in the revolution and construction.

Comrade Kim Il Sung convened the Third Congress of the Workers' Party of Korea in April 1956 for the purpose of laying out a new fighting programme for the Party and the people and energetically organizing and mobilizing the people to the struggle for completing the building of the foundations of socialism as the postwar rehabilitation of the national economy was coming to an end in the main and the socialist transformation of production relations was being triumphantly expedited.

Comrade Kim Il Sung made a report on the work of the Party Central Committee at the Party Congress. In the report, he summed up the great achievements and experiences obtained by our Party in its activities during the period under review and set forth new revolutionary tasks for accelerating the independent unification of the fatherland and socialist construction in the northern half of the Republic and for further strengthening our Party.

He set the new goal of embarking upon the fulfilment of the Five-Year Plan, a prospective plan of a longer-term, from 1957 and elucidated the programmatic tasks of bringing the building of the foundations of socialism to completion and basically solving the questions of food, clothing and housing for the people in this period, thus opening up a new stage in the development of the revolution in the country.

Comrade Kim Il Sung also set forth militant tasks for developing the Party's work of organizational leadership and ideological work including the questions of consolidating the unity and cohesion of the Party, of strengthening the Party life of Party members and the training of their Party spirit, smashing the old patterns of Party work—subjectivism, bureaucratism and formalism—and equipping the Party members and cadres with the revolutionary mass viewpoint, and indicated tasks for further enhancing the people's government's functions and role of the proletarian dictatorship.

At the Congress Comrade Kim Il Sung clarified once again the line of independent unification of the country consistently followed by our Party, and advanced new proposals and concrete measures for its realization. And he gave a clear elucidation of the fundamental principles of our Party's foreign policy—to oppose modern revisionism and firmly defend the purity of Marxism-Leninism, to safeguard the unity and solidarity of the socialist camp and the international communist movement in strict accordance with the principles of proletarian internationalism, give active support to the anti-imperialist national-liberation struggle and strengthen the anti-imperialist, anti-U.S. struggle in the international field.

The report delivered by Comrade Kim Il Sung at the Third Congress of the Workers' Party of Korea provided a powerful ideological-theoretical weapon to our Party's struggle for completing the building of the basis of socialism in the northern half of the Republic and accelerating the cause of the country's unification, and also made a great contribution to the development of the international communist movement and the world revolutionary movement.

Comrade Kim Il Sung was re-elected Chairman of the Party Central Committee at the Party Congress, and led our Party and people along the road of new victory.

The task of completing the building of the foundations of socialism set forth by Comrade Kim Il Sung at the Third Congress of the Workers' Party of Korea was fulfilled through a sharp class struggle against the enemies at home and abroad. At the time the internal and international situation was very complex and many difficulties and trials were lying before our Party and people.

The manoeuvrings of the modern revisionists who had raised their heads within the international communist movement were stepped up further as the days went by and, the imperialists and the international reactionaries, availing themselves of this opportunity, raised noisy "anti-Communist" clamours. The U.S. imperialists occupying South Korea and their stooges intensified their reactionary offensive against the northern half of the Republic as never before. Taking advantage of such a complex situation, the anti-Party, counter-revolutionary factionalists within the Party attacked the Party with the backing of foreign forces. The anti-Party elements in the Party and their supporters—foreign revisionists and great-power chauvinists—were united as one in opposing our Party and went the length of conspiring and manoeuvring to overthrow our Party and Government.

The economic construction of the country, too, was beset with many hardships including the shortage of materials and funds.

How to surmount the created difficulties was a serious question decisive of the fate of our revolution. All these trials and difficulties could be tided over entirely thanks to the seasoned leadership of Comrade Kim Il Sung who enjoys the absolute trust of the whole Party and people and carries the revolution forward victoriously without the slightest vacillation in any stormy weather.

In this difficult period when manifold hardships and trials were lying in the way of the revolution, Comrade Kim Il Sung put forward the wise line of directing the main efforts to socialist economic construction while delivering decisive counterblows to the offensives of all enemies at home and abroad by building up the Party ranks more firmly and uniting the entire people more closely around the Party.

This was a positive and enterprising line for thoroughly crushing all the offensives of the internal and external enemies and for actively pulling through the created difficulties by arousing the entire Party and all the people to activity to fortify our revolutionary positions still more impregnably and bringing about a great upsurge in socialist construction.

Comrade Kim Il Sung organized and directed a political and ideological struggle in the whole Party to oppose factionalism and strengthen the unity and cohesion of the Party.

The entire Party members and working people boundlessly faithful to the Party and the Leader Comrade Kim Il Sung firmly defended the Central Committee of the Party headed by him politically and ideologically and, rallied closely around it, waged a resolute struggle to expose and smash the manoeuvres of the anti-Party, counter-revolutionary factionalists. Thus, they swept away the filth of factionalism following the August 1956 Plenary Meeting of the Party Central Committee.

Through this serious struggle waged under the leadership of Comrade Kim Il Sung, chronic factionalism which had done tremendous harm to our revolution through history was surmounted, the unity and cohesion of our Party further consolidated and the unitary ideological system of the Party firmly established among the whole Party membership and the entire people. This was an event of great significance in the strengthening and development of our Party and the progress of the Korean revolution.

Comrade Kim Il Sung combined the struggle against factionalism for strengthening the unity and cohesion of the Party closely with the struggle against dogmatism, flunkeyism and great-power chauvinism for establishing *Juche,* and against revisionism in defence of the purity of Marxism-Leninism.

He sharply exposed the reactionary nature of factionalism, dogmatism, flunkeyism and revisionism and thoroughly armed the Party members and working people with the ideas of our Party and its lines and policies. And he guided the people to repulse all the pressure exerted by the great-power chauvinists and maintain an independent position and thus thoroughly implement the lines and policies of the Party. As a result, the struggle against dogmatism, flunkeyism and revisionism became more intensified and the political and ideological level of the Party members and working people rose higher.

While organizing and directing the inner-Party ideological struggle for liquidating factionalism and the political struggle of the entire people against the counter-revolutionary moves of the enemy, Comrade Kim Il Sung actively organized and mobilized the revolutionary enthusiasm and creative ability of the masses rallied closely around the Party to socialist economic construction, thereby bringing about a revolutionary upsurge in socialist construction and the great Chollima movement.

He put up a militant watchword, "Let us dash forward at the speed of Chollima!" and aroused the entire Party members and working people to a grandiose struggle to further accelerate socialist construction.

At the December 1956 Plenary Meeting of the Party Central Committee Comrade Kim Il Sung elucidated the national economic plan for 1957, the task for the first year of the Five-Year Plan, and the ways and means of its successful implementation and, after the meeting, visited in person factories and villages in different parts of the country including the Kangson Steel Plant in spite of driving snow and cutting wind, explained in detail to the workers and peasants the difficult conditions in the country and the requirements of the revolution and the intentions of the Party and thus aroused them to the struggle for the "maximum increased production and economization."

Our working class and all the working people who had always faithfully answered the call of the Leader rose as one in the battle to overcome the created difficulties and accelerate socialist construction, upholding his teaching with all their hearts.

As a result, great changes took place and new miracles were wrought in succession on all fronts of socialist construction. Industrial output increased at the remarkable rate of 44 per cent in a year and in agricultural production, too, big bumper harvests were gathered.

Thanks to the revolutionary upsurge resulting from the wise measures taken by Comrade Kim Il Sung, the "anti-communist" offensive of the enemy and the attack of the anti-Party elements were all blown up and those people who had been slandering us hung their heads, too. In contrast, our people were united more firmly around the Leader in high revolutionary spirits and the revolution and construction forged ahead at an extraordinary pace.

This led to a great upsurge of socialist construction and the great Chollima movement in our country.

The great upsurge of socialist construction and the Chollima movement are a concentrated expression of the wisdom of the leadership of Comrade Kim Il Sung and represent a great victory for the revolutionary mass line pursued by him with all firmness and consistency.

In formulating the policies in each stage of development of the revolution, Comrade Kim Il Sung always scientifically reckoned with the prospects of the country's development for the distant future, not only for the present and the near future, and clearly indicated the right course and goal of struggle to the masses on the basis of grasping in good time the aspirations of the people and the matured questions raised by life. And once a policy was established, he carried the adopted line and policy through to the end with indomitable fortitude without falling back even a step in whatever complex and difficult circumstances.

Giving a powerful impetus to the heightened revolutionary spirit of the masses with a strong revolutionary sweep, he solved one question and raised another immediately, and thus led the masses to make continued innovation and continued advance. Along with this, he correctly grasped the main link in the chain of work at each period of socialist construction and solved problems one by one by concentrating efforts on it, thus keeping a firm hold on the whole chain of socialist construction to lead it forward.

The scientific foresight of Comrade Kim Il Sung in working out policies and his staunch fidelity to Marxist-Leninist principle and extraordinary revolutionary sweep in their execution always inspired our people with firm confidence in their work and induced them to advance vigorously along the road indicated by him without any vacillation or hesitation through thick and thin.

Comrade Kim Il Sung always believed in the wisdom and strength of the masses of the people and, whenever new tasks or difficulties arose in the revolution, acquainted the masses with the situation in the country and discussed directly with them how to solve them and tapped and enlisted their inexhaustible creative power in the fulfilment of the tasks.

The Leader always believed in the people, valued them boundlessly and loved them dearly, and the people had an unbounded faith in the Leader, held him in reverence at all times and, convinced that a worthy and happy life, victory and glory could be had only under his leadership, entrusted their destinies entirely to him and fought on tirelessly. The sagacious leadership of Comrade Kim Il Sung and the strength of the entire people united as one around the Leader—this is the source of strength which brought forth the Chollima movement, and is the sure guarantee of all our victories.

Comrade Kim Il Sung took creative measures for inducing the masses to combat passivism and conservatism, bringing into full play the revolutionary enthusiasm and creative power of the masses by adhering firmly to the principle of enhancing the political and ideological consciousness of the masses and combining it correctly with material incentives and for organically combining this with science and technology, and thus further intensified and developed the Chollima movement.

Pointing out that the Chollima movement was the decisive guarantee for the successful building of socialism, Comrade Kim Il Sung defined the movement as our Party's general line in socialist construction.

Comrade Kim Il Sung said as follows:

"...The Chollima movement has become a great revolutionary movement of the working millions of our country, one which sweeps away all that is antiquated and makes constant innovations in all spheres of economy and culture, ideology and morality, and which accelerates socialist construction at an unprecedented rate; the movement has become our Party's general line in socialist construction.

"The essence of this line is to unite the entire working people more closely around the Party by educating and remoulding them in communist ideology and bring their revolutionary zeal and creative talent into full play, so that socialism can be built faster and better."

The Chollima movement which represents the general line of our Party in socialist construction opened up the rightest way to expedite socialist construction in our country to the maximum and furnishes a practical example showing what to draw on, and how, to build socialism and communism.

While leading the Chollima movement vigorously ahead without respite, Comrade Kim Il Sung convened a Conference of the Workers' Party of Korea in March 1958 to take active measures for strengthening the unity and cohesion of the Party ranks and increasing their fighting efficiency and for further hastening socialist construction.

At the Party Conference he set forth the tasks for the different branches of the national economy for the five-year period in accordance with the basic orientation of the Five-Year Plan laid down at the Third Party Congress, and elucidated the concrete ways of their successful implementation.

And he reviewed the results of the previous struggle against factionalism and, drawing on the experiences and lessons gained in this struggle, set forth the tasks of further consolidating the Party's unity and cohesion based on the unitary ideological system of the Party and of developing Party work further still.

Particularly, he emphasized the need of waging a persistent struggle to root up factionalism, parochialism, nepotism and all other unsound ideological elements and the venoms of bourgeois and revisionist ideas spread by the anti-Party factionalists in the ideological field, of strengthening the Party life of the Party members and expanding and serrying the ranks of Party nuclei, in order to strengthen the unity and cohesion of the Party.

On the basis of liquidation of the scummy hangs-over of

factionalism, Comrade Kim Il Sung took measures at the Party Conference for decisively strengthening the unity and cohesion of the Party ranks, thereby opening up a new stage in the development of our Party.

After the Party Conference Comrade Kim Il Sung directed much efforts to the work of further improving and strengthening Party work and further raising the leading role of the Party.

In many speeches including **"On Improving Party Work"** made before the chairmen of the provincial, city and county Party and people's committees in March 1958, **"On the Method of Party Work"** and **"Tasks before the Party Organizations of North Hamgyong Province,"** he gave a clear elucidation of questions of principle arising in strengthening the Party which is the General Staff of revolution, in enhancing the leading role of the Party and firmly building up revolutionary forces, and expounded basic methods and contents of Party work in a concrete way.

Comrade Kim Il Sung said that the firm establishment of the unitary ideological system of the Party in the whole Party and the achievement of the steel-strong unity and cohesion of the Party ranks constituted the source of invincibility of the Marxist-Leninist Party and the decisive guarantee for increasing its militant might and successfully performing revolutionary tasks confronting it.

Pointing out that arming all Party members and working people thoroughly with the lines and policies of the Party is of paramount importance in firmly establishing the unitary ideological system of the Party, Comrade Kim Il Sung said as follows:

"First of all, the Party functionaries should study the policies of the Party and decisions of the Party Central Committee and explain and propagate them to make all Party members have a clear understanding of them. Only when all

Party members know well the policies and decisions of the Party can the one million Party members, from the Chairman of the Party Central Committee down to *ri* Party committee chairman, move in a body, all breathing the same breath and saying the same thing."

Teaching that the revolutionary ranks should be firmly built up, Comrade Kim Il Sung stressed the need, first of all, to solidly build up the ranks of cadres, the backbone of the revolution, and to give them proper education and assistance. He taught that the work with the cadres must be placed first in the work of the Party committee, and expounded the concrete ways and means of improving it.

At the same time, he taught that the ranks of the working class should be built up firmly and the masses of all walks of life be embraced open-mindedly, educated and remoulded to unite them firmly around the Party.

Teaching that the Party organizations should acquit themselves well of the work of economic guidance for the successful fulfilment of the immediate revolutionary tasks, he also offered clear-cut conclusions on questions arising in the Party's guidance of the economic work and in the relationship between the Party functionaries and the administrative and economic workers.

Comrade Kim Il Sung said as follows:

"Relationship between the Party committee chairman and the administrative functionary can be compared to that of the steersman and the oarsman of a boat. The administrative functionary rows in front, while the Party committee chairman, sitting in the stern and taking the tiller, directs the former to the right or to the left, to keep the boat on the right course, so that it may go straight ahead."

Comrade Kim Il Sung taught that Party work should be conducted not by the method of administration and command, or the method of ruling, but primarily by means of education and persuasion so as to bring the Party members and the masses to be mobilized in the revolution voluntarily and consciously.

Saying that whether he works at an administrative organ or a public organization, or in any other place, the Party functionary should be the standard bearer there, not one who issues commands, he indicated the concrete ways and means to do away with the methods of command and administration, with the brandishing of the Party's authority and fame-seeking and formalism and rectify the method and style of Party work.

The teachings of Comrade Kim Il Sung which gave exhaustive answers to the theoretical and practical problems arising in Party work and clearly indicated the direction of work for the Party organizations and Party functionaries, became an important guide and textbook for developing Party work and improving the method and style of work of the functionaries.

Through the struggle for implementing Comrade Kim Il Sung's teachings, our Party turned the entire Party into a powerful combat force armed closely with the great revolutionary ideas of Comrade Kim Il Sung, and rallied its members and the working people firmly around the Party Central Committee headed by Comrade Kim Il Sung. With the improvement of the method and style of Party work, the leading role of the Party rose higher and the Party organizations became able to organize and mobilize the Party members and the working people more energetically to the implementation of the Party's policies.

With a view to consolidating the Party, building up the revolutionary ranks firmly and carrying out the revolution and construction successfully, Comrade Kim Il Sung paid a deep attention to thoroughly acquainting the Party members and working people with the historical roots of our Party and revolution, the glorious revolutionary traditions of the anti-

Japanese armed struggle, and thus making them firmly defend and carry forward the traditions.

His speech, "The Korean People's Army Is the Successor to the Anti-Japanese Armed Struggle," delivered before the men and officers of the 324th Unit of the Korean People's Army in February 1958 while giving on-the-spot guidance to the unit provided a programmatic guide to defending and carrying forward the revolutionary traditions.

In this historic speech and a number of his works Comrade Kim Il Sung gave a scientific elucidation of the immense significance of inheriting the revolutionary traditions and their great vitality in the revolution and construction, their basic contents, the principles that had to be strictly observed in carrying them forward and even the methods of education in the revolutionary traditions.

Comrade Kim Il Sung laid bare and condemned the crimes of the anti-Party, counter-revolutionary factionalists who tried to reject our Party's revolutionary traditions and obscure the unitary ideological system of the Party, and pointed out clearly that we could not inherit all kinds of odds and ends simply because we were carrying forward traditions. Then he said as follows:

"**The only traditions we must inherit are the revolutionary traditions of the Anti-Japanese Guerilla Army that fought in defence of the interests of the working people under the banner of Marxism-Leninism.**"

As he taught, the revolutionary traditions are not made up of all of these and those things that took place in the history of revolution, but only such revolutionary wealth as can make the roots of the Party and revolution and constitute the source of strength in the revolution and construction, can become revolutionary traditions. No revolutionary traditions of a revolutionary Party could be built up in the course of the bourgeois nationalist movement or in such a labour movement as the one in which Right and Left opportunism and factionalism appeared and did a tremendous harm to the revolutionary struggle.

Comrade Kim Il Sung clarified the basic contents of the revolutionary traditions we must carry forward, too.

Comrade Kim Il Sung taught as follows:

"...Our revolutionary traditions consist of the indomitable fighting spirit displayed, and the valuable experiences and achievements gained, by the Korean Communists in their protracted heroic struggle for carving out the way of victory in the Korean revolution under the banner of Marxism-Leninism."

Also, Comrade Kim Il Sung said as follows:

"What does it mean to inherit the revolutionary traditions of the Anti-Japanese Guerilla Army? It means inheriting the ideological system of the Anti-Japanese Guerilla Army and its excellent method and style of work."

Explaining the position and role of the revolutionary traditions in the revolution and construction, Comrade Kim Il Sung taught that the continuation and development of the revolutionary traditions is one of the cardinal problems for victory in the revolution, for victory in socialist and communist construction.

Saying that we owe our victory of today to the glorious revolutionary traditions of the anti-Japanese armed struggle, he taught that the revolutionary traditions will not become outdated even when the Korean revolution is accomplished and communism is fully realized, and that they should be continuously defended, inherited and developed in future, too, for the final victory of the revolution.

Referring to the significance of the education in the revolutionary traditions, Comrade Kim Il Sung taught as follows:

"It plays a most important part in revolutionizing people and establishing the unitary ideological system to conduct the education in the revolutionary traditions profoundly in depth."

Comrade Kim Il Sung taught that only by inheriting the revolutionary traditions and arming the Party members and the working people with them, is it possible to thoroughly establish the unitary ideological system of the Party, revolutionize and *working-classize* the whole society, firmly build up the reserves of the revolution, and raise the revolutionary zeal and activity of the masses to advance the revolution and construction faster and better.

He also taught that only by inheriting and developing the revolutionary traditions and arming ourselves with them, can we thoroughly establish *Juche,* defend the purity of Marxism-Leninism and defend and advance the revolution.

In his historic speech **"The Korean People's Army Is the Successor to the Anti-Japanese Armed Struggle"** and a number of other teachings on the revolutionary traditions, Comrade Kim Il Sung gave an all-round and profound elucidation on the idea and theory concerning the revolutionary traditions, and thus provided a powerful weapon for our Party and people to win victory in the revolution, and made a great contribution to increasing the ideological and theoretical wealth of Marxism-Leninism and the international communist movement.

Comrade Kim Il Sung took steps for further strengthening the people's government and consolidating the state and social system to suit the great socio-economic changes which took place in our country on the basis of the unbreakable political and ideological unity of the masses united firmly around the Party as the socialist revolution and socialist construction got into their strides.

In August 1957, the elections to the Second Supreme People's Assembly were held in our country.

Our people unanimously elected to the Supreme People's Assembly the respected and beloved Leader Comrade Kim Il Sung who always guides them to victory and glory, happiness and prosperity, expressing their feelings of unbounded trust in and reverence for him, and the First Session of the Second Supreme People's Assembly held in September 1957 reappointed Comrade Kim Il Sung Premier of the Cabinet of the Democratic People's Republic of Korea.

At this session Comrade Kim Il Sung made the speech of political programme **"On the Immediate Tasks of the People's Power in Socialist Construction."**

The speech of political programme delivered by Comrade Kim Il Sung who summed up the successes achieved by our people in the revolution and construction over 12 years after liberation and set forth the immediate tasks confronting the Government and the people in expediting the unification and independence of the fatherland and socialist construction in the northern half of the Republic, inspired and encouraged the people to a new victory in the revolution and aroused them more vigorously to the Chollima movement.

Comrade Kim Il Sung saw that the functions of the proletarian dictatorship of the people's government were strengthened and its role as economic organizer and cultural educator steadily enhanced with a view to consolidating the successes achieved in the revolution and construction and accelerating the socialist construction of the country more energetically.

As the revolution and construction progressed successfully in our country, the enemies at home and abroad manoeuvred more desperately to check the onward movement of our revolution. In the meantime, the revisionists within the international communist movement worked hard to weaken the proletarian dictatorship, disseminating their anti-Marxist-Leninist "theory."

It was at that time, i.e., in April 1958, that in his speech **"For the Implementation of the Judicial Policy of Our Party,"** Comrade Kim Il Sung clearly expounded the essence of the proletarian dictatorship and the orientation and ways for its consolidation.

In this speech Comrade Kim Il Sung laid emphasis on further strengthening the proletarian dictatorship under socialism and gave a scientific clarification to the essence of the dictatorship.

Comrade Kim Il Sung taught as follows:

"Today in our era, there are two kinds of dictatorship: one is the dictatorship of the bourgeoisie and the other is the dictatorship of the proletariat.

"...The dictatorship of the bourgeoisie enforces dictatorship over the workers and peasants, while guaranteeing democracy to the landlords and capitalists.... The dictatorship of the proletariat exercises dictatorship over the landlords and capitalists, while guaranteeing democracy to the workers, peasants and broad other sections of the working people. The bourgeois dictatorship is needed for the capitalist system and the proletarian dictatorship for the socialist system."

In his speech Comrade Kim Il Sung made a profound Marxist-Leninist analysis of the essence of laws and their class nature and pointed out that our laws should serve as the weapon of the proletarian dictatorship to defend the socialist system and socialist gains. And he taught that correct enforcement of the state law implied to defend our Party's policy actively and implement it thoroughly, and the functionaries had, accordingly, to study the Party policy strenuously and temper their Party spirit, if they were to enforce the law correctly.

The speech was of great significance, both theoretically and practically, in thoroughly implementing the class line of our Party and strengthening the functions of the proletarian dictatorship of the state.

The implementation of Comrade Kim Il Sung's teaching on cementing the people's power and enhancing the functions of the proletarian dictatorship of the state enabled our people's power, mighty weapon of socialist construction, to strengthen and develop still more and perform more creditably the complicated and difficult revolutionary tasks confronting it.

Thanks to the sagacious leadership of Comrade Kim Il Sung, the socialist transformation of production relations in towns and the countryside was triumphantly completed in our country in August 1958.

As a result of the completion of the socialist transformation of private handicrafts and capitalist trade and industry, along with agricultural co-operativization, the socialist relations of production came to hold undivided sway and the socialist system free of exploitation and oppression was firmly established in the northern half of our country.

The completion of the socialist transformation of production relations in our country represented a great victory for the great idea of *Juche* of Comrade Kim Il Sung and the revolutionary, creative line on co-operativization, an embodiment of the idea, and a materialization of his far-reaching plan for building an advanced socialist society in this land.

It was entirely thanks to the wise leadership of Comrade Kim Il Sung that the socialist transformation of production relations, the most delicate and complicated revolutionary task for reorganizing society, was completed triumphantly, in only four or five short years, in a difficult and complicated period when the country was divided and we were standing face to face with U.S. imperialism, the chieftain of world imperialism, and the severely war-ravaged national economy had to be rehabilitated and constructed.

With the brilliant implementation of the original line for the socialist transformation set forth by Comrade Kim Il Sung, a new avenue was opened up for the socialist transformation of production relations.

In September 1958 the Presidium of the Supreme People's Assembly of the Democratic People's Republic of Korea, expressing the unanimous feelings and wishes of the entire Korean people, conferred the title of Labour Hero of the Democratic People's Republic of Korea on Comrade Kim Il Sung who led to victory the socialist revolution and building of socialism in our country.

Upon the completion of the socialist reorganization of production relations, Comrade Kim Il Sung organized and mobilized the whole Party and the entire people to the struggle for further consolidating and developing the socialist system and, at the same time, for further accelerating socialist construction and victoriously fulfilling the Five-Year Plan by vigorously promoting the technical, cultural and ideological revolutions.

Comrade Kim Il Sung took bold, creative measures for tapping the reserves and potentialities latent in the national economy to the full and speeding up the technical revolution of the country by drawing on the advantages of the triumphant socialist system and the creative power of the masses of the people, with the result that a rapid progress was made in socialist construction.

He concentrated efforts on the work of building a powerful heavy industrial base, particularly on rapidly developing the machine-building and metallurgical industries, which assumed a decisive importance in laying the foundations of socialist industrialization.

Comrade Kim Il Sung put forward the watchword "Iron and machinery are king of industry" at the September 1958 Plenary Meeting of the Party Central Committee and organized and mobilized the entire working people to the struggle for resolving the problem of iron and machinery.

Not only that, he initiated the "machinetool-begets-machinetools movement" to produce machine tools in a movement of the entire masses and thus swiftly strengthened the technical equipment of the national economy and promoted the technical reconstruction.

Comrade Kim Il Sung set forth the creative line of developing the medium- and small-scale local industry in parallel with large-scale industry under central authority for the production of popular consumption goods, so that many local industrial factories were built by turning to account the raw and other materials and labour force remaining unused in the localities, and this made it possible to rapidly expand the light industrial base and fully satisfy the increasing demands of the people for necessaries of life.

Comrade Kim Il Sung actively pushed forward the technical revolution in the countryside by relying on the growing might of heavy industry. On the basis of a scientific analysis of the climate and natural features and the specific conditions of our country where rice growing holds the most important place in agriculture, he set forth and vigorously pushed ahead with the line on the technical reconstruction of agriculture, a line of giving priority to irrigation while carrying on mechanization, electrification and chemicalization. As a result, irrigation networks covered the length and breadth of the rural areas of our country in a short space of time, and great changes took place in all branches of agriculture.

The reality of our countryside where agricultural output steadily grows in spite of continued drought or floods every year, proves how correct his line of technical reconstruction of agriculture was.

Comrade Kim Il Sung unrolled a splendid plan for turning all the hillocks in the country into fruit gardens, and set an example of carrying it into practice in Pukchong and organized a struggle for the generalization of the example throughout the country in a movement of the entire masses, thus turning the whole land in a short space of time into an orchard where all kinds of fruits thrive.

He also set forth the line of radically improving the livelihood of the peasants in the mountain areas through an effective use of the mountains and a comprehensive development of local industry and agriculture in conformity to their natural-economic features, and personally went out to Changsong county, a remotest mountain area in our country, and created a splendid experience in the solution of the matter, paving the way for the even development of livelihood of the people in all parts of the country, whether plain or mountain.

He put forward the tasks of conducting active fishing on the sea all the year round by developing pelagic and deep-sea fishing and combining large-scale and middle- and small-scale fishing, and of decisively improving fish processing. For this purpose, he saw that technical equipment in the domain of fishery was reinforced and the fishing industry placed on a highly scientific basis and that youths went to the sea actively. In this way, he saw to it that a great change was brought about in the development of the fishing industry which has a great significance for the livelihood of the people.

Thanks to the correct economic policy set forth by Comrade Kim Il Sung and his wise leadership, one great innovation after another took place in all fields of the national economy and remarkable progress was made in production and construction in our country.

It is a consistent revolutionary stand inherent in the leadership of Comrade Kim Il Sung to oppose inertia and conservatism, lead the people to make continued innovation and continued advance and steadily carry the revolution forward to new victory and new upsurge.

In this period when a great upsurge began in socialist construction, he promptly perceived that it was passivism, conservatism and mysticism about technique that hampered the onward movement of the revolution, and aroused the masses to crushing them. By so doing, he brought the great upsurge of socialist construction and the Chollima movement onto a higher stage of development.

At the September 1958 Plenary Meeting of the Party Central Committee and a National Meeting of Production Innovators, Comrade Kim Il Sung criticized passivism, conservatism and mysticism about technique which were expressed in failing to believe in the creative ability of the masses, in sticking to the old rated capacities and others' experiences and work norms, and mystifying science and technology, and the remnants of old ideas such as dogmatism and flunkeyism, and taught that the collective innovation movement should be stepped up.

He put up the militant slogan "Let's think boldly and act boldly!" and organized and mobilized the people to the struggle to advance farther the upsurge in socialist construction, and led the masses to new innovations by personally going among the masses to consult them and grasp and solve urgent problems awaiting solution.

In response to the call of the Leader, our working people performed new miracles and innovations every day, shattering all sorts of old and conservative things which hindered the onward movement of the revolution and displaying a high degree of revolutionary zeal and creative initiative, thus smashing old work norms and rated capacities.

In this course all types of modern machinery and equipment including tractors, automobiles, excavators and 8-metre turning lathes were newly turned out in succession in our country and a leap took place in producing and building two or three times as much with the same amount of materials and funds.

Under the wise leadership of the great Leader, each passing day recorded the world-startling miracles and innovations in our country and the Chollima advance continued still more grandiosely.

Comrade Kim Il Sung laid down the cultural revolution, along with the technical reconstruction of the national economy, as one of the basic tasks in socialist construction, and took radical measures for raising the working people's levels of general knowledge, technique and culture, training a large army of technical personnel, improving public health services and hygienic work and rapidly developing science and culture, and thus brought about a great progress in the cultural revolution.

At the direct suggestion and under the personal guidance of Comrade Kim Il Sung, in our country universal compulsory primary education was enforced in 1956, universal compulsory secondary education (seven-year system), the first of its kind in Asia, was introduced in 1958, and completely free education introduced at schools of all levels in 1959 with the general abolition of tuitions. And later, in 1967, universal compulsory nine-year technical education was introduced.

In public health services, too, a rapid stride was made. Thanks to the personal solicitude of Comrade Kim Il Sung and the correct public health policy set forth by him, a system of completely free medical care was introduced and the networks of medical establishments were extended to all villages in the remotest mountainous areas to make it possible to promote the health of the working people, and public health services developed rapidly along prophylactic lines.

Thus, our country has become one of the most advanced countries in the world in public education and health services

Comrade Kim Il Sung saw to it that *Juche* was established in scientific research work to gear it to the solution of practical problems arising in socialist construction. Thus, he made it possible to achieve great successes in the development of science.

Comrade Kim Il Sung also set forth a correct literary and art policy and guided the work for its implementation with meticulous care, thereby speedily developing our literature and art.

He taught that socialist literature and art, the ideological weapon of the working class that has seized power in its hands, should thoroughly oppose all hues of reactionary ideas including bourgeois ideology and revisionism, and serve the revolution and construction, serve the revolutionization and *working-classization* of the whole society.

Comrade Kim Il Sung said as follows:

"**Our literature and art should by no means part from the interests of the revolution and the Party's line, nor should allow those elements which cater to the taste and liking of the exploiting classes. Only revolutionary literature and art which thoroughly rely on the line and policy of the Party can truly enjoy the love of the popular masses and become a mighty weapon of the Party for educating the labouring masses in the revolutionary spirit of communism.**"

Comrade Kim Il Sung taught, in particular, that in literature and art, flunkeyism and dogmatism should be rejected and *Juche* be established, fine traditions of national culture critically inherited and developed to suit the thoughts and feelings of the working people who build socialism, and that literature and art be made a possession of the people themselves and broad masses be made their creators.

Comrade Kim Il Sung originated the revolutionary literary and art thoughts and set forth a creative line on literature and art so as to oppose modern revisionism and Left opportunism and defend the revolutionary principle in literature and art. In many of his writings he creatively developed and enriched the Marxist-Leninist theory on literature and art in their fundamental problems such as of the functions and role of literature and art in the revolution and construction, of the inheritance and renovation of the heritages of national culture, the correlation between ideological content and artistic quality in literature and art, and of types in literature and art.

Thanks to the creative theory of Comrade Kim Il Sung on literature and art and to his wise leadership, the literature and art of our country effloresced and developed as truly Party and popular literature and art, national in form and socialist in content.

Comrade Kim Il Sung pointed the right direction for the question of language and development of linguistics and paid deep attention to the development of our language and letters.

Emphasizing that our people should love and take pride in their fine language and letters, Comrade Kim Il Sung taught as follows:

"**Our language is fluent with its rising and falling inflections and long and short sounds, and has a good intonation, too, and it sounds very elegant to the ear. Our language is so rich in expression that it can express well any complex thoughts and delicate feelings, can stir people, make them cry or laugh. Our language is highly effective for educating people in communist morality, as it can clearly express etiquette. Our national speech is very rich in pronunciation, too. Therefore, our language and letters can express almost freely the pronunciation of the language of any Eastern or Western country.**"

Instructing that our language be refined and developed more accurately and beautifully primarily with words indigenous to our country, Comrade Kim Il Sung clearly elucidated questions of principle that should be a guide to the development of our language.

Comrade Kim Il Sung showed scientific foresight and gave a clear-cut elucidation as to the future of the development of the national language too.

He said that even when the whole world has turned communist, the national characteristics of languages will be preserved for a long time, and taught that the national characteristics should be carried forward and developed to the utmost and, at the same time, the common trend of development of languages of the world peoples should be taken into consideration.

The teachings of Comrade Kim Il Sung concerning the linguistic question furnished a programmatic guide to the development of language and letters in our country.

When the socialist reorganization of production relations was completed in towns and the countryside, Comrade Kim Il Sung lost no time to advance the line of all-round communist education and energetically promoted the ideological revolution, not only reckoning with the present but also foreseeing the distant future of the revolution and construction.

Comrade Kim Il Sung taught as follows:

"**To build socialist society it is necessary to remould the minds of people while laying the material and technical foundations. Even though the socialist reorganization of production relations has been completed and up-to-date techniques are introduced, we cannot say that we have built socialism completely unless we remould people, the masters who run society and handle technology.**"

Comrade Kim Il Sung taught that to educate and remould the working people along communist lines is a lawful requirement of socialist and communist construction and an important task of the dictatorship of the proletariat.

Particularly, he stressed that the ideological education of the working people came to the fore as an especially important question under the conditions of two opposing social systems existing in North and South Korea and the enemy carrying on vile manoeuvres against socialism.

Comrade Kim Il Sung taught that all people, to the exclusion of very few confirmed hostile elements, could be educated and remoulded on communist lines under the conditions in which the socialist system had been established in the country and the unitary ideology of our Party was firmly prevailing in the whole society, and that they should all be taken along to communist society, and he vigorously promoted the work of educating and remoulding the masses, while giving definite precedence to the ideological revolution before all other work.

He taught that the education and remoulding of the masses on communist lines is, in the final analysis, aimed at revolutionizing and *working-classizing* them and bringing them up into revolutionaries and Communists faithful to the Party and the cause of revolution, and, accordingly, in conducting the ideological education of the working people, the education in the Party's policies and the revolutionary traditions, above all, should be strengthened, and communist education with class education as its main content and the education in socialist patriotism should be carried on.

The work of Comrade Kim Il Sung **"On Communist Education"** published in November 1958 provided a programmatic guide to the communist education of the working people.

In this and a number of other works Comrade Kim Il Sung made a deep analysis of the great role played by the thoughts and consciousness of the working people in the building of socialism and communism and clearly indicated the main content and ways of communist education.

Comrade Kim Il Sung taught as follows:

"In order to reach the eminence of socialism as early as possible, we must arm the working masses firmly with communist ideology. Unless we conduct ideological education and wage ideological struggle in a thoroughgoing way, we cannot ensure the advance of the revolution, nor can we consolidate the victories we have already won.

"We must root out the remnants of the obsolete feudal and capitalist ideologies which still remain in the minds of the working masses.

"The revolution we are carrying on is a struggle to shatter all that is outmoded and to create things that are new. The struggle between the new and the old, between progress and conservatism, between activeness and passivism, between col-

lectivism and individualism, and in general between socialism and capitalism—such is the content of our revolutionary struggle. The cause of socialist construction can win victory only by sweeping away all the outdated and corrupt things that block our advance."

Elucidating the main content of communist education, Comrade Kim Il Sung taught the necessity for arming the working people with our Party's policies, for educating them in the spirit of loyalty to the Party, inspiring them with firm confidence in the superiority of the socialist system and in the inevitability of its triumph, making them have a clear understanding of the reactionary nature of the capitalist system and the inevitability of its downfall, and thus bringing them to strive actively to defend the socialist system and further consolidate and develop this system.

He also taught that the working people should be brought to oppose individualism and selfishness and acquire the spirit of loving collectivism and labour, and should be equipped with socialist patriotism and proletarian internationalism and with the revolutionary ideas of uninterrupted innovation and continued advance.

Comrade Kim Il Sung taught that class education was the keystone of communist education.

He taught that the strengthening of class education was posed as a very urgent question in view of the fact that the socialist and communist revolution is accompanied by a fierce class struggle against imperialism and all shades of reactionary classes, particularly in view of the fact that our country is divided into the North and the South and is standing opposed to U.S. imperialism, the chieftain of world imperialism. Also, after giving a scientific analysis to the fact that new generations who have had no taste of exploitation and oppression nor undergone the trials of the revolutionary struggle, are emerging as masters of society in the socialist countries and the fact that people may forget their previous lot and slide into indolence and laxity and get weary of the revolution as the revolution assumes a protracted nature and their living standards rise, he taught that the question of class education acquired special importance in communist education.

Stating that class education in the countries where the revolution triumphed only in a part of their territory and in the socialist countries where the revolution emerged victorious earlier under the conditions in which imperialism remained in existence, was a question of great importance for the international communist movement at the present time, Comrade Kim Il Sung said as follows:

"**In all socialist countries the work of class education should be energetically conducted to carry their revolution to the end and fulfil the world revolution to the end. Strengthening of class education among the working people, it can be said is an important task assigned to all the Communists of our era by the cause of the world revolution.**"

Comrade Kim Il Sung not only gave a clear and intelligent account of the main content of communist education with class education as its keystone, but also taught that communist education should always be conducted on the basis of strengthening the education in the revolutionary traditions and in close combination with this.

He also taught that communist education should be conducted with the work places as its bases, its principal method being education through influence by the medium of positive examples.

The work of Comrade Kim Il Sung "**On Communist Education**" and his teachings concerning communist education clearly pointed to the new road to be followed by our Party in its work of ideological education and furnished a powerful ideological and theoretical weapon for rearing the Party members and working people into Communists and turning the whole society Red.

While energetically accelerating the ideological revolution in our country, Comrade Kim Il Sung made great efforts, as an important part of the ideological revolution, to rear the rising generations into fine builders of socialism and communism, into men of a new, communist type who are developed in an all-round way.

In a number of works including **"On the Duty of Educational Workers in the Upbringing of Children and Youth,"** and **"Let Us Educate the Students into True Reserves of Socialist and Communist Construction,"** Comrade Kim Il Sung newly defined the principle of education of the rising generations under socialism, particularly of school education, and the orientation of its development, and solved it successfully.

Pointing out that the proper education and training of successors to the revolution is an important revolutionary work which decides the destiny of the revolution and guarantees its victory and that, accordingly, it is a lofty task of the Communists, Comrade Kim Il Sung emphatically taught that the role of the educational establishments had to be enhanced in the education of children and youth.

Comrade Kim Il Sung taught that the educational establishments under socialism are important organs which fulfil the educational-cultural function of the state of the proletarian dictatorship, and hold an important place in tne conduct of the ideological revolution.

Comrade Kim Il Sung said as follows:

"**The major foundation for bringing up people into revolutionaries should be laid in school education. The educational establishments ranging from kindergartens to primary schools, middle schools, higher technical schools and institutions of higher education are one of the fundamental means in conducting the ideological revolution. In other words, the** educational establishments, as one of the organs which directly fulfil the educational-cultural function of the state, are an important weapon of ideological education."

Comrade Kim Il Sung taught that the primary task of educational institutions under socialism is to bring up Communists who will fight against exploitation and oppression for society, the people and the working class, and, therefore, that the class principle of the working class should be thoroughly observed and *Juche* should be established firmly in school education.

The educational thoughts and lines set forth by Comrade Kim Il Sung, who, by creatively developing the Marxist-Leninist theory on education, newly raised and brilliantly solved the theoretical and practical questions arising in the education of children and youth and in school education such as of the position and role of school education and its orientation and contents under socialism, constituted a programmatic guide in bringing up children and youth, successors to the revolution, into true revolutionaries, to carry on the revolution generation after generation, revolutionize and *working-classize* the whole society and firmly ensure victory for socialism and communism.

In accordance with the line laid down by Comrade Kim Il Sung, the ideological revolution was promoted vigorously and the education in the Party's policies and the revolutionary traditions and communist education with class education as its main content were intensified, so that the revolutionary ardor and creative activity of the working people were brought into fuller play and the Chollima movement was developed in depth to turn into the Chollima workteam movement.

As the Chollima workteam movement which organically combined the collective innovation movement with the work of educating and remoulding people was widely organized and unfolded, a new trait of working, studying and living in a communist way under the motto "One for all and all for one" began to take shape in an all-round way among the working people and there took place a big change in the work of educating and remoulding the masses.

The new circumstances and conditions in our country—where the socialist reorganization of production relations was completed to establish the undivided sway of the socialist economic form, the productive forces developed rapidly, the volume of production increased sharply, and the political enthusiasm and creative activity of the masses rose immensely—made it imperative to improve the system of work at the Party, state and economic organizations and the methods and style of work of the functionaries in an all-round way to fit in with the new circumstances and conditions.

Comrade Kim Il Sung perceived this urgent demand in good time and gave instructions at the December 1959 Plenary Meeting of the Party Central Committee to decisively improve the system and methods of work to suit the new circumstances. Subsequently, in February 1960, he gave the historic on-the-spot guidance to the village of Chongsan-ri, Kangso county, for 15 days.

Comrade Kim Il Sung obtained a deep, first-hand knowledge of all work of the county and the village and had concrete discussions with the masses, and thus explored the way of improving the work of the Party, state and economic organizations to suit the developing realities and the new changed circumstances.

Through the on-the-spot guidance to Chongsan-ri and Kangso county and in his speeches **"For the Correct Management of the Socialist Rural Economy"** made at a general membership meeting of the Chongsan-ri Party organization, **"On Improving the Method of Work of the County Party Organization to Fit in with New Circumstances"** made at a plenary meeting of the Kangso county Party committee and **"On the Lessons Drawn from the Guidance to the Work of the Kangso County Party Organization"** made at an Enlarged Meeting of the Presidium of the Party Central Committee, he gave comprehensive clear-cut answers to the urgent questions awaiting solution in the management of the socialist rural economy and in the work of the Party and the state.

The Chongsan-ri spirit and Chongsan-ri method is the most correct guiding idea and guiding method for the work of the Party and state and for economic work under socialism, which was created anew by Comrade Kim Il Sung and the model of which was supplied by him personally.

Comrade Kim Il Sung said as follows:

"The essentials of the Chongsan-ri method are that the higher organ helps the lower, the superior assists his inferiors and always goes down to work places to have a good grasp of the actual conditions there and find correct solutions to problems, and gives priority to political work, or work with people, in all activities to give play to the conscious enthusiasm and creative initiative of the masses so as to ensure the fulfilment of the revolutionary tasks. This method is not only an effective method of work enabling us to carry out the immediate revolutionary tasks successfully in a deep-going manner but a potent method of education that enhances the ideological and political levels and practical ability of the functionaries and revolutionizes the masses."

He taught that the Chongsan-ri method should be thoroughly embodied to improve the work with people and make all people active. In other words, he instructed, all Party members should be roused to action in such a way as one person rouses ten to action and ten persons rouse a hundred and a hundred men a thousand in order to make the whole Party a living organism and the Party members should mobilize the entire masses to perform the revolutionary tasks with success.

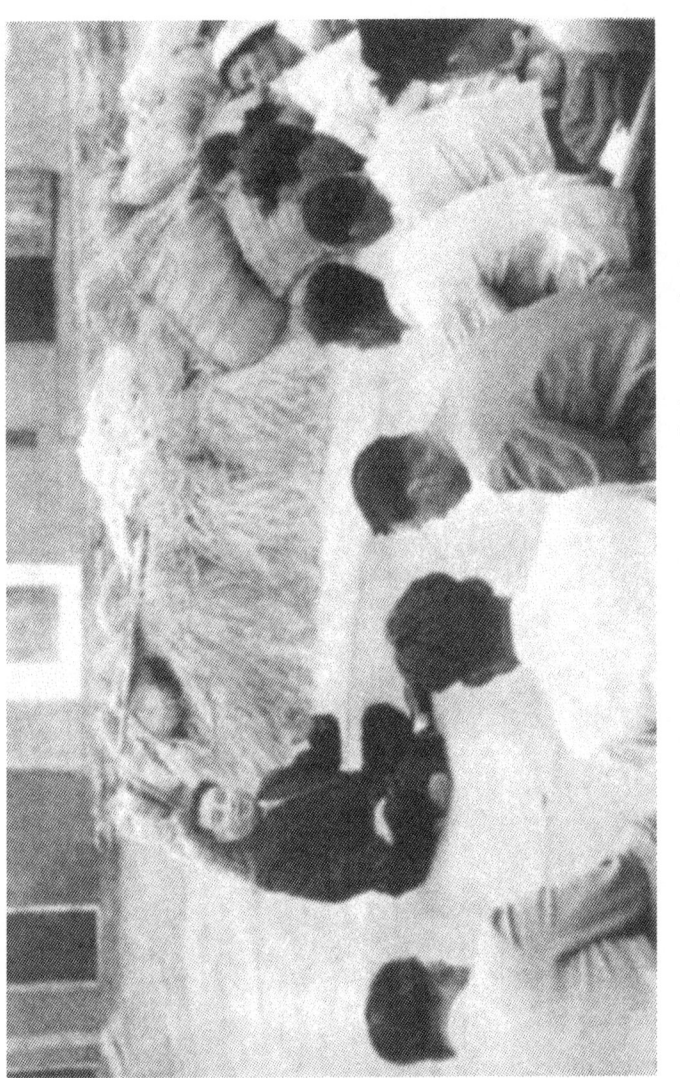

Comrade Kim Il Sung chatting with farmers during his on-the-spot guidance to Chongsan-ri, Kangso county, South Pyongan Province

The Chongsan-ri method is a genuine Party method and a communist method of guidance of the masses. It contains all the fundamental principles and methods of Party, state and economic guidance.

The Chongsan-ri spirit and Chongsan-ri method which gives comprehensive answers to the fundamental problems of Party, state and economic guidance in socialist and communist construction, furnishes a theoretical and practical example of the Marxist-Leninist Party's revolutionary guidance.

The revolutionary mass viewpoint and revolutionary mass line of Comrade Kim Il Sung who firmly believes in the strength of the masses of the people and settles all revolutionary tasks by relying on them, underlies the Chongsan-ri spirit and Chongsan-ri method which constitutes the great source of all innovations and victories and a powerful theoretical and practical weapon for the building of socialism and communism.

In the whole course of the arduous anti-Japanese armed struggle and all the complicate and hard struggles since the liberation, Comrade Kim Il Sung has always been among the people, shared joys and sorrows with them, consulted with them about state affairs, and enlisted their inexhaustible strength and wisdom in tiding over the difficulties and leading the revolution and construction to victory.

To what extent Comrade Kim Il Sung always goes and works deep among the people, is well demonstrated by his on-the-spot guidance.

Up to now he has personally given on-the-spot guidance to more than 80 per cent of all the cities and counties (districts) of the country. He gave on-the-spot guidance to the village of Chongsan-ri alone as many as 40 times or more.

Indeed, there is almost no place in our country which has not been visited by Comrade Kim Il Sung, whether towns or farm villages, factories or enterprises, schools or scientific and cultural institutions, lumbermen's settlements up in deep mountains or fishermen's hamlets on the seashore.

He mapped out the Party's lines and policies on the basis of overall study and understanding, through his on-the-spot guidance, of what the masses were aiming for and how matters stood down below, and organized and guided their thorough implementation; he directed state affairs after a concrete study and analysis of the realities.

Further, in the course of his on-the-spot guidance he shows parental care and kindly looks after every aspect of the livelihood of the people throughout the country—from the dietary life of the workers and farmers and the shoes of the children in the streets to the health of scientists and dresses and school supplies of pupils and students, and resolved urgent problems awaiting solution.

The Chongsan-ri spirit and Chongsan-ri method is the embodiment and development of the revolutionary mass line in conformity to the new reality of socialist construction—a line which Comrade Kim Il Sung, who personifies the revolutionary method and popular style of work, has been firmly adhering to ever since the days of anti-Japanese armed struggle.

The Chongsan-ri spirit and Chongsan-ri method has a firm grip on the hearts of the millions for its correct reflection of the urgent requirements of the revolutionary development and for the might of personal example set by Comrade Kim Il Sung in practice.

With the carrying into effect of the Chongsan-ri spirit and Chongsan-ri method which was created by Comrade Kim Il Sung, the old system, method and style of work which had hampered the onward movement were crushed and a new revolutionary system, method and style of work were fully established in all domains of Party, state and economic guidance.

With Party work thoroughly turned into work with people, the intentions of the Party came to be accepted readily by the masses and the Party's policies carried out more effectively.

As the Chongsan-ri method penetrated deep into the masses, the work of educating and remoulding the working people was converted into a work of the masses themselves and developed into a mass movement for ideological remoulding.

In January 1961, a year after the guidance in Chongsan-ri, Comrade Kim Il Sung personally guided a general membership meeting of the Rihyon-ri Party organization, Sungho district, and delivered the historic speech "The Main Thing in Party Work Is to Educate, Remould and Unite All People."

In this speech, Comrade Kim Il Sung set forth the tasks for carrying through more thoroughly the Chongsan-ri spirit and Chongsan-ri method.

Pointing out, above all, that after the generalization of the Chongsan-ri spirit and Chongsan-ri method the Party organizations and Party members confidently undertook a most difficult work, the work of educating and remoulding people and were bringing into firm unity the masses of all walks of life, Comrade Kim Il Sung taught as follows:

"Since our Party organizations have become invincible militant ranks of devoted communist fighters who are able enough to tackle this kind of work, we have nothing to fear, and no difficulty whatever could block our path ahead....

"This achievement we have gained is dearer than gold or millions of tons of rice, and cannot be bartered for anything."

In the course of generalizing the Chongsan-ri method, the Party's leading role was further enhanced and our revolutionary ranks were rapidly reinforced. All this gave a more powerful impetus to the great upsurge of socialist construction and the Chollima movement.

Under the wise leadership of Comrade Kim Il Sung the Five-Year Plan was carried out in two years and a half in gross industrial output value and was fulfilled or overfulfilled in four years in all indices, too, amidst the great upsurge of socialist construction and the swift advance of the Chollima movement.

In 1960 our industrial output was 1.3 times higher than the level envisaged in the Five-Year Plan, the total value of industrial output was 3.5 times that in 1956 and 7.6 times greater than in the pre-liberation year 1944. In the four years of the fulfilment of the Five-Year Plan, grain output went up by 32 per cent and great success was achieved in the technical revolution in the countryside, too.

With the fulfilment of the Five-Year Plan, the historic task of laying the foundations of socialism was accomplished triumphantly in the northern half of our country and our country turned into a socialist industrial-agricultural state with the firm foundations of an independent national economy.

Socialist relations of production came to hold undivided sway in town and country, and there were laid the heavy industrial base with the machine-building industry as its core and the light industrial base, and agriculture, too, was put on a firm foundation of production. The people's livelihood improved and all people were freed from worries about food, clothing and housing.

Under the wise leadership of Comrade Kim Il Sung our people laid the solid foundations of an independent national economy in a short space of time, and thus firmly ensured the independence and political sovereignty of the country and have come to possess a formidable defence power to frustrate any aggressive acts of the enemy at one blow, and become able to consolidate rock-firm the revolutionary base of the northern half of the Republic which represents the decisive guarantee for the unification of the country and for the nation-wide victory of the Korean revolution.

This clearly proved the wisdom and correctness of the leadership of Comrade Kim Il Sung who set forth the line of building an independent national economy and the line of economic construction for the priority growth of heavy industry with simultaneous development of light industry and agriculture and saw to their thorough implementation through the strictest economy in the revolutionary spirit of self-reliance.

The great victory won by our people in successfully building the foundations of socialism on the war debris in spite of all the difficulties and trials, further cemented their conviction that there can be no unconquerable fortress for them and they can fulfil whatever difficult and complex tasks with flying colours, when they march forward under the wise leadership of Comrade Kim Il Sung, united firmly around him.

While pushing ahead actively with the revolution and construction in the northern half of the Republic after the war, Comrade Kim Il Sung correctly set forth the strategic and tactical line for the South Korean revolution and the unification of the country and the fighting tasks for each period, and unswervingly led our people to the struggle for their successful realization.

Showing the road ahead of the South Korean revolution, Comrade Kim Il Sung said as follows:

"**The basic contradiction in South Korean society at the present stage is the contradiction between U.S. imperialism and its accomplices—landlords, comprador capitalists and reactionary bureaucrats—on the one hand, and the workers, peasants, urban petty bourgeois and national capitalists on the other.**

"**To attain freedom and liberation, therefore, the South Korean people must drive out the U.S. imperialist forces of aggression and overthrow the landlords, comprador capitalists and reactionary bureaucrats who are in league with them. U.S. imperialism, above all, is target No 1 of the struggle of the South Korean people.**"

Teaching that the basic task of the South Korean revolution is to blow up the colonial rule of U.S. imperialism, secure the democratic development of South Korean society and achieve the country's unification in unity with the socialist forces in the northern half, he called upon all the patriotic forces in the southern half to unite and wage an all-people struggle against the U.S. imperialist aggressors.

Comrade Kim Il Sung advanced the invariable principle of unifying the country independently on democratic principles free from the interference of outside forces and exerted efforts to put it into effect.

After the war he put forward the most correct and reasonable proposals for independent, peaceful unification of the country and carved out new phases for the unification of the country.

The fundamental policy of our Party and Government set forth by Comrade Kim Il Sung for independent, peaceful unification of the country was to set up a unified government through free all-Korea elections based on democratic principles under the conditions in which the U.S. imperialist aggression troops would be made to withdraw from South Korea and interference of any outside forces precluded.

Comrade Kim Il Sung taught as follows:

"...Our country should be unified peacefully according to the democratic will of the Korean people themselves with no interference from any other country. Our country which is divided into the North and the South should be unified through nation-wide elections held on universal, equal and direct suffrage by secret ballot, with no pressure and restriction from without, under the conditions where free activities of all political parties are assured in North and South Korea."

Being an expression of the unanimous will of the entire Korean people, the line set forth by Comrade Kim Il Sung for independent, peaceful unification gained an active support and approval of the progressive peoples throughout the world, not to speak of the Korean people.

To consolidate peace in Korea and create a favorable atmosphere for the country's unification, Comrade Kim Il Sung put forward a number of reasonable proposals on the questions of expelling the U.S. imperialist aggression forces from South Korea and reducing the North and South Korean armies, of realizing economic and cultural exchanges, free travels and correspondence between the North and the South, establishing a confederation of the North and the South, and so on.

He also made proposals and suggested relief measures for rehabilitating the South Korean economy devastated by the colonial rule of the U.S. imperialists and stabilizing the livelihood of the people in the southern half who are in rags and suffering from hunger.

The reasonable and fair proposals advanced by Comrade Kim Il Sung for the independent, peaceful unification of the country greatly inspired the South Korean people in their struggle against the U.S. imperialists and the Syngman Rhee puppet clique.

The South Korean people who drew courage and strength from our Party's line for the unification of the country laid down by Comrade Kim Il Sung and from the triumphant progress made in socialist construction in the northern half under his leadership, rose at last in the April 19th Popular Uprising in 1960 and overthrew the regime of the puppet Syngman Rhee, the old stooge of the U.S. imperialists, dealing a mortal blow to the colonial rule of the U.S. imperialists.

Alarmed by the ever mounting struggle of the South Korean people for the unification of the country following the April 19th Popular Uprising, the U.S. imperialists established a military fascist regime in South Korea.

In the light of the changed situation, Comrade Kim Il Sung vigorously aroused the North and South Korean people to a more positive struggle to further strengthen the revolutionary base of the northern half, firmly build up the revolutionary forces in South Korea and actively meet the great event of the unification of the country.

Thus, the South Korean people waged an unremitting struggle, upholding the correct line of Comrade Kim Il Sung on the South Korean revolution and the unification of the country.

Comrade Kim Il Sung has never forgotten even a moment all the Korean citizens abroad including the 600,000 Korean citizens in Japan, and constantly directed paternal solicitude to them, guiding their struggle for democratic, national rights and freedom along the right path.

Comrade Kim Il Sung gave the right orientation in the patriotic movement of the Korean citizens in Japan and their struggle for democratic, national rights, thereby enabling them to frustrate all the suppression and persecution by the Japanese reactionary forces and fight successfully in defence of their national rights as overseas citizens of the Democratic People's Republic of Korea.

In May 1955 the Korean citizens in Japan, upholding the line of struggle set forth by Comrade Kim Il Sung, formed the General Association of Korean Residents in Japan (Chongryon), which is truly their own organization.

The formation of Chongryon as an organization of the citizens of the Democratic People's Republic of Korea in Japan was an historic event which marked an important turning-point in the life of the Korean citizens in Japan and in the development of their patriotic activities.

Deeply concerned for the education of the children of the Korean citizens in Japan, he not only pointed the right direction for the development of their democratic, national education, but also sent enormous sums of educational aid funds, thus enabling the Korean citizens in Japan to conduct democratic, national education with success.

Also, according to the unanimous will of the Korean citizens in Japan and the entire Korean people, he opened the way for the repatriation of the Korean citizens from Japan. As a result, in 1959 Korean citizens in Japan began returning to their dear homeland—the Democratic People's Republic of Korea—and thus the returnees have come to lead a new happy life in the bosom of the Leader.

That is why the Korean citizens in Japan regarding it as the greatest honour and happiness to have Comrade Kim Il Sung as their Leader and live and fight under his leadership as citizens of the Democratic People's Republic of Korea, vigorously waged the struggle for the independent unification of the country and the defence of their democratic, national rights with great national pride and confidence, even though they were living in the alien land.

While always leading the revolution and construction in our country to victory, Comrade Kim Il Sung waged an active struggle for the advancement of the international communist movement and the world revolutionary movement.

When modern revisionism made its appearance in the international communist movement, he saw through it in good time and waged a resolute struggle against it in defence of the purity of Marxism-Leninism, firmly adhering to the revolutionary principles of Marxism-Leninism and the stand of *Juche,* and put up a stubborn struggle against dogmatism, too. And he advanced the most correct line for safeguarding the unity and solidarity of the socialist camp and the international communist movement on the principles of Marxism-Leninism and proletarian internationalism and of complete equality, independence, mutual respect, non-interference in each other's internal affairs and comradely co-operation, and waged a principled struggle for the implementation of the line.

Particularly, he resolutely fought in defence of independence against the manoeuvrings of great power chauvinists to force their erroneous lines upon others and interfere in the latter's internal affairs, set forth the principled line of defending the socialist camp as a whole, not any particular country, and waged a resolute struggle against all attempts to split the socialist camp.

Comrade Kim Il Sung also waged a determined struggle to strengthen the international solidarity and unity with the peoples of the countries in Asia, Africa and Latin America, give an active support to the anti-imperialist, national-liberation movement of the peoples in these areas and to the revolutionary movement of the peoples in different countries, to oppose the imperialist policy of aggression and war and promote world peace and the progress of mankind.

He sharply exposed and criticized the modern revisionists for their illusions about U.S. imperialism, the chieftain of imperialism, and taught that only when the revolutionary forces of the world unite and strike blows at the U.S. imperialists and bind them hand and foot everywhere they set foot, can peace be really safeguarded and the revolutionary cause of the people be accomplished.

The activities of Comrade Kim Il Sung who, holding aloft the revolutionary banner of Marxism-Leninism, waged a principled struggle for the unity and cohesion of the socialist camp and the international communist movement, for victory in the revolutionary struggle of the peoples of all countries and for world peace, earned him a broad support among the Communists and the revolutionary peoples throughout the world. Numerous Communists and revolutionary peoples of the world have thus come to trust and respect Comrade Kim Il Sung still more profoundly.

7

Upon the successful fulfilment of the task of building the foundations of socialism set forth at the Third Congress of the Workers' Party of Korea, Comrade Kim Il Sung put forward the new strategic task of further advancing socialist construction in the northern half of the Republic and organized and mobilized the whole Party and the entire people to its fulfilment.

The Fourth Congress of the Workers' Party of Korea, a congress of victors and a congress of unity, was convened in September 1961 under the circumstances in which the whole country, standing at a great turning-point in the development of the revolution, was seething with labour upsurge and creative enthusiasm.

In his report on the work of the Party Central Committee to the Congress, Comrade Kim Il Sung summed up in an all-round way the brilliant successes achieved by our Party in the socialist revolution and building of socialism in the period under review, and put forward the magnificent programmatic tasks of the Seven-Year National Economic Plan for scaling the eminence of socialism.

Pointing out that the Seven-Year Plan would mark the decisive period in the socialist construction of our country, Comrade Kim Il Sung said as follows:

"**The fundamental task of the Seven-Year Plan is to carry out all-round technical reconstruction and cultural revolution** and to radically improve the people's livelihood relying on the triumphant socialist system. We must carry out socialist industrialization, equip all branches of the national economy with up-to-date techniques, and decisively raise the material and cultural standards of the entire people, and thus attain to the eminence of socialism."

Comrade Kim Il Sung placed great stress on the need to firmly adhere to, and continue to thoroughly carry out, the revolutionary lines and policies—the line of building an independent national economy, the basic line of postwar economic construction, the Chollima movement which represented the Party's general line in socialist construction, and the great Chongsan-ri spirit and Chongsan-ri method—whose validity has been confirmed beyond doubt in the course of practical struggle.

Comrade Kim Il Sung reaffirmed the line for the South Korean revolution and independent unification of the country and set forth in an all-round way the fighting tasks of the North and South Korean people on the basis of a deep analysis of the features of the developments in South Korea and the experiences of the protracted struggle for the accomplishment of the cause of the unification of the country.

He summed up the successes and experiences obtained in the period under review in the work of firmly building up the ranks of the Party and raising its leading role, and set forth the fighting tasks for applying the Chongsan-ri spirit and Chongsan-ri method more effectively, for decisively raising the cadres' level of leadership and conducting, on an all-Party and all-mass scale, the work of uniting the masses through education and remoulding.

He also gave teaching to further heighten the functions of the proletarian dictatorship of the people's government and the role of the working people's organizations, the transmission belts of the Party.

In the report, Comrade Kim Il Sung elucidated the through-and-through anti-imperialist, proletarian internationalist foreign policy of our Party for opposing revisionism and dogmatism, for defending the unity and solidarity of the socialist camp and the international communist movement, and giving active support and encouragement to the struggle of the Asian, African and Latin American peoples against imperialism and colonialism for freedom and national independence and to the revolutionary struggle of the international working class.

The report of Comrade Kim Il Sung to the Congress infused our Party members and working people with the boundless pride and confidence of a victor and furnished a powerful ideological and theoretical weapon for inspiring them to a new battle.

The report to the Congress, which made a profound analysis and generalization of the experiences and achievements gained by our Party in the course of carrying out the original lines and policies of Comrade Kim Il Sung and which clarified the fighting tasks ahead, made a valuable contribution to enriching the treasure-house of Marxism-Leninism and the experiences of the international communist movement.

Comrade Kim Il Sung was re-elected Chairman of the Party Central Committee at the Congress.

Immediately after the historic Fourth Congress of the Workers' Party of Korea, Comrade Kim Il Sung organized and mobilized the whole Party and the entire people to the implementation of its decisions.

One of the important questions whose solution was indispensable to the acceleration of socialist construction and to the carrying out of the programmatic tasks of the Seven-Year Plan was to improve and strengthen the state guidance of the economy and the management and operation of enterprises to fit in with the character of the socialist economy and the requirements of the constantly developing realities.

The question of improving the direction and management of the socialist economy was a very urgent task whose early solution was indispensable for the building of socialism and communism.

No one, however, had ever given a definite answer to the question of how to direct and manage the socialist economy, and there was no experience to bring in from anywhere to draw on in its solution.

Comrade Kim Il Sung originally solved this question point by point from the position of *Juche* on the basis of profound thinking and theory, firm revolutionary stand and of a scientific analysis of the socialist economic system.

At the Second Enlarged Plenary Meeting of the Fourth Central Committee of the Party in November 1961, Comrade Kim Il Sung taught that the guidance of the economy and the management and operation of enterprises should be improved and strengthened by applying the Chongsan-ri method scrupulously. He personally went out to a locality and tackled the matter. In the course of the personal on-the-spot guidance to the Taean Electrical Machine Factory in December 1961, he radically improved the old system of management of the factory and created the Taean work system, a new socialist system of industrial management.

In the new system of work, Comrade Kim Il Sung laid down the principle that the factory be managed under the collective leadership of the Party committee, and established a system of guidance of production to intensify the technological guidance of production and give comprehensive direction in production. And he established a material supply system under which the higher units supply the lower ones with materials and a new supply-service system.

Comrade Kim Il Sung said as follows:

"The Taean work system is radically different from the old system of work; it is an advanced work system with many factors of communist management of enterprises. This new system of work is an excellent embodiment of the principle of collectivist, communist life: 'One for all and all for one.' "

The Taean work system created by Comrade Kim Il Sung is a communist system of guidance and management of the socialist economy, and a new revolutionary system of economic management capable of bringing the advantages of the socialist economic system into full play.

As Comrade Kim Il Sung said, the introduction of the Taean system, a new system of industrial management, enabled economic organizations and enterprises to perform all their work under the collective leadership of the Party committees and carry out their revolutionary tasks by giving precedence to political work and rousing the masses to activity, and enabled the higher organ to help the lower, the superior to assist his inferior, those who are versed in work to teach the less versed, all people to co-operate in a comradely way and all workshops, factories and branches to closely co-operate with each other so as to develop co-operative production and run the economy rationally on scientific lines in accordance with the objective laws of economy.

Comrade Kim Il Sung established the line of unified and detailed planning in the Taean work system, and thus brought about a radical change in the planification of the socialist economy.

The unified and detailed planning implies that the state planning organs and planning cells all over the country form a single system of planification to secure complete unity in planification under the unitary centralized leadership and see that all cogs of the managing activities of enterprises gear squarely with each other down to details.

This is the most revolutionary and scientific way of planification making it possible to thoroughly meet the demands for plan and balance in socialist economic management and steadily develop the economy at a high tempo by intensifying the centralized, planned guidance of the state, by strengthening discipline in the fulfilment of plans, following the mass line in planification and enlisting all reserves to the maximum.

The introduction of the unified and detailed planning further strengthened the functions of state organs as economic organizers and eliminated the subjectivism of state planning bodies and the departmentalism and localism of the producers in planning so that truly realistic, scientific and active plans could be drawn up by properly combining the intentions of the state with the creative initiative of the producers.

Indeed, the unified and detailed planning represents an original measure which has given clear answers to the fundamental problems whose solution is essential to planification.

After creating the Taean work system Comrade Kim Il Sung radically revised the system of guidance in socialist agriculture.

In the field of the rural economy he established a new system of agricultural guidance with the county co-operative farm management committee as its pivot and concentrated under it agro-technicians and state enterprises in the service of agriculture. The establishment of the new system of agricultural guidance made it possible to direct agriculture by the industrial method of management, render material and technical assistance from the state to co-operative farms more effectively and strengthen the leading role of the property of the entire people decisively in relation to co-operative property.

He also originated the sub-workteam management system which is the most rational form of labour organization that brings into full play the advantages of the socialist system of agriculture and which is a cell of collective life for cultivating the communist ideas among the peasantry and a form of production organization at the basic unit.

With the sub-workteam management system generally in-

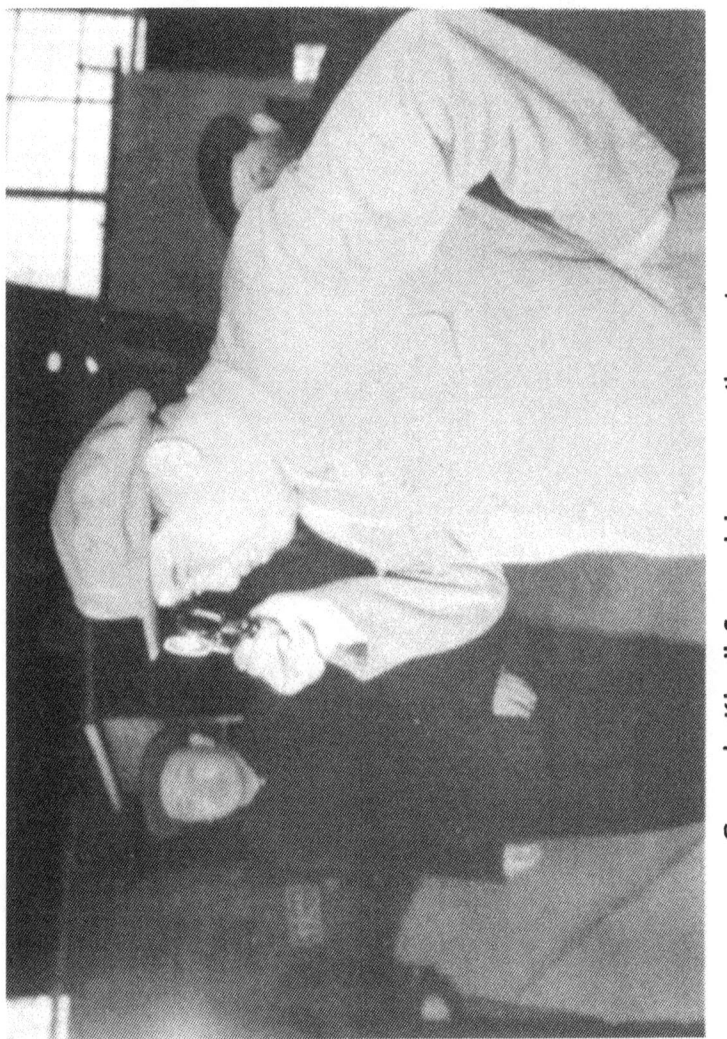

Comrade Kim Il Sung giving an on-the-spot guidance at the Hwanghae Iron Works

troduced in the rural areas of our country, a most scientific system of agricultural management came to fully cover the lowest, basic units.

Only after Comrade Kim Il Sung created the Taean work system and the new agricultural guidance system, the question of guidance and management of the socialist economy which was raised as an urgent question in the course of socialist and communist construction internationally, was solved excellently in a Marxist-Leninist way.

After he created the new system of work of guidance and management of the socialist economy, Comrade Kim Il Sung taught that to thoroughly carry it into operation the functionaries' ideological viewpoints and methods of work should be rectified, and at the Tenth Plenary Meeting of the Fourth Central Committee of the Party he took measures to raise the functionaries' level of guidance to keep up with the requirements of the developing realities and the new system of work.

And to solve this question, he personally guided Party meetings of Ministries and Bureaus and induced the leading functionaries to raise their Party spirit, working-class spirit and popular spirit. After that, he went down to the Hwanghae Iron Works with leading functionaries of Ministries and Bureaus and personally showed an example of putting into practice the revolutionary method of work required by the Taean work system.

In the course of the guidance, Comrade Kim Il Sung taught that those who come down to give guidance and those who receive it should co-operate. And he indicated one by one the principles and procedures for converting the guidance into a work of the Party committee and concrete ways for the upper bodies to give help to the lower units in a Party-like and political way.

The on-the-spot guidance of Comrade Kim Il Sung at the

Hwanghae Iron Works is another live example of the method of teaching the inferiors, his traditional work method of giving general assignments and then delving into one specific point to create a model and generalize it.

Upholding the teaching of Comrade Kim Il Sung a vigorous struggle was waged in the whole Party to enhance Party spirit, working-class spirit and popular spirit and, in this course, a radical change took place in the ideological viewpoint and work attitude of the leading functionaries and Party members.

For the successful carrying out of socialist economic construction, Comrade Kim Il Sung saw to it that the Taean work system was thoroughly carried into operation in economic management and, at the same time, he grasped in good time the urgent questions arising in socialist construction and took creative measures for their solution.

He completely established a unified planning system for the national economy of the country as a whole and, subsequently, reorganized the banking system which plays an important role in the development of the national economy.

He also reorganized the trading system to meet the requirements of the ever-improving material and cultural life of the people, and established a well-organized land administration system which is of great importance for taking good care of the natural resources of the country and for more assiduously managing the economic life of the country.

While improving the guidance and management of the economy, Comrade Kim Il Sung directed great attention to further improving and strengthening Party work by thoroughly applying the Chongsan-ri spirit and Chongsan-ri method to it in accordance with the basic line laid down at the Fourth Congress of the Party.

In the course of giving on-the-spot guidance to Party organizations in South Hwanghae Province early in 1962,

Comrade Kim Il Sung acquired a grasp of how things stood with Party work as a whole and, on this basis, called the Third Enlarged Plenary Meeting of the Fourth Central Committee of the Party in March 1962 where he took steps for the improvement of Party work.

In his concluding speech **"On Improving and Strengthening the Organizational and Ideological Work of the Party"** made at the meeting, Comrade Kim Il Sung clarified the essentials and contents of Party work and taught that the Party organizations should put an end to the practice of taking upon themselves to do administrative work, concentrate their efforts on Party work and build up the Party into a revolutionary, militant living organization, an active Party.

Pointing out that Party work is designed to firmly build up and consolidate the Party, steadily expand and develop it, properly arouse its organizations to activity to make it fully display its combat function as a Marxist-Leninist Party, he gave detailed teachings on improving and strengthening the inner work of the Party—the work with Party members and cadres, with Party cells and Party committees.

Saying that the main link in Party work lies in giving the Party members correct guidance in their Party life, Comrade Kim Il Sung taught:

"A Party member belongs to a Party organization from the very day of admission and must fulfil the tasks assigned by the Party organization.

"The organizational life of a Party member begins from the moment he joins the Party organization. Organizational life in the Party means activities of the Party members to fulfil the tasks assigned them by the Party. It represents the political life and revolutionary activities of the Party members. We always say that the traits required of a revolutionary should be acquired, and the revolutionary is not an extraordinary man. If a Party member, abiding by the Party Rules,

efficiently carries out the revolutionary tasks assigned him by the Party, it can be said that he fulfils the duties of a revolutionary."

Comrade Kim Il Sung also instructed that what is important in the guidance of Party life is to give proper assignments to the Party members so that they may execute the tasks given by the Party well in accordance with the duties stipulated in the Rules, and thus make the entire Party display activity, and, to this end, he taught, the Party cells to which the Party members belong and the Party committees at all levels should be built up firmly and their fighting efficiency enhanced.

Further, Comrade Kim Il Sung emphasized that all the Party organizations, while concentrating their efforts on Party work, should further enhance their role as steersmen in relation to the administrative and economic work, and gave detailed explanation as to the direction of work and functions of the Party committees at all levels and their departments.

The teachings of Comrade Kim Il Sung at the enlarged plenary meeting served as a programmatic guide to the development of the work of our Party.

While firmly building up the Party, the General Staff of the revolution, and enhancing its fighting efficiency, he took a series of creative measures for improving the work of the toiling people's organizations—the transmission belts of the Party—in conformity to the new circumstances of socialist construction in order to enhance their role.

Comrade Kim Il Sung who personally guided the Fifth Congress of the Democratic Youth League of Korea in May 1964, clarified the duties and role of the youth organization for the present stage of socialist construction, and saw to it that it was renamed League of Socialist Working Youth to suit its duties and role.

Subsequently, he called the Ninth Plenary Meeting of the Fourth Central Committee of the Party in June 1964 where he newly defined the duties and role of the trade unions under socialism and indicated concrete tasks for improving their system and method of work as a whole in conformity to the needs of the developed realities.

Particularly, at the plenary meeting Comrade Kim Il Sung set forth the line of newly organizing the Union of Agricultural Working People.

His creative line for organizing the Union of Agricultural Working People was the most sagacious line to unite all the working people in the rural areas without exception in the political organization and educate, remould and rear them into conscious socialist and communist builders under the changed circumstances after socialist co-operativization, it was a further development of the theory of Marxism-Leninism concerning the role of the transmission belts of the Party in the building of socialism and communism.

Comrade Kim Il Sung also gave programmatic teachings on the duties of the Women's Union organizations and on the need to enhance their role in the period of socialist construction, and gave meticulous guidance in the work of the Women's Union, showing deep solicitude for it.

He personally attended, and guided the work of, the National Meeting of Mothers held in November 1961 and, subsequently, the Third National Congress of the Democratic Women's Union and the National Meeting of Nursery Governesses and Kindergarten Workers, and elucidated programmatic tasks of the Women's Union organizations and women for each period.

The working people's organizations in our country such as the General Federation of Trade Unions, the Union of Agricultural Working People, the League of Socialist Working Youth and the Democratic Women's Union have been built up as reliable transmission belts of our Party, as firm political organizations which, no matter how complex and difficult the circumstances may be, are capable of coping with any difficult tasks with honour in response to the call of the Leader, and they have firmly armed the entire working people with the revolutionary ideas of Comrade Kim Il Sung—the unitary ideology of the Party—and rallied them more closely around the Leader.

Comrade Kim Il Sung taught that the level of leadership by the cadres, the basic nuclear force of the Party, should be decisively raised in order to thoroughly embody the Chongsan-ri spirit and Chongsan-ri method in all fields of Party work and social life and successfully carry out revolutionary tasks, and he took measures for the solution of the matter.

With a view to raising the level of the cadres and the entire working people to keep abreast of the rapidly developing realities, he set it as a task of the entire Party to study and, particularly, the cadres at the county level and upwards to raise their level to that of the college or university graduate in the shortest possible time.

Comrade Kim Il Sung taught that what was important in raising the level of the cadres and working people was to strengthen the education in the Party's policies and, at the same time, to heighten their technical and practical qualifications for their respective domains.

Referring to the significance of the education in the Party's policies, Comrade Kim Il Sung taught as follows:

"**Our Party's policies are Marxism-Leninism applied in the concrete practice of the Korean revolution and a guide to all our actions. When you know them, you are as good as in possession of a yardstick. You can measure all phenomena by this yardstick. Only whe you judge whether what you are going to do conforms to the Party's policies or not and which road you should take to carry out the Party's policies, can you distinguish between right and wrong, maintain principles and correctly settle the matters in hand.**"

In order to raise the level of the cadres and working people, Comrade Kim Il Sung saw to it that all cadres assumed responsibility for the education of their inferiors, and established a system of cadres' education and training under which the cadres could study while working. And he provided the cadres with all conditions for regular study and even set the study-hours for them, so that all cadres could rapidly raise their politico-theoretical level and practical qualifications.

In 1962 the U.S. imperialists, making frenzied preparations for a new war in South Korea, became more rampant in their aggressive provocations against the northern half of the Republic and, internationally, provoked the Caribbean crisis against the Republic of Cuba and further expanded their aggressive war in South Viet Nam.

To cope with such situation Comrade Kim Il Sung called the Fifth Plenary Meeting of the Fourth Central Committee of the Party in December 1962 and set forth the new line of carrying on economic construction and defence upbuilding in parallel.

While reorganizing economic construction in keeping with the prevailing situation and continuously developing it, he took a series of important measures to more thoroughly implement the military line of our Party which, being a full embodiment of the self-defensive principle in national defence, has as its basic contents the training of the whole army into a cadre army, its modernization, the arming of the entire people and fortification of the whole country.

Thus, our self-defence capacity has further increased and full preparations have been made to cope with the manoeuvres of the enemy for war provocation.

With the development in depth of socialist construction in our country, life called for a scientific elucidation on the final solution of the rural question.

Under socialism the rural question is one of the fundamental questions whose solution is indispensable to the building of socialism and to the preparations for transition to communism.

No one, however, had ever given a clear answer to this question and, more, some countries had failed to give full scope to the advantages of the socialist agricultural system. Meanwhile, the imperialists and their servants, taking advantage of the hardships which some socialist countries were undergoing in the solution of the rural question, hurled malignant calumnies and slanders at the socialist agricultural system.

Like this, the socialist rural question was a difficult and complicated question and a burning question whose solution was urgent.

In February 1964 Comrade Kim Il Sung, a great Marxist-Leninist, made public his historic work **"Theses on the Socialist Rural Question in Our Country"** in which he gave a scientific elucidation concerning the final solution of the socialist rural question.

In the Theses he scientifically analyzed and summed up the brilliant successes and experiences gained by our Party in the building of the socialist countryside in the past and, on this basis, gave a deep and extensive explanation as to the essentials and contents of the rural question under socialism and the basic principles and ways for its final solution.

In the Theses Comrade Kim Il Sung made it clear that under socialism the peasant and agricultural questions become a matter of developing the productive forces of agriculture to a high level, making the life of the peasants bountiful, abolishing the backwardness of the countryside left over by the exploiter society, and gradually obliterating the distinctions between town and country, on the basis of the continuous strengthening of the socialist system established in the countryside. And he clarified the basic principles to be adhered to imperatively for the solution of the rural question, saying:

"Firstly, the technical, cultural and ideological revolutions should be thoroughly carried out in the rural areas;

"Secondly, the leadership of the working class over the peasantry, the assistance of industry to agriculture and the support of the towns to the countryside should be strengthened in every way;

"Thirdly, the guidance and management of the rural economy should be steadily brought closer to the advanced level of management of industrial enterprises, the links between the property of the entire people and co-operative property should be strengthened, and co-operative property should be steadily brought closer to the property of the entire people."

In the Theses, Comrade Kim Il Sung formulated in a classic manner the original thought that the Marxist-Leninist Party should continue with the revolution for the victory of socialism and communism even after the establishment of the socialist system.

Comrade Kim Il Sung said as follows:

"The revolution must be continued to achieve the full-scale construction of socialism and to prepare for the gradual transition to communism.

"The very fact that the distinctions between town and country and the class distinction between the working class and the peasantry remain even after the liquidation of the exploiting classes and the completion of socialist transformation, shows that the revolution should be carried forward and that the revolution in the rural areas, in particular, should be carried out more thoroughly."

Comrade Kim Il Sung defined the ideological, technical and cultural revolutions as the central revolutionary tasks to be carried forward continuously in the countryside and gave concrete teachings concerning the ways and means for their implementation.

Pointing out that the leadership of the working class over the peasantry, assistance of industry to agriculture and support of towns to the countryside should be strengthened in every way, he taught that this was one of the essential conditions for obliterating differences between town and country.

Proceeding from this, he stressed that the Party and the state should continuously strengthen their assistance to the countryside so that the burdens of the co-operative farms and the peasants might be systematically lightened, and that the peasants, too, like the workers, should be provided with all conditions for production and livelihood in the future by the state and the whole society.

This idea of Comrade Kim Il Sung is an embodiment of the most thoroughly revolutionary stand of the working class to lead the peasantry to communist society and an expression of his boundless loyalty to the historical mission of the working class.

His idea is a creative development and perfect elaboration of the Marxist-Leninist theory on the worker-peasant alliance corresponding to the historical conditions of the period of socialist and communist upbuilding.

In the Theses, Comrade Kim Il Sung also put forward the questions of the direction and management of socialist agriculture, of the development of co-operative property and correlation between the property of the entire people and co-operative property as one of the basic questions in building the socialist countryside and in socialist construction as a whole, and as an important question of principle for erasing class distinctions between the working class and the peasantry, and indicated clear-cut ways to its solution.

He taught that the large-scale agricultural co-operative farming equipped with modern technique should be directed by the industrial method of management like industry. Stressing that the system of co-operative economy in agriculture, displaying its great superiority, gives a powerful stimulus to the development of the productive forces, Comrade Kim Il Sung also gave an instruction that the potentials and possibilities of the system of co-operative farming should be tapped and utilized to the maximum and co-operative property developed and perfected further in line with the strengthening of the material and technical basis of the rural economy and the rise in the peasants' level of culture, thoughts and consciousness. He pointed out that along with this, the questions of the correlation between the two types of property and the bond between industry and agriculture should be solved correctly.

Comrade Kim Il Sung said as follows:

"...The questions of the correlation between the property of the entire people and co-operative property and of the ties between industry and agriculture must be solved correctly. What is of prime importance in this connection is to organically link the two types of property in such a way as to strengthen the direct production ties between industry and agriculture and constantly enhance the leading role of property of the entire people over co-operative property."

The original ideas of Comrade Kim Il Sung concerning the bond between industry and agriculture and correlation between the two types of property clearly indicate the most scientific Marxist-Leninist way to increase political and ideological influence of the working class on the peasantry, introduce industry's machine technology, advanced method of industrial management and production culture in agriculture in a better way, and to give effective assistance from towns to the countryside, and thus consolidate and develop co-operative property to bring it closer to the property of the entire people, facilitating and accelerating the process of gradual welding of co-operative property into property of the entire people.

In the Theses he also further developed the idea set forth by himself already at the Changsong Joint Conference of Local Party and Economic Functionaries in August 1962 and, on this basis, defined the county as the regional unit for giving direct, unified and comprehensive leadership to the rural work and to the local affairs as a whole, as the base for accelerating the ideological, technical and cultural revolutions in the countryside and as the base for linking towns with the countryside and bringing the support of towns to the countryside, and put forward the task of increasing the role of the county.

He also set forth concrete tasks to strengthen the material and technical foundations of socialist agriculture and to swiftly improve the livelihood of the peasantry.

The Theses opened up broad vistas before our people of abolishing differences between town and country and class distinctions between the working class and peasantry and of building a socialist countryside, rich and civilized, where everyone will enjoy a happy life.

The Eighth Plenary Meeting of the Fourth Central Committee of our Party adopted the **"Theses on the Socialist Rural Question in Our Country"** as a great programme of our Party in the building of a socialist countryside.

The **"Theses on the Socialist Rural Question in Our Country"** which comprehends all the brilliant plans of Comrade Kim Il Sung concerning the solution of the rural question, is a great programmatic document which scientifically indicated the road to the final solution of the rural question for the first time in the history of the development of Marxism-Leninism.

The Theses blew up the slanders of the imperialists and reactionaries against the socialist system of agriculture and demonstrated the real advantages of this system. The Theses also defended the purity of Marxism-Leninism in the solution of the rural question and developed it from a new angle, and it is making a tremendous contribution to the cause of socialist and communist construction.

As soon as the Theses was published, a great number of Communists and revolutionary people the world over highly appraised the Theses as the "most correct text-book for the solution of the socialist rural question" and "a valuable Marxist-Leninist document which has provided a scientific solution to the basic question of socialist and communist upbuilding."

Comrade Kim Il Sung took epochal steps for abolishing agricultural tax in kind and strengthening the assistance of the state to the countryside to put into practice the tasks provided in the Theses.

On the initiative of Comrade Kim Il Sung, the Third Session of the Third Supreme People's Assembly held in March 1964 adopted a historic law on completely abolishing agricultural tax in kind in the years from 1964 to 1966, on carrying on capital construction and house building in the countryside with state funds and supplying the countryside with major production equipment and farm machines at state expenses.

In the rural areas of our country the ideological, technical and cultural revolutions have made brisk headway, capital construction and house building have been carried out on a large scale with state funds in accordance with the tasks laid down in the Theses, and the look of the countryside has changed beyond recognition today. Irrigation, mechanization, electrification and chemicalization have been promoted rapidly in the countryside and agricultural tax in kind has been abolished once and for all. Our countryside in the old society where ignorance and darkness, exploitation and poverty had prevailed for thousands of years, has been turned into a socialist countryside in the era of the Workers' Party led by Comrade Kim Il Sung, a countryside, rich and civilized, free from exploitation and oppression and all sorts of levies and taxes and knowing no crop failure.

While energetically carrying forward socialist construction in the northern half of the Republic, Comrade Kim Il Sung mapped out a clear-cut line of struggle for positively paving the way for the unification of the country and the revolution in South Korea.

At the Eighth Plenary Meeting of the Fourth Central Committee of the Party in February 1964, he set forth the strategic line and fighting tasks for advancing the cause of the country's unification and the revolution in South Korea.

He scientifically analyzed the situation created in our country and the balance of forces between revolution and counter-revolution, defined the revolutionary forces in the northern half of the Republic, the revolutionary forces in the southern half and the international revolutionary forces as three major revolutionary forces essential for the accomplishment of the cause of the unification of the country, and set forth the line and fighting tasks for strengthening them in every way, thereby brightly illumining the road of struggle lying before the North and South Korean people.

Particularly when the U.S. imperialists and Pak Jung Hi puppet clique were hastening towards the "final conclusion" of the "ROK-Japan talks" and the Japanese militarists were becoming pronounced in their machinations to resume aggression, Comrade Kim Il Sung sharply analyzed and exposed the reactionary nature of the "ROK-Japan talks" and vigorously aroused the South Korean people to the struggle against it.

In March 1964 broad segments of patriotic youths, students and people in South Korea rose in a mass demonstration struggle against the traitorous acts of the Pak Jung Hi puppet clique who were selling out South Korea to the U.S. and Japanese imperialists as a dual colony and against the U.S. imperialists and the manoeuvres for resumption of aggression by the Japanese militarists who were seeking to worm into South Korea with the backing of the U.S. imperialists.

Horrified at the struggle of the enraged youths, students and people, the U.S. imperialists and Pak Jung Hi puppet clique made frenzied efforts to stamp out their struggle by brutal repression and conciliatory and deceptive tricks.

According to the policy set forth by Comrade Kim Il Sung,

the Third Session of the Third Supreme People's Assembly expressed full support and solidarity for the patriotic struggle of the youths, students and people of South Korea who turned out in a struggle, and appealed for the immediate formation of a nation-wide united anti-U.S., anti-Japanese, national-salvation front.

And it put forward concrete proposals to restore the severed bonds of national affinity, realize economic exchanges between the North and the South, and offer an enormous volume of relief goods for South Korea to tide over its economic crisis.

The South Korean youth, students and people, boundlessly encouraged by the sagacious policy for struggle and deep solicitude of Comrade Kim Il Sung, the great Leader of the 40 million Korean people, waged a valiant struggle for over 70 days in the teeth of the enemy's harsh suppression, hitting hard at the U.S. and Japanese imperialists and their stooges.

Comrade Kim Il Sung clearly indicated the line for the South Korean people to raise their fighting spirit continuously to combat the U.S. imperialists' manoeuvres for another war and the troop dispatch to South Viet Nam, overthrow the tyrannical military fascist rule and win democratic rights and freedom and, further, to develop their revolutionary movement to the struggle for seizing power.

He taught that in South Korea the main force of the revolution—the basic classes that could be mobilized to the revolution and a Marxist-Leninist Party rooted deep among them—should be built up solidly before anything else, and the work of the united front should be strengthened to win over the masses of all social strata to the side of the revolution.

He induced the South Korean people to concentrate their efforts on preparations for actively greeting the decisive hour of the revolution by preserving the revolutionary forces from the enemy's suppression and, at the same time, by constantly building up and expanding those forces in the course of the struggle, and provided for clear strategic and tactical principles to be abided by in aligning revolutionary forces and carrying forward the revolution.

Comrade Kim Il Sung said as follows:

"It is necessary... to develop the revolutionary movement, properly combining diverse forms and ways of struggle—the political and economic struggles, the violent and non-violent struggles, the lawful and unlawful struggles—to suit the obtaining subjective and objective situations....

"The revolutionary organizations and revolutionaries in South Korea must do their best to constantly accumulate and expand the revolutionary forces through a positive struggle against U.S. imperialism and its hirelings."

The strategic and tactical lines and tasks put forth by Comrade Kim Il Sung for the South Korean revolution and the unification of the country offered the possibility for the South Korean revolution to develop rapidly along the rightest path even under the circumstances in which the Right and Left opportunists who made their appearance within the international communist movement were manoeuvring most outrageously.

These strategic and tactical lines and tasks immediately got a grip on the hearts of the people and revolutionaries in South Korea, swiftly brought them to unite and aroused them with a sweeping force to an ever more active anti-U.S., national-salvation struggle including the armed struggle.

It was thanks to the deep concern and brilliant strategy and tactics of Comrade Kim Il Sung that the South Korean revolution and the cause of the country's unification triumphantly pulled through the difficulties and made a steady progress.

When our people, under the correct leadership of Comrade Kim Il Sung, were fighting with great revolutionary enthusiasm for socialist construction in the northern half and the unification of the country, the imperialists headed by the U.S. imperialists were further aggravating the international situation, while endeavouring more and more desperately to suppress the growing revolutionary movement of the peoples.

And many complex questions arose within the socialist camp and the international communist movement.

This situation placed obstacles in the way of the development of the world revolutionary movement and also affected the revolution and construction in our country.

Comrade Kim Il Sung who always actively opened up the way for our revolution and is fighting energetically for the development of the international communist movement and the world revolution, correctly analyzed the prevailing situation and the state of affairs within the international communist movement and mapped out a positive and revolutionary policy to cope with them.

In October 1966 Comrade Kim Il Sung convened a Conference of the Workers' Party of Korea.

In his report **"The Present Situation and the Tasks of Our Party"** delivered at the Party Conference, Comrade Kim Il Sung gave a comprehensive and profound scientific analysis and correct Marxist-Leninist assessment of the present international situation, and elucidated the line of internal and external activities of our Party for energetically pushing ahead with the revolution and construction in our country and promoting the international communist movement and the world revolutionary movement as a whole to suit the prevailing situation.

He elucidated the basic strategy of the world revolution to counter the U.S. imperialist policy of aggression and war provocation.

Comrade Kim Il Sung taught as follows:

"The basic strategy of the world revolution today is to direct the spearhead of attack mainly on U.S. imperialism."

Saying that today the U.S. imperialists are resorting to the strategy of swallowing up primarily the divided or small countries one by one while refraining as far as possible from worsening their relations with big countries, Comrade Kim Il Sung said as follows:

"In the present situation, the U.S. imperialists should be dealt blows and their forces be dispersed to the maximum in all parts and on all fronts of the world—in Asia and Europe, Africa and Latin America and in all countries, big and small— and they should be bound hand and foot everywhere they set foot so that they may not act arbitrarily. Only in this way can we succeed in foiling the strategy of the U.S. imperialists to destroy the international revolutionary forces including the socialist countries one by one by concentrating their forces in this or that area and country."

Emphasizing that all forces should be concentrated on the struggle against U.S. imperialism, he set forth in the report the strategic line of achieving joint anti-imperialist action and forming a united anti-imperialist front.

Comrade Kim Il Sung taught as follows:

"The attainment of joint anti-imperialist action and a united anti-imperialist front is the acutest question of principle in the international communist movement today. It concerns the fundamental questions of whether the U.S. imperialist policy of aggression and war can be checked or not, whether the socialist camp can be defended or not, whether the national-liberation movement can be stepped up or not and whether world peace and security can be safeguarded or not."

The basic strategy of world revolution and the strategic line of achieving joint anti-imperialist action and forming a united anti-imperialist front advanced by C o m r a d e Kim Il Sung, threw light on the most correct way to ride out the complex situation of the present time and energetically advance the world revolution.

In the report he reaffirmed the anti-imperialist, proletarian internationalist position of our Party to fight against U.S.

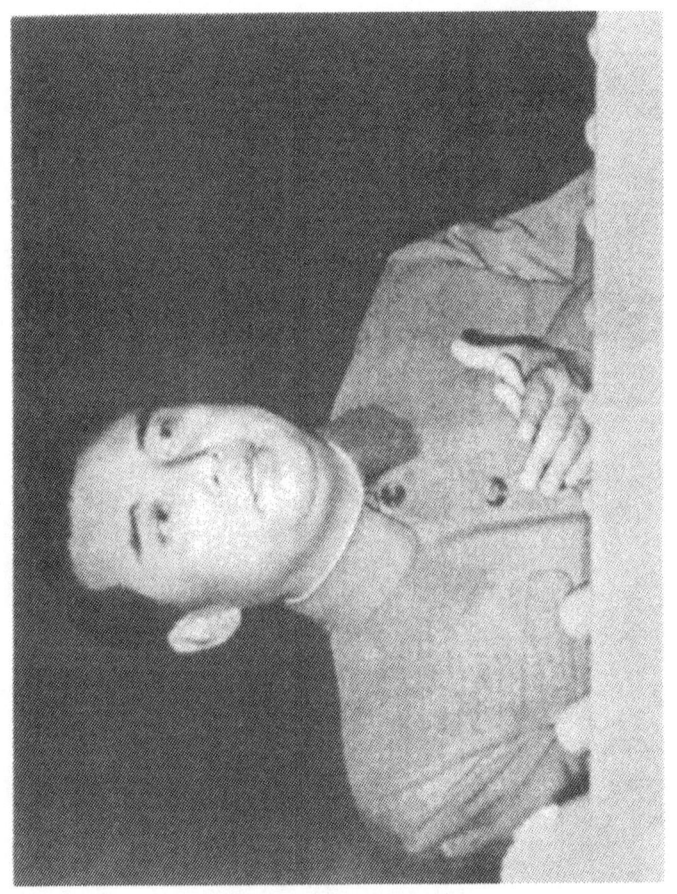

Comrade Kim Il Sung delivers a report at a conference of the Workers' Party of Korea

imperialism and, at the same time, its allies—Japanese and West German militarism, positively assist the Vietnamese people who are heroically fighting against U.S. imperialism, defend and aid in the Cuban revolution and actively support the anti-imperialist, anti-colonialist struggle of the Asian, African and Latin American peoples and the revolutionary struggle of the working people in capitalist countries.

Comrade Kim Il Sung also gave a profound analysis to the true nature and harmfulness of Right and Left opportunism, clearly accounted for the revolutionary stand to actively fight against them on two fronts and set forth the most correct ways and means to overcome Right and Left opportunism and restore the unity and cohesion of the socialist camp and the international communist movement.

He taught that only by overcoming Right and Left opportunism and defending the purity of Marxism-Leninism can the unity of the socialist camp and internatinonal communist movement be achieved. And he taught that the struggle against Right and Left opportunism is closely linked with the struggle for the unity of the socialist camp and the cohesion of the international communist movement, and clarified the principle of uniting while fighting and fighting while uniting.

Comrade Kim Il Sung said as follows:

"We should not commit the Leftist error of rejecting solidarity for fighting opportunism, nor should we commit the Rightist error of giving up the struggle against opportunism for defending solidarity."

Especially, he taught that the socialist camp is an integral whole which is united on the common political and economic basis and knitted together by the same goal of socialist and communist construction. And he pointed out that no one can liquidate it at one's discretion, and one can neither draw renegades into this camp nor exclude certain countries from it at will, and taught that the brotherly parties should fight in defence of the socialist camp as a whole. At the same time, he taught that the complicated questions which have arisen between brotherly parties are, in any case, internal affairs of the socialist camp and international communist movement and, therefore, should be settled by means of an ideological struggle guided by a desire for unity.

Pointing out further that opportunism could be overcome in the practical revolutionary struggle as well as in the ideological struggle, he taught that the united anti-imperialist front and joint anti-imperialist action should be achieved.

Comrade Kim Il Sung taught that the Communist and Workers' Parties of all countries should maintain independence.

He taught that only when each party has independence can it successfully carry on the revolution in its country and also contribute to the world revolution, and can the unity and co-operation of the fraternal parties be truly voluntary, solid and comradely.

Particularly, he stressed that in order to maintain independence, one should resolutely reject flunkeyism and greatpower chauvinism, and uphold one's conviction in Marxism-Leninism unwaveringly under whatever circumstances.

Comrade Kim Il Sung taught as follows:

"**It is not on instructions from anyone nor to curry favour with him that the Communists are engaged in the revolution. The Communists carry on the revolution out of their own faith in Marxism-Leninism for the emancipation of the working class and the working people in their own countries, for the great cause of the international working class. It is a noble trait of the Communists to adhere to their conviction and fight unyieldingly for its sake.**"

In the next part of the report Comrade Kim Il Sung set forth strategic lines for further consolidating the revolutionary base of the northern half politically, economically and militarily, which is a sure guarantee of victory for our revolution.

Comrade Kim Il Sung defined, first of all, the strategic line of carrying on economic construction and defence upbuilding in parallel as an unshakable line of the Party, and said as follows:

"It is of paramount importance in our revolutionary struggle and constructive work today to reorganize the whole work of socialist construction in line with the requirements of the prevailing situation and, especially, to carry on the building of economy and defences in parallel so as to further increase the defence capacities to cope with the enemy's aggressive manoeuvres."

This revolutionary line is the only correct line for taking in hand and tackling equally all of the questions of strengthening defence capacities, consolidating the economic foundations and improving the people's livelihood with the firm conviction that an aggressive war provoked by the imperialists headed by the U.S. imperialists might delay our economic construction, but could never check our progress towards socialism and communism, while taking full account of the danger of war which might be unleashed by them.

This revolutionary line indicated by Comrade Kim Il Sung clarified the most revolutionary Marxist-Leninist stand and attitude of opposing the Right and Left deviations in the attitude towards imperialism and the war it might provoke and of coping with imperialist aggression, and gave a scientific answer to the fundamental question of how to defend and carry forward the revolution and construction under the conditions in which imperialism remains.

Setting forth the task of firmly building up the revolutionary ranks politically and ideologically to further strengthen the revolutionary base of the northern half, Comrade Kim Il Sung also elucidated in the report the creative line of correctly combining the political and ideological unity of the masses of the people with the class struggle.

This line elucidated by Comrade Kim Il Sung is based on a scientific clarification of the basic motive power propelling the development of socialist society and of the characteristics of the class struggle under socialism.

He made it clear that in socialist society where the exploiting classes have been liquidated, the unity and co-operation of the working class, co-operative farmers and working intellectuals make the basis of social relations and that the political and ideological unity of the masses of the people based on the worker-peasant alliance and their common aspirations and enthusiasm to build socialism and communism under the leadership of the Party constitute the basic motive power propelling the development of socialist society and the decisive factor accelerating socialist construction.

Also, he elucidated that under socialism, too, the class struggle is continued, and laid stress on the proper combination of the two factors—the class struggle and the political and ideological unity of the masses of the people.

Comrade Kim Il Sung said as follows:

"One may commit a Leftist error if he emphasizes class struggle only and overstates it, forgetting that the alliance of the working class, peasantry and intelligentsia constitutes the basis of social relations under socialism.... In contrast, one may commit a Rightist error if he sees only the political and ideological unity of the masses of the people and absolutizes it, oblivious of the fact that under socialism, too, there exist hostile elements, the outmoded ideological survivals remain and class struggle continues."

This teaching of Comrade Kim Il Sung clearly shows the most correct way to accelerate the revolution and construction by thoroughly isolating and suppressing the handful of hostile elements and educating and remoulding the broad masses and rallying them more firmly around the Party on the basis of categorically opposing the Right and Left deviations manifested in emphasizing and absolutizing either political and ideological unity of the popular masses or class struggle and of properly combining them.

In the report Comrade Kim Il Sung also gave a scientific analysis of the class essence and contents of the building of socialism and communism and set forth the creative line of revolutionizing and *working-classizing* the whole society.

He taught that it is necessary for the revolutionization and *working-classization* of the whole society to elevate the leading role of the working class, increase its revolutionary influence, enhance its ideology, organization and culture, serry its ranks more closely and thus make the working class a more revolutionary and cultured class and enable it to perform its role better as the leading class.

He stressed that for the revolutionization and *working-classization* of the peasantry which hold an important place in the revolutionization of the whole society, it was necessary to energetically push ahead with the technical, cultural and ideological revolutions in the countryside, continuously strengthen the guidance and assistance to the countryside by the Party and state of the working class, and steadily bring cooperative property close to property of the entire people, while developing the two forms of property in organic combination.

Comrade Kim Il Sung paid deep attention to the revolutionization of the intelligentsia.

The policy of Comrade Kim Il Sung on the revolutionization and *working-classization* of the intellectuals proceeds from the deep care for and trust in them shown by him who, attaching faith to the national and democratic revolutionary spirit of the intellectuals of our country already from immediately after liberation, has positively embraced and educated them and led them along the most correct path to make them faithfully serve the revolutionary cause of the working class.

The line of revolutionizing the intellectuals set forth by him is a genuinely Marxist-Leninist, revolutionary line which is antipodal both to the Right deviation of failing to see the danger of the old ideological survivals and educate the intellectuals in a revolutionary way, and to the Left deviation of suspecting and rejecting the intellectuals, exaggerating the danger of the old ideological survivals in their minds.

Comrade Kim Il Sung set forth the concrete task of intensifying political and ideological work among the working people in order to accelerate the process of the revolutionization and *working-classization* of the whole society and solidly build up the revolutionary ranks.

Particularly in this connection, he taught that the education in the Party's policies and the revolutionary traditions should be strengthened and the communist education with class education as its main content and the education in socialist patriotism be intensified.

Comrade Kim Il Sung indicated the creative line of revolutionizing and *working-classizing* all members of society and thus clearly expounded the historical necessity of firmly maintaining the leadership of the working class in the course of building socialism and communism and elucidated for the first time the way for the abolition of classes and transition to a classless society systematically and scientifically.

Comrade Kim Il Sung gave a new, all-round definition of the historical mission of the dictatorship of the proletariat and its functions as well.

Comrade Kim Il Sung said as follows:

"**The historical mission of the dictatorship of the proletariat lies not only in liquidating the exploiting classes and putting down their resistance but in remoulding all the working people to** *working-classize* **them, thus gradually eliminat-**

ing all class distinctions. In our society where the exploiting classes have been wiped out and the socialist system triumphed, an important task of the dictatorship of the proletariat is the work of educating and remoulding the working people and *working-classizing* the whole society."

Comrade Kim Il Sung defined it as the basic form of the class struggle under socialism to revolutionize and *working-classize* the workers, peasants and working intellectuals through education and remoulding for the purpose of their unity and solidarity.

Referring to the forms of class struggle under socialism in his subsequent works, Comrade Kim Il Sung taught as follows:

"...In socialist society there is a form of class struggle to enforce the dictatorship upon the enemy at home and abroad, together with the basic form of class struggle to revolutionize and remould the workers, peasants and labouring intellectuals by the method of co-operation aimed at their unity and cohesion."

Proceeding from this, he taught that although the dictatorship of the proletariat under socialism should wage the class struggle and dictatorship should be exercised over the handful of hostile elements in conformity with its historical mission, the struggle against the survivals of obsolete ideas in the minds of the working people for their revolutionization and *working-classization* should be waged entirely by means of persuasion and education, for it is an internal affair of the working people who advance hand in hand to realize their common ideal and a task raised for educating and remoulding all the working people and leading them along to communist society.

The thought of Comrade Kim Il Sung which gave a new, all-round definition of the historical mission of the proletarian dictatorship and the characteristics of the class struggle under socialism indicates the most correct and wise way of overcoming the outdated ideological remnants in the minds of the working people and educating and remoulding them on communist lines, while guarding against both the Right deviation of weakening the proletarian dictatorship's functions for suppression of hostile elements, underestimating the danger of the survivals of outmoded ideas and neglecting the struggle against them, and the Left deviation of exaggerating the danger of the survivals of outmoded ideas to a fault, identifying the struggle against them with the struggle for repressing the hostile elements.

Comrade Kim Il Sung, on the basis of a profound scientific analysis of the present situation in South Korea, set forth once again the basic line and concrete fighting tasks for developing the South Korean revolution and the struggle for the unification of the country.

Comrade Kim Il Sung's report **"The Present Situation and the Tasks of Our Party"** is not only a programmatic document which brightly illumines the road ahead of the Korean revolution but a great classic document which further develops Marxism-Leninism at the present age and makes a great contribution to the development of the international communist movement and world revolution.

Comrade Kim Il Sung's work **"The Present Situation and the Tasks of Our Party"** wins absolute support and sympathy from the Communists and the revolutionary peoples on an international scale.

At the Party Conference, Comrade Kim Il Sung reassumed the heavy responsibility of General Secretary of the Party Central Committee by the unanimous will of the entire Party.

In May 1967 Comrade Kim Il Sung made public an immortal work, **"On the Questions of the Period of Transition from Capitalism to Socialism and the Dictatorship of the Proletariat."**

Comrade Kim Il Sung at writing

In the work he, firmly adhering to the stand of *Juche,* profoundly analyzed the propositions of the founders of Marxism-Leninism on the question of the transition period, linking them with the historical circumstances of their times and the premises they had started from, creatively applied them to the concrete reality of today and developed them, thus giving a most scientific and all-round elucidation to the question for the first time, overcoming all sorts of Right and Left deviations in dealing with it.

Comrade Kim Il Sung said as follows:

"...The questions of the transition period and the dictatorship of the proletariat as defined by the classics were perfectly correct under the historical circumstances of their times and the premises they had started from.

"Our present reality, however, demands us to develop them creatively and not apply them perfunctorily. We carried out the socialist revolution under the conditions where we had taken over very backward productive forces of a colonial agrarian country, and are building socialism under the circumstances where capitalism still exists as a considerable force in the world.

"We must take into account such specific realities of ours in order to give correct solutions to the questions of the transition period and the dictatorship of the proletariat. Bearing this point in mind, I consider it to be excessive to regard the transition period in our country as the period up to the higher phase of communism, I deem it right to regard it as the period up to socialism. But it is wrong to believe that the transition period will come to a close as soon as the socialist revolution has come off victorious and the socialist system is established."

Defining the transition period as up to complete victory of socialism, Comrade Kim Il Sung taught us that when we push ahead with socialist construction and thoroughly win over the former middle classes to the side of the revolution, when we eliminate the distinctions between the working class and the peasantry and build a classless society, we shall be able to say that the tasks of the period of transition from capitalism to socialism have been accomplished.

Saying further that the transition period will not immediately be followed by the higher phase of communism even when it is over and a classless society is built, he elucidated that even after the close of the transition period, the revolution and construction must be continued in order to enter the higher phase of communism.

The thought and theory of Comrade Kim Il Sung concerning the transition period represent another immortal feat in the development of the theory on scientific communism.

Also given in the work is a new, all-round account of the question of the dictatorship of the proletariat.

On the basis of scientific elucidation of the essentials of the transition period and the proletarian dictatorship, Comrade Kim Il Sung made it clear that the transition period and the dictatorship of the proletariat will not perfectly correspond to each other in their periods, and even with the end of the former the latter will exist much longer as long as the revolutionary struggle of the working class continues.

Comrade Kim Il Sung said as follows:

"...**If a classless society is materialized and the complete victory of socialism is achieved in our country, i.e., if the tasks of the transition period are accomplished, will the dictatorship of the proletariat become no longer necessary? We never can say so. Even when the transition period is over, the dictatorship of the proletariat must be continued up to the higher phase of communism, to say nothing of the necessity of having it during the whole period of transition.**"

Comrade Kim Il Sung also proved that even if the higher phase of communism is realized in one country, the dictatorship of the proletariat will still be needed under the conditions in which the revolution has not been accomplished on a worldwide scale.

The ideas of Comrade Kim Il Sung that the working class should firmly maintain the dictatorship of the proletariat till the accomplishment of its revolutionary cause, constitute a decisive blow to all sorts of opportunist ideological trends of the present time which consist in rejecting the dictatorship of the proletariat, denying the class nature of the socialist state and clamouring about the withering away of the state.

Comrade Kim Il Sung's work **"On the Questions of the Period of Transition from Capitalism to Socialism and the Dictatorship of the Proletariat"** constitutes a great contribution to the development of the international communist movement and the theory on scientific communism as a classic work which has perfected the theory concerning the class struggle.

Comrade Kim Il Sung who has always shown deep concern for the development of the world revolution, wrote the work **"Let Us Intensify the Anti-Imperialist, Anti-U.S. Struggle"** in August 1967 and the work **"Great Anti-Imperialist Revolutionary Cause of Asian, African and Latin American Peoples Is Invincible"** in October 1968, thus actively inspiring the people who have risen in the struggle for finally doing away with the colonial slave system of imperialism.

In these treatises he summed up the experiences of the revolutionary peoples of the world in the anti-imperialist, anti-colonialist struggle and, on this basis, clarified again the revolutionary and scientific strategic and tactical lines to intensify the anti-imperialist, anti-U.S. struggle and the national liberation struggle in colonies.

In these works, Comrade Kim Il Sung made a most correct appraisal of the world-historical significance and role of the anti-imperialist, anti-colonialist struggle of the peoples of the three continents. It is pointed out in the work **"Let Us Inten-**

sify the Anti-Imperialist, Anti-U.S. Struggle" that the anti-imperialist, anti-colonialist struggle of the Asian, African and Latin American peoples is a sacred struggle for liberating themselves and, at the same time, is a great struggle for cutting the life line of world imperialism, and that this struggle, as well as the revolutionary struggle of the international working class, constitutes one of the two major revolutionary forces of our times.

He pointed out that any illusion about the possibility of the imperialists making a gift of independence to the colonial peoples should be dissipated, and explained that the oppressed peoples can liberate themselves only through a struggle. Then he branded and strongly denounced all the tendencies to avoid or to be afraid of the struggle against imperialim as acts of helping the imperialist policy of aggression and war.

Saying that so long as imperialism plunders and oppresses small and weak nations by force, it remains an inalienable right of the oppressed nations to fight against the aggressors with arms in their hands, Comrade Kim Il Sung taught:

"**The struggle must continue till all shades of colonialism are wiped off the face of the earth once and for all, till all the oppressed and humiliated nations build their independent states and achieve social progress and national prosperity.**"

Pointing out that the revolution cannot develop of itself but can be advanced and brought to maturity only through an active and hard struggle of the revolutionaries, Comrade Kim Il Sung taught:

"**It is the task for the revolutionaries of each country to lay down a scientifically-motivated, careful way of struggle on the basis of a correct assessment of the internal and external situation and a proper calculation of the balance of forces between friend and foe, accumulate and build up the revolutionary forces by rearing the nuclear elements and awakening the masses of the people in the trying crucible of the revolu-**

tion, unfolding an active struggle and yet going around the snags and avoiding unnecessary sacrifices at ordinary times, and make full preparations to meet the great revolutionary event. And once the revolutionary situation is created, they should not miss the opportunity to rise without delay in a showdown to shatter the reactionary regime."

Comrade Kim Il Sung made it clear that the forms and methods of revolutionary struggle, too, are determined not by the wishful thinking of individuals but always by the subjective and objective situation created and by the extent to which the reactionary ruling classes offer resistance.

In the works he stressed again that in order to fight against imperialism, the spearhead of attack should be directed first of all against U.S. imperialism, the chieftain of world imperialism, and, for that purpose, joint anti-U.S. action should be achieved and a united anti-U.S. front be formed.

He taught that only by forming a broadest possible united anti-U.S. front and isolating U.S. imperialism thoroughly and by administering blows to U.S. imperialism with united strength everywhere it stretches its tentacles of aggression, is it possible to disperse and weaken the force of U.S. imperialism to the last degree and lead the people to knock down U.S. imperialism with overwhelming power.

Saying that particularly the small countries should discard flunkeyism which implies depending on big countries in the anti-imperialist, anti-U.S. struggle, Comrade Kim Il Sung taught that even small countries can defeat big enemy, if they establish *Juche,* unite the masses of the people and valiantly rise and fight without fearing sacrifice.

The works "**Let Us Intensify the Anti-Imperialist, Anti-U.S. Struggle**" and "**Great Anti-Imperialist Revolutionary Cause of Asian, African and Latin American Peoples Is Invincible**" are winning the warm approval of the revolutionary peoples of the world with each passing day, for they express the unanimous desire and will of the oppressed peoples who are waging a struggle.

After the Party Conference Comrade Kim Il Sung organized and mobilized the whole Party and the entire people to the struggle for carrying out the decisions of the Party Conference.

For the implementation of the decisions of the Party Conference, Comrade Kim Il Sung concentrated efforts, first of all, on the work of strengthening the Party and firmly building up the revolutionary ranks politically and ideologically.

He set it as the most important task to equip the Party members and the working people more thoroughly with the unitary ideology of the Party.

Pointing out that firm establishment of the Party's unitary ideological system is the basic principle in the building of a Marxist-Leninist Party and the decisive guarantee for the successful carrying out of the revolution and construction, Comrade Kim Il Sung gave an account of our Party's unitary ideology as follows:

"**The unitary ideology of the Party is the ideas of our Party run through with the principle of *Juche* in ideology, independence in politics, self-sustenance in the economy and self-defence in national defence. The ideas of our Party and the policies of our Party are Marxism-Leninism creatively applied to our realities, which leads the Korean revolution to completion and the Korean people to socialism and communism along the most correct road.**"

He taught that only when the entire Party members and working people have been firmly armed with the unitary ideology of our Party, can they thoroughly establish *Juche*, firmly safeguard the revolutionary traditions and successfully fight against all sorts of unhealthy ideological trends.

Comrade Kim Il Sung taught that in order to establish the unitary ideological system of the Party, a vigorous struggle should be waged to strengthen the education in the Party's policies and the revolutionary traditions among the Party members and the working people and thoroughly eliminate all unhealthy ideological venoms such as Right and Left opportunism, flunkeyism towards great powers, capitalist ideas, feudalistic Confucian ideas, factionalism, parochialism and nepotism.

Through the struggle to establish the unitary ideological system of the Party, the revolutionary traits were built up thoroughly in the whole Party and among the entire people of thinking and acting according to the ideas and will of Comrade Kim Il Sung no matter when and where and unconditionally accepting the policies of the Party without the slightest vacillation in any storm and defending and carrying them through to the end; and the whole Party and all the people were united more firmly around Comrade Kim Il Sung.

Comrade Kim Il Sung energetically organized and unfolded the struggle to follow out the new revolutionary line of the Party of carrying on economic construction and defence upbuilding in parallel, while guiding the work of strengthening the Party and closely serrying the revolutionary ranks.

Comrade Kim Il Sung energetically organized and unfolded the work of arming the Party members and working people with the unitary ideology of the Party and, at the same time, the work of opposing passivism and conservatism and bringing into full play the revolutionary enthusiasm and creative activity of the working people, and thus gave rise to a new great revolutionary upsurge in all fields.

He smashed to pieces the bourgeois and revisionist sophistry that when the economy is developed and its scale is expanded, the rate of its progress cannot be increased, and infused firm confidence and inspiration in our working people who are making continued advance and uninterrupted innovation, free from inertia and standstill.

While giving on-the-spot guidance to the Ryongsong

Machine-Building Plant and other factories and enterprises in the Hamhung area in June 1967, Comrade Kim Il Sung kindled the flames of struggle against passivism and conservatism revealed in implementing the revolutionary line of the Party on carrying on economic construction and defence upbuilding in parallel and for bringing about new innovations. And he actively supported the bold initiatives of our heroic working class with faith in their inexhaustible creative power, and inspired them to put those initiatives into practice.

The on-the-spot guidance given by Comrade Kim Il Sung marked a great revolutionary turn in inducing the working people throughout the country to burn away passivism and conservatism and bring about a new labour upsurge in the struggle for implementing the Party's revolutionary line of carrying on economic construction and defence upbuilding in parallel.

Boundlessly inspired by the teachings of the Leader, the working people of the whole country displayed high revolutionary enthusiasm and creative initiative to make new innovations and miracles in all fields of the national economy that were unthinkable in the past. The working people at a large number of factories and enterprises in various parts of the country fulfilled their yearly plans more than three months ahead of schedule. In 1967 the total value of industrial output increased by 17 per cent as compared with the previous year and grain output by 16 per cent.

In defence upbuilding, too, the munitions industry has developed rapidly and the Party's military line has been thoroughly implemented, which has as its basic content the training of the whole army into a cadre army, its modernization, arming of the entire people and fortification of the whole country.

Our heroic People's Army has grown and strengthened into a cadre army each of whose members is a match for a hundred, into a powerful modernized revolutionary army; the entire people have been armed; and every region of the country turned into an impregnable fortress. Thanks to the establishment of an all-people, nation-wide defence system with the People's Army as its core, our Party and people are in a position to frustrate at every step the U.S. imperialist aggressors' military provocations which have been intensified more than ever before and to firmly defend the security of the country and the revolutionary gains.

Great successes scored in the course of strengthening the Party, of firmly building up the revolutionary ranks and energetically promoting economic construction and defence upbuilding, gave ample proof of the correctness of the line set forth by Comrade Kim Il Sung at the Party Conference and the wisdom of his leadership.

Under the circumstances in which all the Party members and working people, upholding the decisions of the Party Conference, were making a new revolutionary upsurge in all domains of socialist economic construction and defence upbuilding, elections of deputies to the Fourth Supreme People's Assembly were held in November 1967.

The elections clearly testified to our people's absolute support for and deep trust in Comrade Kim Il Sung and our Party and the Government of the Republic led by him and again demonstrated to the whole world the monolithic political and ideological unity of the entire people closely united around the respected and beloved Leader Comrade Kim Il Sung.

The First Session of the Fourth Supreme People's Assembly held in December 1967 reappointed Comrade Kim Il Sung Premier of the Cabinet of the Republic in accordance with the unanimous desire of our people.

At the session Comrade Kim Il Sung announced the historic Political Programme of the Government of the Republic, **"Let Us Embody More Thoroughly the Revolutionary Spirit of**

Independence, Self-Sustenance and Self-Defence in All Fields of State Activity."

Making an overall review in the Political Programme of the brilliant successes scored in the revolution and construction thanks to the correct policies of our Party and the Government of the Republic, he solemnly declared that the Government of the Republic would thoroughly implement, in future too, the revolutionary line of independence, self-sustenance and self-defence in all fields of state activity, and, proceeding from the general tasks of our revolution, set forth the political, economic, cultural and military tasks confronting the Government of the Republic as follows:

"Firstly. The Government of the Republic will implement with all consistency the line of independence, self-sustenance and self-defence to consolidate the political independence of the country, build up more solidly the foundations of an independent national economy capable of ensuring the complete unification, independence and prosperity of our nation, and to increase the country's defence capacities so as to safeguard the security of the fatherland reliably by our own force, by splendidly embodying our Party's idea of *Juche* in all fields....

"Secondly. In order to put an end as early as possible to the present misfortunes of our people caused by the artificial partition of the territory and split of the nation, liberate the people in South Korea and realize the unification of the fatherland, the Government of the Republic will firmly prepare the people in the northern half of the Republic morally and materially so that they can always support the South Korean people in their sacred anti-U.S., national-salvation struggle and meet the great revolutionary event actively....

"Thirdly. The Government of the Republic, under the leadership of the Workers' Party of Korea, will wage a vigorous struggle to revolutionize and *working-classize* all members of society including the peasants and intellectuals by further stepping up the ideological and cultural revolutions and enhancing the leading role of the working class....

"Fourthly. The Government of the Republic will see to it that the functionaries of the state and economic organs eliminate bureaucracy and establish the revolutionary mass viewpoint, in order to enhance the functions and role of the people's power and actively organize and mobilize the broad masses of people for the revolution and construction....

"Fifthly. The Government of the Republic will consolidate the foundations of the independent national economy of the country, further improve the people's livelihood and fulfil the sacred task of freeing the working people from arduous labour by continually holding to the policy of the Workers' Party of Korea for socialist industrialization and struggling to carry out the technical revolution in all fields of the national economy....

"Sixthly. The Government of the Republic, adhering firmly to the idea of *Juche* of the Workers' Party of Korea, will fight on stubbornly to step up the development of the country's science and technology and build socialist culture....

"Seventhly. The Government of the Republic will do all it can to further increase the defence capabilities of the country and build up the defence posture of the whole country and the entire people to cope with the obtaining situation....

"Eighthly. The Government of the Democratic People's Republic of Korea, while continuing to hold fast to the line of building an independent national economy by enlisting its own potentials and domestic resources to the maximum under the banner of self-reliance, will establish economic relations and develop foreign trade with other countries on the principles of proletarian internationalism, complete equality and mutual benefit....

"Ninthly. The Government of the Democratic People's Republic of Korea will fight actively in defence of the interests and national rights of all the Korean compatriots abroad....

"Tenthly. From the first days of the founding of the Democratic People's Republic of Korea, we have consistently affirmed that we would promote friendly relations with all countries which oppose imperialist aggression, respect the liberty and independence of our people and desire to establish state relations with our country on an equal footing, and we will, in the future too, continue to hold fast to this principle in the field of foreign policy."

The Political Programme of the Government of the Republic announced by Comrade Kim Il Sung is a guide to state activity which brilliantly embodies the idea of *Juche* in the internal and external policies of the Government of the Republic, and a programmatic document which brightly illumines the road of victory ahead of the Korean revolution.

In the Political Programme, Comrade Kim Il Sung defined it as a question of fundamental significance for the revolution and construction to establish *Juche* by generalizing the practical experiences of the revolution in our country.

Comrade Kim Il Sung said as follows:

"**Whether or not *Juche* is established is a question of key importance on which depends the victory of our revolution, a vital question which decides the destinies of our nation.**"

In the Political Programme he pointed out that only by firmly establishing *Juche* can each country repudiate flunkeyism and dogmatism and creatively apply the universal truth of Marxism-Leninism and the experience of other countries in conformity to its historical conditions and national peculiarities and solve its own questions entirely for itself on its own responsibility by discarding the spirit of relying on others and displaying the spirit of self-reliance and, accordingly, carry on its revolutionary cause and construction work with success.

Comrade Kim Il Sung again taught in the Political Programme that the principle should be firmly adhered to of studying and analysing the realities of Korea and solving all problems arising in the revolution and construction independently in accordance with the idea of *Juche.*

Comrade Kim Il Sung declared that in order to consolidate political independence, we would shape all policies of the country independently, conduct all matters on our own judgment and conviction in conformity to our actual conditions, and would allow no one to violate or insult the rights and dignity of our nation.

Expounding profoundly that the line of building an independent national economy consistently followed by our Party and Government was a thoroughly revolutionary line of economic construction which conforms to the lawful requirements of the building of socialism and communism, he emphasized that in future too, our Party and Government would continue to adhere to the principle of self-reliance and the line of building an independent national economy and would implement them more thoroughly.

He taught that a nation can secure political independence, make the country rich, strong and advanced and achieve national prosperity only when it has built an independent national economy.

He also taught that as long as national distinctions remain and the states exist, a comprehensive, independent national economy should be built with each national state as a unit. Only then is it possible to lay firm material and technical foundations of socialism and communism, rapidly develop science, technology and culture, steadily enhance the technical and cultural standards of the working people, bringing them up into a new type of men developed in an all-round way.

He also said that the building of a developed independent national economy is the basic guarantee for enabling nations to do away with economic backwardness which is the actual basis of inequality between them, and to achieve national prosperity and to build socialist and communist society successfully.

Comrade Kim Il Sung's profound idea and theory concerning the building of an independent national economy clearly indicate the most correct way to build socialism and communism successfully and eradicate national inequality as well as class distinctions.

In the Political Programme, Comrade Kim Il Sung clarified again the independent and principled foreign policy of the Government of the Republic, gave a new explanation of the significance of economic co-operation between the states and of the world socialist market and expounded the fundamental position to be maintained by the socialist states in foreign trade relations.

Comrade Kim Il Sung stressed that the socialist countries should maintain the class stand in foreign trade and direct primary concern to consolidating and developing the world socialist market and, proceeding from the political interests of the victory of the common cause of opposing imperialism and colonialism and building socialism and communism, display the lofty spirit of proletarian internationalism and completely renounce hidebound national selfishness in mutual economic relations.

At the same time, he taught that the socialist countries should develop economic relations on the principle of complete equality and mutual benefit with the newly-independent countries of Asia and Africa which have cast off the yoke of imperialism and achieved political independence, and the developed socialist countries, in particular, should give more unselfish material assistance, with no political strings attached, to the economically backward countries which are striving for socialism against imperialism.

The basic ideas which run through the Political Programme are the great idea of *Juche* of Comrade Kim Il Sung

Comrade Kim Il Sung's great idea of *Juche* is the most correct guiding idea to carry on the revolution and construction successfully.

The Political Programme of the Government of the Republic "**Let Us Embody More Thoroughly the Revolutionary Spirit of Independence, Self-Sustenance and Self-Defence in All Fields of State Activity**" which fully embodies Comrade Kim Il Sung's idea of *Juche* is a powerful weapon for arousing our people dynamically to a new struggle for greater victory and firmly guaranteeing the victory.

The Political Programme has become an inspiring banner which infuses an indomitable revolutionary will and strength in the entire Korean people who are fighting for the complete unification and independence of the country and for the victory of the socialist and communist cause, and a terrible bomb which gives shivers, terrors, and anxiety to U.S. imperialism and its henchmen, the enemy of the revolution.

Internationally, the Political Programme has further increased confidence in victory and courage of the revolutionary peoples who are fighting valiantly in opposition to imperialism and gave a more powerful impetus to their anti-imperialist struggle.

The Political Programme cast a new light on the theoretical and practical questions whose solution is urgent in the building of socialism and communism and thus made an outstanding contribution to the development of Marxist-Leninist theory.

Today the Political Programme of the Government of the Republic, which embodies the great idea of *Juche* of Comrade Kim Il Sung, enjoys the unquestioned support not only of the Korean people but also of the true Communists and revolutionary peoples of the whole world, and has called forth a big echo on an international scale.

A great number of revolutionaries and revolutionary peoples of the world have highly appraised the Political Programme of the Government of the Republic as a "document which made a most important and most decisive contribution to Marxism-Leninism," a "classic in the theory about socialist construction" and a "textbook for the politicians of the whole world."

The Political Programme of the Government of the Republic, which has made a great contribution to further developing and enriching Marxism-Leninism, displays its great vitality ever more clearly as time passes on.

Early in 1968, a tense situation was created in our country owing to the intensified manoeuvres of the U.S. imperialists to provoke another war.

The situation became more acute as the U.S. imperialists raised frantic war clamours particularly in January 1968 when their armed spy ship "Pueblo" which was sent to intrude deep into the territorial waters of our country and perpetrate a grave provocation, was captured by the Navy of our heroic People's Army.

A serious state of affairs was engendered in our country owing to the reckless row of war provocation by the U.S. imperialists, which threatened the outbreak of a war at any moment; and the world's attention was focussed on Korea.

Comrade Kim Il Sung seriously warned the U.S. imperialist aggressors, who were making frenzied war clamours in connection with the seizure of the "Pueblo," as follows:

"If the U.S. imperialists continue to try to solve this matter by means of threat and blackmail by mobilizing their armed forces, they will get nothing therefrom. If they get anything it will be only corpses and death.

"We do not want war, but are never afraid of it. Our people and People's Army will return retaliation for the 'retaliation of the U.S. imperialists, all-out war for all-out war."

This warning struck terrors into the enemy's heart and inspired our people with firm confidence in the victory of the

Comrade Kim Il Sung among People's Army soldiers

revolution and fighting will to annihilate the enemy, and greatly encouraged them and drove them forward to the grandiose struggle for defending the country and further propelling socialist construction.

After the seizure of the "Pueblo," the U.S. imperialists tried to threaten our people with "retaliation" like a thief shouting "stop thief!"

But the scoundrels could not frighten our a-match-for-a-hundred people who are armed with the great revolutionary ideas of Comrade Kim Il Sung.

Unable to get out of the fix before the firm attitude of the Government of the Republic based on the principled and resolute stand of Comrade Kim Il Sung, before the indomitable determination and invincible might of our people, closely rallied around the Leader, and before the definite arraignment of the peoples of the world, the U.S. imperialists at last went down on their knees before the Korean people in December 1968 and made an apology for their aggressive acts and signed the letter of apology which guaranteed that they would not repeat such crimes.

This was a brilliant victory of the self-defence line of our Party set forth by Comrade Kim Il Sung, the great Leader of the revolution, and another great victory achieved by our people in the anti-imperialist, anti-U.S. struggle.

This smashed to pieces once again the "myth" about the "mightiness" of the U.S. imperialists, inflicting upon them an ignominious defeat, and it widely demonstrated the might of our Republic and infused infinite conviction and valour in the revolutionary peoples of the world who have risen in the anti-imperialist, anti-U.S. struggle.

While scrupulously organizing and leading all work so that preparations might be made in full to cope with the ever intensified manoeuvres of the U.S. imperialists for unleashing another war, Comrade Kim Il Sung took a series of measures for further raising the flames of the great revolutionary uplift on all fronts of economic construction and defence upbuilding and for further accelerating the Chollima march.

Our heroic working class and the working people, rallied more firmly around the respected and beloved Leader Comrade Kim Il Sung, have waged revolutionary struggles, sparing minutes and seconds and doing two- or three-fold work ready to frustrate the enemies at one sweep in case they dare pounce upon us, and smashed all stagnation and conservatism, and marched on and on, and struggled and marched ahead in the Chollima spirit.

As a result, a great number of factories and enterprises throughout the country achieved remarkable successes fulfilling their yearly plans ahead of schedule before the 20th anniversary of the founding of the Republic, and wrought world-startling prodigies and innovations day in, day out.

In September 1968 our people celebrated with pomp and splendor the 20th anniversary of the Democratic People's Republic of Korea, our glorious fatherland, overflowing with the high pride and honour and with infinite emotion and joy of having Comrade Kim Il Sung as the Leader and having won great victories in the revolution and construction under his wise leadership in the majestic circumstances in which the spirit of creation and progress was vibrating and flames of great revolutionary upswing were rising in every nook and corner of the country.

At the celebration of the 20th anniversary of the Republic Comrade Kim Il Sung made a historic report: "**The Democratic People's Republic of Korea Is the Banner of Freedom and Independence for Our People and the Powerful Weapon of Building Socialism and Communism.**"

In the report Comrade Kim Il Sung scientifically analyzed and summed up the great exploits and the rich theoretical and practical experiences gained by our people in the revolution and construction under the banner of the Republic over the last 20 years, and set forth new programmatic tasks of the struggle to win complete victory of socialism in the northern half, to hasten the South Korean revolution and the cause of unification of the country, to frustrate the world strategy of the U.S. imperialists and promote the cause of the international revolution as a whole.

In the report Comrade Kim Il Sung gave a new Marxist-Leninist explanation, above all, on the question of the complete victory of socialism on the basis of a profound scientific analysis of the essence of the socialist system, of the characteristics of its socio-economic and class relations, the historical missions of the proletarian dictatorship, the law of the development of socialist society, etc., and elucidated the historical tasks for their materialization.

Comrade Kim Il Sung taught as follows:

"A society—where the hostile classes persist in insidious manoeuvrings, the corrosive action of old ideas continues, there still remain distinctions between towns and the countryside and the class distinctions between the working class and peasantry, the industrialization of the country has not been realized fully and the material and technical basis of socialism has not been laid firmly—cannot yet be called a completely triumphant socialist society.

"In order to achieve the complete victory of socialism and accomplish the historical cause of the working class, the socialist state must further strengthen its role as a weapon of class struggle, weapon of the building of socialism and communism. In other words, the socialist state should strengthen the dictatorship of the proletariat, carrying on the class struggle on the one hand and vigorously pushing ahead with the building of socialist economy on the other."

To continue with the revolution after the triumph of the socialist system and win the complete victory of socialism,

Comrade Kim Il Sung taught, it is necessary to intensify the dictatorship over the class enemies, carry out the ideological revolution thoroughly and revolutionize and *working-classize* the whole society, solve the rural question once and for all and eliminate the distinctions between town and country, the class distinctions between the working class and the peasantry, carry out the socialist industrialization of the country, and firmly build up the material and technical basis of socialism. He further taught that to carry out these tasks properly, the proletarian dictatorship should be maintained firmly in the whole period of transition, the dictatorship over the hostile elements, the ideological revolution and economic work should be promoted all alike to seize the ideological and material fortresses. Further, he gave a clear Marxist-Leninist elucidation to the essence of the proletarian dictatorship and stressed the need to properly combine the dictatorship with democracy, the class struggle with the strengthening of unity and solidarity of the popular masses.

The profound theory and correct policies on the complete victory of socialism, as elucidated by Comrade Kim Il Sung. are a comprehensive, further development of the Marxist-Leninist theory concerning the transition period, class struggle and the proletarian dictatorship.

In the report, Comrade Kim Il Sung gave a new, scientific explanation also on the question of winning the final victory of socialism on the basis of a profound analysis of the historical experiences and the prospects of socialist construction.

Teaching that the final victory of the world revolution would be won in the course of the socialist revolution breaking out and winning the complete victory in a number of countries and the socialist camp being gradually extended, strengthened and developed, Comrade Kim Il Sung said that the class alliance of the socialist countries and the unity and solidarity of the socialist camp should be consolidated and the might of the camp be made invincible in order to win the final victory of socialism.

In shedding a new, clear light on the out-and-out revolutionary and scientific way to the complete victory of socialism and to its final victory, Comrade Kim Il Sung has given to the revolutionary peoples of the world a powerful weapon for the brilliant fulfilment of the historic cause of the working class against Right and Left opportunism under the complicated circumstances of today.

In the report, Comrade Kim Il Sung also made clear the unshakable stand, combat strategy and policy of our Party and Government for more vigorously unfolding the anti-imperialist, anti-U.S. struggle to smash the U.S. imperialists and further develop the world revolution as a whole at the present time.

Pointing out that U.S. imperialism is today target No. 1 in the struggle of the peoples of the whole world, he taught that in order to defeat U.S. imperialism, the broad anti-imperialist forces should jointly deal a blow at U.S. imperialism and put pressure on it in Asia and Europe, Africa and Latin America, in all countries, big and small, in all areas and all lands to which U.S. imperialism has stretched out its claws of aggression.

He emphasized here, in particular, that should the peoples of small countries engaged in the revolution join their forces and resolutely fight, firmly convinced of victory, they could lay low U.S. imperialism on every front with overwhelmingly superior force.

Elucidating the anti-U.S. combat strategy that all should join in mutilating U.S. imperialism everywhere in the world, Comrade Kim Il Sung taught as follows:

"**The peoples of all countries making revolution should tear limbs off the U.S. beast and behead it all over the world. The U.S. imperialists appear to be strong, but when the peoples** of many countries attack them from all sides and join in mutilating them in that way, they will become impotent and bite the dust in the end."

This superb principled strategy, which embodies Comrade Kim Il Sung's great thought concerning the world revolution, is the only correct line under the present situation for further developing the anti-imperialist, anti-U.S. struggle, which has given the revolutionary peoples of the world great encouragement and firm confidence in the victory of the revolution.

In the report Comrade Kim Il Sung again declared the consistent stand of the Government of the Republic concerning the South Korean revolution and the independent unification of the country, and clarified the correct strategical and tactical lines and measures for further accelerating the nationwide victory of our revolution.

Comrade Kim Il Sung taught that the South Korean people should actively wage the struggle for driving the U.S. imperialist aggressors out of South Korea and smashing their colonial rule, and conduct this struggle in close combination with the struggle for seizing power. He further taught that in the revolutionary struggle in South Korea all forms of struggles—political and economic, legal and illegal, violent and non-violent, small-scale and large-scale—should without exception serve as preparations for the decisive battle for seizure of power, and this decisive battle can be crowned with victory only by violent methods.

Touching upon the issue of the unification of the country, Comrade Kim Il Sung emphasized that it can be realized only when the U.S. imperialist aggressors have been driven out from the territory of our country and the South Korean puppet regime has been smashed, and he said as follows:

"**When U.S. imperialism is driven out and the people's democratic revolution is crowned with victory in South Korea and the people take power into their own hands, our cause of** national unification will be achieved by the united strength of the socialist forces in the northern half and the democratic forces in South Korea."

This line set forth by Comrade Kim Il Sung is the most correct line which accords fully with the desire of our people and interests of the nation and enjoys wholehearted support from the peoples the world over.

The historic report delivered by Comrade Kim Il Sung at the 20th anniversary celebration of the founding of the Democratic People's Republic of Korea is a brilliant historic document which gave a profound Marxist-Leninist analysis, review and generalization of the results and experiences gained by our Party and people in building a new society, and is a great programmatic document which showed clear prospects and fighting tasks for consolidating and developing our socialist system, for achieving the complete victory of socialism and expediting the revolution in South Korea and unification of the country.

The report is also a superb revolutionary document which explicates the strategy and line of the struggle for frustrating the world strategy of U.S. imperialism at the present stage, accelerating its final downfall and achieving victory for the international revolutionary cause as a whole.

The report which logically systematizes and comprehends the profound thoughts, scientific theories and distinguished lines on the revolution and construction is a great Marxist-Leninist document of classical significance.

As soon as the report of Comrade Kim Il Sung at the 20th anniversary celebration of the founding of the Democratic People's Republic of Korea was made public to the world, numerous revolutionaries and revolutionary peoples of the world expressed absolute support and sympathy for it, appraising it highly as a "great programmatic document of principle on the socialist revolution and socialist construction as a whole," a "Communist Manifesto of the mid-twentieth century" and a "great Marxist-Leninist document of classical significance at the present times."

The entire Korean people who have read this historic report which illumines the bright path to victory in the revolution, are fighting on with redoubled courage along the glorious road of struggle, the road of victory and progress indicated by the wise Leader Comrade Kim Il Sung, filled with boundless respect for and trust in the Leader, who always guides them along the golden road of victory and honour, with a swelling sense of pride and happiness to have him as the Leader.

In March 1969, Comrade Kim Il Sung, the great Marxist-Leninist and brilliant Leader of revolution, published his scientific work **"On Some Theoretical Problems of the Socialist Economy"** which gave answers to important, theoretical and practical problems awaiting elucidation in the building of socialism and communism in the present era.

In this work Comrade Kim Il Sung threw a new, Marxist-Leninist light and set forth formulae on important theoretical and practical problems urgently calling for solution in the building of socialism and communism and on fundamental questions of the socialist political economy—the correlation between the scale of the economy and the rate of development of production, the means of production in the form of commodity and the use of the law of value, and the peasant market and the way of abolishing it in socialist society.

The publication of Comrade Kim Il Sung's brilliant work **"On Some Theoretical Problems of the Socialist Economy"** marked a great historic event in developing our revolution, in building socialism and communism and advancing the Marxist-Leninist theory of economy.

In the work Comrade Kim Il Sung first clarified brilliantly, and furnished incontestable theoretical and practical proof of, the great truth that socialist society has unlimited potentialities to develop the economy continuously at a high rate, and that the further socialist construction advances and the stronger the economic basis grows, the greater the potentialities become.

Comrade Kim Il Sung taught as follows:

"Socialist society has unlimited potentialities to incessantly develop the economy at such a high rate as is inconceivable in capitalist society, and the further socialist construction advances and the stronger the economic basis grows, the greater become these potentialities."

On the basis of demonstrating the new law-governed process of development of the socialist economy, Comrade Kim Il Sung taught that the rate of growth of production in socialist society is so high that it is inconceivable in capitalist society, and cast a new, full light on the conditions and ways of principle for effecting it.

He taught that in socialist society, all the labour resources and natural wealth of the country can be used most rationally, and production can be boosted steadily according to plan, and that this possibility of production growth will ever increase according as the balances between the branches of the national economy are rationally preserved and the country's economy is kept in better shape with the strengthening of the economy-organizing functions of the state of the proletarian dictatorship and the rise of the level of economic management of the functionaries.

And he pointed out that in socialist society technology develops rapidly by making use of the unrestricted possibility of development of the productive forces offered by the production relations of socialism, and, with this, labour productivity increases constantly and production develops at a high rate.

In particular, Comrade Kim Il Sung clarified that the decisive factor giving a strong impetus to the development of the production forces in socialist society is the high revolutionary zeal of people, and taught that the more the Party and state of the proletariat, in conformity to their proper functions, strengthen the ideological revolution among the working people and gradually eliminate the survivals of old ideologies from their minds, the more the working people will devote their talents and energies to their work for the development of socialist production.

On the basis of a profound analysis of the advantages inherent in socialist society and the practical experiences of building socialism in our country, Comrade Kim Il Sung scientifically testified to the fallacy and injustice of the theory that in socialist society the reserves for increased production diminish gradually and production cannot be kept rising at a high rate with the development of the economy and expansion of its scale.

In the work Comrade Kim Il Sung also gave comprehensive Marxist-Leninist answers for the first time to the questions of the use of the commodity-money relations, especially to the problems of the means of production in the form of commodity and the use of the law of value in socialist society.

By his brilliant ability for scientific insight and on the basis of the rich practical experiences in our country, Comrade Kim Il Sung gave a clear scientific and theoretical elucidation of the reason why there exists the production of commodity in socialist society and of when the means of production is a commodity and when not, and then, for the first time in history, gave an intelligent and clear-cut theoretical answer to the question that the means of production exchanged between the state enterprises assumes the form of commodity and here the law of value operates in form.

Comrade Kim Il Sung taught as follows:

"**Firstly, when a means of production turned out in the state sector of ownership is transferred to co-operative ownership or** vice versa, it is a commodity in either case and, therefore, the law of value operates here; secondly, a means of production which is exchanged within the bounds of co-operative ownership, between co-operative farms, between producers' co-operatives or between the former and the latter, is equally a commodity and here, too, the law of value operates; thirdly, in the case of export the means of production is a commodity and it is dealt at the world market price or at the socialist market price....

"It would be right to say that the means of production which are transferred between the state enterprises according to the plans of equipment and material supply and of co-operative production are not commodities, but assume the form of commodity, and that, accordingly, in this case the law of value does not operate in substance as in the case of commodity production, but in form."

Giving a scientific explanation also to the reason why the means of production which are transferred between the state enterprises, are not commodities but merely assume the form of commodity, Comrade Kim Il Sung taught that it is so because the state enterprises are relatively independent and deliver the means of production on the principle of equivalent compensation, and the independence of the state enterprises in management and the principle of equivalent compensation have something to do with the specific feature of socialist society which is a transitional one, that is, the productive forces and the communist consciousness of people have not yet developed to a high degree and labour has not yet become life's prime requirement for the people.

Comrade Kim Il Sung also scientifically elucidated the question of making use of the law of value in the production and circulation of commodities and, especially, the question of properly fixing the prices of commodities on the basis of correct reckoning with the requirements of the basic economic law of socialism and the law of value, and also in principles arising thereof.

In his work **"On Some Theoretical Problems of the Socialist Economy"** Comrade Kim Il Sung expounded in a comprehensive way the problem of the peasant market in socialist society which had so far remained without any elucidation, the concept of the peasant market, the origin of *Jang* (market—Tr.), the character of the peasant market as a backward form of trade, the survivals of capitalism in the peasant market, the reason why the peasant market exists in socialist society and its role, the way to abolish it and all other problems; and he raised the utterly new questions of the withering away of the circulation of commodities and of the transition from socialist trade to the supply system, giving a brilliant explanation to its law-governed process.

Here, in particular, he put forth the original idea that the peasant market and the underhand dealings will disappear and trade will go over finally to the supply system only when the productive forces have developed to such an extent that all kinds of goods required by the people can be sufficiently turned out and supplied and co-operative property has grown into property of the entire people. This furnished a clear, scientific explication to the question as to how the production of commodities will disappear and in what form the distribution of goods will be done after its disappearance.

Comrade Kim Il Sung's work **"On Some Theoretical Problems of the Socialist Economy"** which gave a perfect and flawless scientific, theoretical elucidation of the fundamental problems of the socialist economy for the first time in history on the basis of profound and plain logic and indisputable facts and illumined the only correct way to solve those problems, is a great classic document concerning the problem of the socialist economy, a programmatic document and an outstanding Marxist-Leninist document from which the state of the dictatorship of the proletariat should take guidance in drawing up and executing the economic policy.

This work also furnishes a brilliant example for creatively developing Marxism-Leninism and defending its purity in the domain of the economic theory of socialism, and constitutes a decisive blow to the reactionary economic theory of bourgeoisie and the economic theory of opportunism.

Comrade Kim Il Sung's distinguished theory which brilliantly illumines the victorious way to socialism and communism, has inspired boundless confidence, fighting spirit and courage in the Korean people who are waging a heroic struggle for the complete victory of socialism and the nation-wide victory of our revolution; and it has imbued the revolutionary peoples of the world aspiring after socialism and communism with the righteousness of the communist cause and deep confidence in its victory and with great encouragement.

A great number of publications of the world have highly appraised this work as a "historic document which marks a milestone of new epoch-making significance in the development of socialist economic theory" and a "programmatic document which a state of the proletarian dictatorship should adhere to in formulating its economic policy."

Under the sagacious and outstanding leadership of Comrade Kim Il Sung, the Korean people have won glorious victories in the revolution and construction through storms over the last nearly half a century.

It was thanks to the great revolutionary ideas and theory of Comrade Kim Il Sung, the scientific lines and policies set forth by him and to the great exploits and a wealth of experiences accumulated by him that our Party and people have traversed the most correct and straight way in the revolution and construction and come to have an invincible theoretical and practical weapon which enables them to tide over any difficulties and trials in their onward march.

The Korean people are filled with the conviction that they are bound to win victory when they, under the leadership of Comrade Kim Il Sung, advance along the road of victory indicated by him.

This is a rock-firm conviction and will of our people based on their experience of life gained in the course of over 40 years during which they have fought and won victories under the wise leadership of Comrade Kim Il Sung.

A brilliant victory and glory is always in store for the Korean people who, armed firmly with the great revolutionary ideas of the respected and beloved Leader Comrade Kim Il Sung, the great Marxist-Leninist, strategic genius of the revolution and one of the outstanding leaders of the international communist and world revolutionary movements, are fighting and advancing under his wise leadership, and the unification of the country and the cause of socialism and communism in Korea will surely be accomplished.

* * *

Comrade Kim Il Sung, the great Leader of the 40 million Korean people, has led the Korean revolution to victory for over 40 years and performed really immortal exploits.

Comrade Kim Il Sung put forth scientific revolutionary lines and policies and led the Korean revolution along the right path by creatively applying Marxism-Leninism to the realities of our country, and thereby opened up a new great era of revolution which marked a radical turn in the communist movement and the anti-Japanese national-liberation struggle in Korea; and he has established a powerful socialist state in this land overridden by the aggressors for a long time and brought about epoch-making changes in all domains of the political, economic and cultural life of our people.

In the grimmest period of Japanese imperialist rule,

Comrade Kim Il Sung organized and waged the heroic anti-Japanese armed struggle, thus demonstrating to the whole world the honour and spirit of our nation and establishing the glorious revolutionary traditions of our Party and people.

Comrade Kim Il Sung led our people to defeat the heinous Japanese imperialists and achieve the restoration of the fatherland. He victoriously guided the Fatherland Liberation War of the Korean people to crush the aggression by U.S. imperialism, chieftain of imperialism, who had boasted themselves of being the "mightiest" in the world, and defended the independence of the country and the freedom of the people.

Comrade Kim Il Sung founded the Workers' Party of Korea on the basis of the organizational and ideological preparations for the founding of the Party made during the anti-Japanese armed struggle, and has strengthened and developed it into an invincible Marxist-Leninist Party; he established the first state of the dictatorship of the proletariat in our country and has strengthened and developed it amid the fierce struggle against the enemies at home and abroad; and he founded the People's Army, the reliable defender of the revolution, and has strengthened and developed it into a revolutionary armed force which is a cadre army and modernized, each of its members being a match for a hundred.

Comrade Kim Il Sung has originated the only correct revolutionary theory to lead the revolution in our country along the rightest path to victory, established a well-regulated system of the dictatorship of the proletariat such as the Party, the state and the working people's organizations, and leads it as a whole.

Comrade Kim Il Sung, leading the Party and the people, triumphantly carried out in a brief span of time the anti-imperialist, anti-feudal democratic revolution and the socialist revolution in the northern half of the Republic, and thereby set up a most progressive socialist system free from all sources of exploitation in our country, built a powerful independent national economy in our country which had been reduced to ruins owing to the destruction by Japanese and U.S. imperialism, and developed science, education and culture to brilliant efflorescence.

Comrade Kim Il Sung has solved theoretical and practical questions newly arising after the establishment of the socialist system in a most correct and original way, thus successfully paving the way to the complete victory of socialism and to communism in our country.

Comrade Kim Il Sung has also mapped out the most correct lines and policies for the South Korean revolution and the unification of the country, and is leading the North and South Korean people in implementing them to accelerate the nation-wide victory of the Korean revolution.

Indeed, the course of the development of the Korean revolution is the course of brilliant victory for the great revolutionary ideas of Comrade Kim Il Sung and his seasoned leadership.

Thanks to the long unyielding revolutionary struggle and wise leadership of the respected and beloved Leader Comrade Kim Il Sung, the Korean people were liberated from all kinds of exploitation and oppression, abolished centuries-old backwardness and penury and are now leading a free and happy life as masters of the country and society.

It is thanks to the superb leadership of Comrade Kim Il Sung that the Korean people have become an invincible people who have the most revolutionary Party, people's government and the revolutionary army each member of which is a match for a hundred, have become a people possessed of the advanced socialist system, a powerful economy and a resplendent culture, and are living in an era of victorious advance of the revolution, in an era of national prosperity for the first time in their history.

Comrade Kim Il Sung, adhering firmly to the revolutionary principles of Marxism-Leninism, is exerting all his efforts to develop the international communist movement and the world revolution as a whole.

He has indicated the most correct line for overcoming Right and Left opportunism in the international communist movement and for the solidarity of the socialist countries and the unity of the international communist movement, and is fighting with all consistency to carry it out.

Also, holding high the banner of anti-imperialist, anti-U.S. struggle, he is fighting devotedly to frustrate the policy of aggression and war of the imperialists headed by the U.S. imperialists, and advance the revolutionary struggle of the Asian, African and Latin American peoples.

Comrade Kim Il Sung has given correct answers to all questions of principle arising not only in the revolution and construction of our country but in the international arena at the present times, thus making a great contribution to the development of the international communist and world revolutionary movements.

The immortal exploits performed by Comrade Kim Il Sung in leading the Korean revolution to victory in the teeth of grave difficulties, his tremendous contributions to the development of the international communist movement and world revolution, the great revolutionary ideas, original theories and methods contained in his brilliant works, and experiences accumulated by him—all these constitute a priceless asset and rich treasure for the victory of the cause of socialism and communism.

At the same time, they have served to defend the purity of Marxism-Leninism and further enrich its ideological and theoretical treasure-house.

The glorious revolutionary history of Comrade Kim Il Sung constitutes, indeed, the source which infuses indomitable strength, courage and confidence into the entire Korean people, and the peoples who are fighting for the independence and prosperity of their countries, for their freedom and happiness and for the cause of socialism and communism, and which imbues them with revolutionary zeal and wisdom; it constitutes a revolutionary textbook that illuminates the road to victory.

Comrade Kim Il Sung is the brilliant Leader of the revolution who is possessed of unwavering fidelity to the revolutionary principle and an unyielding will not to be shaken under any stresses and storms, an extraordinary revolutionary sweep to constantly advance the revolution by surmounting whatever difficulties and trials, scrupulousness in carefully analyzing all things and phenomena, keen perspicacity to penetrate below the surface of any complex circumstances and situation to steer the right course through them easily, and of an unusual ability of leadership.

As he set forth *Juche*-motivated revolutionary lines and policies and has led our people undeviatingly along the straight road of victory, the Korean revolution has been able to beat back the desperate attack of the imperialists, frustrate the subversive machinations of the renegades, repulse the pressure of great-power chauvinism and overcome the obstacles caused by the lags which have been bequeathed by history, and to win the great victory of today by finding its way through the raging storms.

The revolutionary history of Comrade Kim Il Sung is filled with shining examples of boundless love for the people and the popular method and style of work.

Comrade Kim Il Sung is not only the great Leader of the revolution but a teacher and benevolent father who shows the road of revolution and construction to the people and looks after all aspects of their life, and a close comrade who shares sweets and bitters with our people.

He is always among the people, regards their sufferings as his own and looks after them with a warm fatherly love.

He has always consulted personally with the workers, peasants and other sections of the working people on the state affairs and mobilized their strength and wisdom and, relying upon them, led the revolution and construction to victory.

For his great exploits in the struggle for the advancement of the Korean revolution and world revolution, Comrade Kim Il Sung now enjoys absolute trust and respect not only of the Korean people but also of numerous revolutionaries and revolutionary peoples of the world.

The Korean people feel immensely happy and honoured to have Comrade Kim Il Sung as their Leader and to live, work and fight as his revolutionary soldiers, and they speak of it proudly to the whole world.

Our Party members and working people are doing all they can to train themselves into true soldiers of Comrade Kim Il Sung, revolutionaries who are firmly equipped with the Marxist-Leninist world outlook and have the indomitable revolutionary spirit and will by studying the history of the great revolutionary activities of Comrade Kim Il Sung and learning from him.

Our people are filled with a firm determination to uphold, in future too, as in the past, the leadership of Comrade Kim Il Sung and fight as revolutionary soldiers boundlessly loyal to him.

Invincible are the Korean people who are under the wise leadership of the respected and beloved Leader of the 40 million Korean people Comrade Kim Il Sung, the peerless patriot, national hero, ever-victorious iron-willed brilliant commander and one of the outstanding leaders of the international communist and working-class movements.

www.ingramcontent.com/pod-product-compliance
Lightning Source LLC
Chambersburg PA
CBHW021802220426
43662CB00006B/153